Teaching about the Future

Other books by Peter C. Bishop and Andy Hines:

ConsumerShift: How Changing Values Are Reshaping the Consumer Landscape, A. Hines

Managing Your Future as an Association, A. Hines, J. Coates, J. Jarratt & J. Mahaffie

Thinking about the Future: Guidelines for Strategic Foresight, A. Hines & P. Bishop

2025: Scenarios of US and Global Society as Reshaped by Science and Technology, A. Hines, J. Coates & J. Mahaffie

Teaching about the Future

Peter C. Bishop
University of Houston, USA

and

Andy Hines
University of Houston, USA

Sociological Imagination by C. Wright Mills and Amitai Etzioni (1999), 371 words from page 1 and 155 words from page 4. By permission of Oxford University Press, Inc.

First published 2012 by
PALGRAVE MACMILLAN

Palgrave Macmillan in the UK is an imprint of Macmillan Publishers Limited, registered in England, company number 785998, of Houndmills, Basingstoke, Hampshire RG21 6XS.

Palgrave Macmillan in the US is a division of St Martin's Press LLC, 175 Fifth Avenue, New York, NY 10010.

Palgrave Macmillan is the global academic imprint of the above companies and has companies and representatives throughout the world.

Palgrave® and Macmillan® are registered trademarks in the United States, the United Kingdom, Europe and other countries.

ISBN 978–0–230–36349–6

This book is printed on paper suitable for recycling and made from fully managed and sustained forest sources. Logging, pulping and manufacturing processes are expected to conform to the environmental regulations of the country of origin.

A catalogue record for this book is available from the British Library.

A catalog record for this book is available from the Library of Congress.

10   9   8   7   6   5   4   3   2   1
21   20   19   18   17   16   15   14   13   12

Printed and bound in Great Britain by
CPI Antony Rowe, Chippenham and Eastbourne

To the faculty, students, graduates, and administrators in the University of Houston System who have contributed to this new discipline of Strategic Foresight over the last 35-plus years.

Contents

List of Tables

List of Figures

Preface

This book is the product of more than 35 years of accumulated experience of the faculty teaching foresight on the Graduate Program in Futures Studies, first at the University of Houston-Clear Lake (UHCL) and now at the University of Houston (UH). The program was established by Dean Calvin Cannon and Chancellor Alfred Neumann in 1975. Dean Cannon's rationale for establishing this program in that new university was simple, "We study the past, don't we? Why can't we study the future?" And from that simple thought came the first official degree in foresight.

Dean Cannon hired two academic futurists to staff the program: Jib Fowles, a sociologist and communications professor from the New School for Social Research, where he studied with Alvin Toffler for a time, and Chris Dede, a futurist of educational technology who drafted his own futures degree at the University of Massachusetts. These faculty then hired Oliver Markley from Stanford Research Institute to turn the program into a more applied and professional direction. Peter Bishop started teaching in the program in 1983, coming from Michigan State University with degrees in sociology and social change. Andy Hines took his degree from the program in 1990 and has now returned to UH to teach and prepare students as professional futurists.

The curriculum for the futures program has evolved over that time, but it has remained remarkably stable over the last ten years. Dr Bishop started putting courses online in 2001, requiring a new level of specificity in what students had to learn and do in each course and each class. It is now time to share that curriculum with the rest of the futures community and with educators in general.

Foresight appeared in public first in France in the 1950s and then in the US and elsewhere in the 1960s. Since then, hundreds of futures courses have been taught around the world. But that number pales in comparison with the number of courses taught about the past, that is, history. There are still only a dozen or so graduate degrees in the world and no doctoral program yet. So it is unfortunate that in times of intense change, where creativity and innovation are required for competitive success, little knowledge of how to anticipate and influence the future is provided for students. It's not the teachers' fault. They were not taught about the future either.

Table P.1 History of the Houston Futures program

Year	Event
1975	University of Houston-Clear Lake (UHCL) establishes the Futures program
	Jib Fowles and Chris Dede join as charter faculty
1978	Oliver Markley joins faculty from the Stanford Research Institute
1983	Peter Bishop starts teaching in Futures program
1996	Wendy Schultz joins faculty as Visiting Professor
2000	World Future Society holds annual conference in Houston, and annual "Best of Houston" session featuring student work begins
2001	Alumni Retreat proves instrumental in founding of Association of Professional Futurists the following year
2001	Chris Jones joins faculty and World Futures Studies Federation Secretariat is hosted by the program
2001	Program begins putting courses online (one per semester until entire curriculum online)
2005	Andy Hines joins as Lecturer, as program moves to UH main campus
2007	UH Main campus re-approves the program
2007	Hines & Bishop publish *Thinking about the Future*
2008	Students earn first of three APF Student Papers Awards: Charles Kennedy (2008), Darko Lovric (2009), Elizabeth Chapman (2010)
2009	35th Anniversary Celebration
2009	Certificate program in Strategic Foresight begins

This is where this book comes in. The University of Houston has been teaching and preparing professional futurists for decades. Now it is time to expand that mission to educators everywhere. The authors believe that it is possible to include futures thinking into every discipline at every level of education, particularly high schools, colleges, and professional schools. In fact, it is our vision that, in the long run, teaching about the future is as common as teaching about the past. The past is where the record of human achievement and failure appear; the future is where people will live as time goes on. Should they not get equal time? Should not every high school and college student who takes a course in world history also take a course in world futures? Should they not learn to envision, plan, and execute plans to create change toward a more preferable future? Of course they should.

So this book contains the UH foresight curriculum from start to finish. It contains approximately one chapter for every course in the curriculum. It is also the basis of a week-long Certificate in Strategic Foresight course, a day-long Introduction to Foresight course and other training programs offered in organizations every year. Our students, clients, and professional colleagues suggest that this approach brings it all together. It integrates the best of what futurists around the world have been teaching in a common-sense and practical approach.

Teachers may not be able to teach everything in this book. It could be a textbook for an introductory course in foresight, which would be fine. But more importantly, it contains ideas and approaches that could be incorporated in history, social science, science, and even mathematics courses. Teaching about the future is not a big mystery. People use foresight every day. Why not explicitly teach students to use their natural human instinct to anticipate, plan, and influence their own future and the future of their organizations and communities. What greater mission could we as teachers have than to *really* prepare students for the future!

Purpose

This work is a conceptual description of the field as developed and taught by the University of Houston's Graduate Program in Futures Studies. It is the basis of our curriculum, which has adapted and evolved over the last 37 years in response to new developments in the field and changes in the marketplace for foresight. A consistent theme over this time, among the foresight community in general and foresight educators in particular, has been the need for a consistent and comprehensive description of the field – for someone to bring it all together. This is our attempt at doing so. And our hope is that others will adopt this description as a basis for a standard curriculum. We have shared it with several other programs over the years in that hope. This publication will help us to reach a much wider audience. We will be happy even if we are just able to nudge the field in a common direction.

A secondary purpose of the book is to support the training that the program has been doing in addition to the Master's Degree program. We have supplemented the Master's program with a range of other offerings: extension courses, a week-long Certificate course, a day-long Introduction to Foresight course, a Futurizing Your Teaching Practice course for teachers, and a Futures Summer Camp for students. Our participants will benefit from a big-picture yet detailed overview of the field.

A third purpose is to give secondary and college teachers an approach to futures that they can use in their classes. The book will be more conceptual, but they should be able to read it through, or at least select chapters so they might use some of the ideas in their classes.

Finally, the book could, in the future, be adopted as a text in a college introductory course. It will certainly be used in our Introduction to Foresight course.

Acknowledgements

No great thing is created by one person alone or in any short period of time. And the Graduate Program in Futures Studies at the University of Houston is no exception. Today's curriculum has been inspired by and drawn upon the collective wisdom of its superb faculty over the years: Jib Fowles, Chris Dede, Jim Bowman, Fred Kierstead, Jim Coomer, Wendy Schultz and Chris Jones, and the current faculty including Terry Grim, Draper Kaufman, and Cindy-Frewen-Wellner.

We are grateful to Shirley Ezell for bringing the program to the attention of Dean William Fitzgibbon, of the College of Technology at the University of Houston, who invited the authors to re-establish the program there in 2007 under the leadership of Ezell and Department Chair Carole Goodson.

Thanks to the program's Advisory Board members for providing valuable "real world" feedback: Joel Barker, Clem Bezold, Napier Collyns, Tom Conger, Christian Crews, Ted Gordo, Dominique Jaroula, Jennifer Jarratt, Oliver Markley, Pero Micic, Amy Oberg, Dave Rejeski, Paul Saffo, Wendy Schultz, and Lee Shupp.

Also, thanks to our many professional colleagues who have helped the program over the years in many different ways, whether visiting for a lecture, offering an internship or job to a student, and the like.

Finally, and perhaps most important, thanks to the students and alumni who have each left their mark on the program in some important way – without you, none of this happens.

Introduction

Foresight is fundamentally about the study of change. Of course, futurists are not the only ones who study change. Scientists study change in physics (the motion of bodies), astronomy (the formation of stars and planets), chemistry (chemical reactions), biology (the evolution of species), and in a whole host of other disciplines. The social sciences also study change at the personal level (psychology), at the group, organizational and societal levels (sociology), and at the cultural level (anthropology). In fact, two disciplines are particularly concerned with change: history studies change in the past; journalism chronicles change in the present. And that is where foresight fits in. Most people think of time as flowing from the past (history), through the present (journalism), and into the future. Therefore, just as historians study the past and journalists the present, so futurists study the future. It is interesting that history is an ancient discipline and journalism has been around a long time. Why don't we have an academic discipline that studies the future?

Oh yeah! The future hasn't happened yet. Can futurists study something that doesn't exist? On the face of it, that's a big problem. Of course, historians study something that doesn't exist either – the past. It did at one time, but it doesn't exist anymore.

The big difference between history/journalism and foresight, however, is that history and journalism have direct evidence of the changes they are describing. Historians have artifacts (tools, books, buildings) from which they can infer what life was like in the past; journalists have statements, statistics, and their observation of events to describe change in the present. How can a futurist infer what is going to happen in the future when the people there have not yet created the artifacts and statistics to use as evidence?

Why teach the future?

It is disappointing that so few people teach about the future when, in fact, people will live the rest of their lives there. Almost everything people do is intended to understand or to influence the future. But where is the future in our educational systems? A fair amount is studied about the past – as it should be – but why not study an equal amount about the future?

> We should teach as much about the future as
> we do about the past

There are two answers to that question – one professional and the other epistemological. The professional answer is that teachers do not teach what they do not know. Since they were never taught about the future, how can they be expected to teach their students about the future? The more important and deeper answer, for most people, is that the future is unknowable. You cannot teach things you cannot know. But that is a fallacy. The future is knowable in exactly the same way that next week's weather is knowable or next week's stock market or next week's ball scores. They can be known as a set of possibilities, as plausible alternative futures, any one of which has a significant chance of occurring. Granted, knowing a set of possibilities is not as satisfying as *really knowing* what will happen. But when really knowing is impossible, is it not better to know something about the future (its possibilities) than to ignore it and know little or nothing?

People and organizations change when the world changes and when they aspire to do something significant, if not great. The world is changing and at an accelerating pace. And with this change comes the need to learn new skills. The current model of public education was created to prepare students for the industrial age. Be on time, stay in formation, do the work, accept supervision and, most of all, know the right answer. These skills made the workers of yesterday's factories and bureaucracies successful.

But now, gone is the majority of factory employment and going are offices wedded to rigid procedures and command-and-control processes. The pace of the world has quickened, driven by fast-paced information flows. Flattened organization, networked workers and collaborative technologies facilitate flexibility and quick response to the information age.

Teaching the future to gifted and talented students

Mary Tallent-Runnels (2005) makes the case for teaching the future to gifted and talented students

- Gifted learners have said they love to think about the future, and this love increases as they become older (Torrance, 1978).
- They are more interested in global issues than other students and sometimes feel helpless to do anything about these issues (Galbraith, 1985; Tallent-Runnels & Mullen, 2004).
- They have the potential for intense social, moral, and ethical concerns (Passow, 1988).
- Gifted learners worry about the future, because they are sensitive to world problems (Passow, 1988).
- They also can be more morally sensitive than others – a trait that is essential to the welfare of our society (Silverman, 1994).
- When supported and guided in positive directions, these qualities can empower them to successfully manage change (Carroll, 1991) and to cope with problems in general and change the future (Torrance, 1974).
- Finally, many believe that gifted youth will become our world leaders and ultimately solve our global problems. Therefore, we must help them develop their leadership abilities and learn to think ahead to the world they will lead (Passow, 1988; Roeper, 1988) ... They can become change agents and set realistic goals as they lead others (Carroll, 1991).

As the world environment changes so do the skills for success. The successful will be those who have mastered the basics of change, how to anticipate it, how to manage uncertainty and ambiguity, and ultimately how to proactively create the changes necessary to bend the future to more preferable outcomes. And the time to teach these skills is now (Bishop & Strong, 2010, 105).

The problem of prediction

The problem of making statements about the future is, of course, the problem of prediction. People learn to make predictions when they observe the consequences of change. The baby that repeatedly throws the cup to the floor is engaged in a primitive form of prediction. What will happen? Will Mommy keep picking it up? How many times? Dan Barry, former astronaut and Head of Faculty at Singularity University, famously described watching his two-month-old son discover his foot – wiggle, wiggle, laugh; wiggle, wiggle, laugh. The capacity to make predictions is formalized in science class with swinging pendulums, rolling balls down inclined planes, melting ice cubes and predicting the outcomes. Each prediction is a statement about what is expected to happen in the future, and then one checks to see whether or not it happens as expected. One is right if one measured the initial variables accurately, put them in the right equations and did the math correctly. If the prediction does not compute, one has to go back and do it again. Professional scientists do the same thing. They keep repeating the experiment until they can predict the outcome.

People also need to predict the future in the world at large so they use the same process. They believe that all they need to do is understand the laws that govern human behavior and predict what will happen. But that the process does not seem to work as well in the world as it did in the lab. Most predictions about human behavior are almost always wrong. What good is this prediction thing if it didn't tell what was going to happen? Bummer!

Prediction does not work very well in the world of human affairs because there is not a good, scientific theory of human behavior. In fact, there are many theories in psychology, anthropology, sociology and the like. All work to some extent, but they fail just as often. So there is *uncertainty* when predicting the outcome of a process involving human beings. Uncertainty is the reason that the predictive process developed in the lab does not work in the world. Uncertainty is not bad in itself. It's just very inconvenient when it comes to predicting behavior. In fact it might even be good because it makes people cautious as they approach something new, whether it is an unfamiliar dog or a new stock tip. What is not generally appreciated is outcomes in the world involving people are and should be less certain than outcomes in "hard" sciences.

One can reduce the uncertainty in the lab to very small quantities over time – first by developing and using more precise measurements and secondly by developing and using better theories. Uncertainty is still there, but it is quite small. It can be reduced to very small quantities with lots of time and money, but it cannot be eliminated. For example, the official mass of the electron is $9.10938188 \times 10^{-31}$kg. That's just over nine-billionths of a billionth of a billionth of a gram!

But it is still uncertain to about a millionth of a per cent. Plus or minus 0.000001% is good enough for most people! In that case, one can ignore the uncertainty and go ahead with predictions of the future using that number.

Technically, one makes an assumption when doing so. One assumes that the mass of the electron is *exactly* that number. That is a pretty good assumption because it almost is. One doesn't have to worry about the millionth of a per cent uncertainty in most calculations. So one predicts the future with confidence and usually gets pretty good results.

What happens when the same reasoning is used in making predictions in the human world? Is the uncertainty in the human world equivalent to millionths of a per cent? Hardly! Compared to the physics lab, the human world is awash in uncertainty. Just look at today's newspaper. It contains lots of facts about what happened yesterday, but only random speculation about what will happen tomorrow. People are so far from predicting the future state of the world – even by one day – that it is ridiculous to even try.

And that is why most people do not like to think about the future. It is why there are no courses or departments on foresight in our schools. It is why cultures are blind to the future. Ironically and tragically, however, the future is where people are headed and where they will spend the rest of their lives. That is why they come to work or to school every day – to understand and change the future – yet they are ill-equipped for the task. They have never had any explicit training in change or the future, and they are trying to use an inappropriate mechanism of prediction that they learned in science. It doesn't work. People must come to understand and influence the future better than they have. Indeed their very lives depend on it.

The future(s)

Since one cannot predict, does that mean giving up on thinking about the future? Certainly not, but the approach has to be modified. One must first give up the possibility of predicting the future on any consistent basis. Sometimes predictions do turn out to be true either because of a lucky guess or because the world operated according to known rules during some brief period. But one is not lucky very often, and one does not know when these periods will be so most of the time cannot count on being lucky.

However, rather than not thinking about and preparing for the future altogether, futurists reject the basic assumption that the future of human affairs is predictable. Instead, they modify it by saying that while it is true that people cannot know *the* future – the one that will ultimately become the present – they may be able to know the *futures*, the set of plausible futures that one future is drawn from. In this conception, the future is multiple not singular. One is not looking for the *real* future amidst a bunch of imposters, but describing all the plausible futures as a set. The future is understood by mapping the range of plausible futures and preparing for the whole range.

Admittedly, that solution is not entirely satisfactory. People want to know the one future, they want to be certain, and they want to be right. If they are, they can prepare more precisely for that one future. But that knowledge is impossible for all the reasons given above. Given that, would it not be better to know something about the future rather than to know nothing? When the weather turns bad and one has to keep driving, one does not close one's eyes and refuse to look down the road because one cannot see very far anyway? Of course not. In fact, a driver looks harder, straining to pick up any clue of what lies ahead. They think of the possibilities – a curve, a pothole, a car stalled in the middle of the road – and prepare for all of them. Is one angry or sad that none of those possibilities occurred? That the forecast of possibilities was wrong? Of course not! One is happy to have gotten through that stormy drive without incident. By the same token, one should not try to be "right" about the future. Being prepared for whatever does occur is a lot more important.

So, in the same way, futurists look more carefully at the signs leading to the future, because they can't predict accurately. It's a harder job to deal with multiple possibilities, and the result is less satisfactory, but it is better than closing one's eyes and hurling oneself blindly into the future.

Most people's image of the future is a line, or a road, or a river, or even a rollercoaster (depending on how thrilling they think the ride will be!).

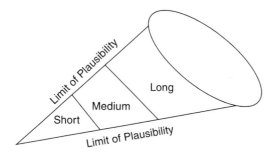

Figure I.1   Plausible options increase in the future
Source: Based on Charles Taylor, Army War College.

It is a continuous strip of time leading from now to then. A better image, given our inability to see the road ahead, is a cone, an expanding set of plausible futures. The cone is relatively narrow in the short-run. One is pretty sure of what will happen next because the number of plausible alternatives is low. But as one moves into the medium and long term, the range expands revealing some interesting, challenging, even exciting futures.

Futurists are those who survey and explore the full range of plausible futures and share what they find. They help people expand their narrow focus on one future to a broader range of other possibilities. The key underlying principle is that the future is actually a set of futures from which a subsequent present will be drawn.

Be prepared

The purpose of forecasting, and even of prediction, is not just to know the future as an abstract description but rather to prepare for it. The objective is not just to know what will happen but to be ready whatever does happen. Almost none of the plausible futures will actually occur. But when one does, one is happy to have made adequate preparations. That's success from a futures point of view. The objective is not to be too right (which is impossible), but rather not to be wrong – not to be surprised. Surprise means inadequate preparation, late response, risk of failure, even chaos or panic. Preparing for the full range of plausible futures is the objective of foresight, reducing the element of surprise.

Foresight is not even that unusual in daily life. Most people buy insurance against catastrophic loss – such as of life, health, or home. They consider a range of plausible futures, albeit negative ones, and prepare for their occurrence. They are not expected to predict which year their house will burn down or which month they will go to the hospital. They realize that predicting those things is impossible. So they carry insurance the whole time. They don't get to the end of the year and kick themselves because they didn't use their medical or auto insurance that year. In fact, they are happy that those bad things did not happen. And they don't try to guess whether they will need the insurance the next year; they pay up and feel comfortable that they are covered no matter what happens.

People in dangerous occupations think this way all the time. It's their way of staying alive. The police officer on the street or the soldier in combat is continuously thinking about what could go wrong, how they might be surprised, because they know they are in danger when they are surprised.

People would be much better prepared for their organizational or work futures if they applied that same logic. They don't have to predict what is going to happen as long as they are covered for all the things that could happen. But is it possible to prepare for everything? Actually, not. The full range of possible futures is infinite. People can't consider them all, much less prepare for them. Therefore, futurists narrow the range to that of plausible futures, ones that have more than a negligible chance of occurring.

If one could assign a minimum probability to a plausible future, they would know for sure which were plausible and which were not, but probabilities here are quite subjective. Rather, futurists say that a plausible future is one that has a *story* that makes sense. One can see how it might actually occur. An alien landing on the lawn of the White House, though great for Hollywood, lacks plausibility. But a coming economic crisis or a serious terrorist attack on the Internet or a breakthrough in cancer research – those all have stories that people can accept. They can see them appearing on the front page of the newspaper. They might even have information that makes those futures more likely.

The line between possible and plausible is subjective, for sure. It comes down to whether reasonable people with open minds will accept the story as plausible, whether they have a foundation for believing that the story could come true. Foundations of stories are used in courtrooms and fiction all the time. Lawyers and writers have to prepare their listeners for the appearance of a character or an event. When they don't, one's natural reaction is "Where did that come from?" They do not have to believe the story is probable, but only that it could actually happen. The sum of all such stories is the range of plausible futures.

Treating the future as a set of plausible outcomes rather than one future to be discovered is one of the two major assumptions on which futurists differ from other forecasters. The other is that people do have some influence over parts of the future that actually occurs. Most forecasters describe the future independent of their actions or the actions of their clients. That is a fine, even necessary, analytical device to be able to construct the forecast in the first place. Otherwise one might find oneself in an infinite recursion of "what if ... and then what if they ... and then what if

---

Key assumptions of foresight

1. The future is a set of plausible outcomes rather than one future to be discovered
2. People do have some influence over which future actually occurs.

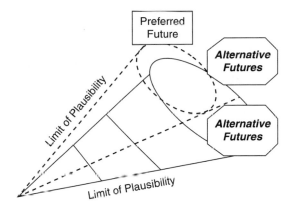

Figure I.2 Shifting the cone
Source: Based on Charles Taylor, Army War College.

we ..." and on and on. One has to start somewhere, and a world changing without people's intervention is as good a place as any.

But one ought not to stop there because the world, or parts of it, is sensitive to people's actions. Even though people may not be able to control the future, as in selecting the exact future they want, they do have the ability to influence what happens. Influence is like power; it bends the trajectory of the future toward the future one prefers. The more influence one has, the more one gets what one wants. Or to put it in forecasting terms, influence bends the development of the future into areas that are more preferable and away from areas that are less preferable.

Imagine the future

People's degree of influence over the future is the product of two quantities: their inherent ability to influence the future and the effort they choose to expend. The ability to influence the future varies by the domain or topic area. One might have a lot of influence over the future in some domains, like family or workplace, and relatively little in others, such as national or world affairs. Secondly, one can choose to make an effort to influence the future in a particular domain or not. Of course, those who do not make an effort will have no influence over the future at all. They must accept the future that other forces create.

Our years of experience teaching and consulting about the future have persuaded us that most people do not believe they have much influence over the future. They feel powerless, at the mercy of unseen and impersonal forces over which they have no control. Such feelings are understandable. The world is large and complicated. People are bathed in media that show other people and events that have little relation to their world or their needs. The future seems to be something that will be handed to them, whether they like it or not.

On the other hand, a focus on national and world events obscures the fact that everyone does have a sphere of influence, a part of the world in which they have some influence. While that influence is never absolute, even over one's own behavior sometimes, at least one has some power to create a future that is better than if no effort were expended at all. And that is the reason that people work, save money, take time with their kids, even get up in the morning – to exert their influence on the world.

And that is where futurists come in, as do many other people who work toward a better world. The message from every motivational speaker in the world is that people have more influence over the future than they think. Some will even go so far as to say that one can have whatever future one wants. They may believe that, but futurists don't. There are constraints; no one's influence – even leaders of nations or the world's richest people – is absolute. Everyone must deal with part of the world that is beyond their control. Nevertheless, most people have more influence over the future than they are exercising at the moment.

The power for people to influence their future is related to the quality of their vision. A vision is a concrete image of a preferred future state. It is a picture of how one wants things to be. The more attractive and more concrete the vision, the more it motivates one to expend effort to work toward it.

Visions work the same for groups (organizations, communities and societies) as they do for individuals. They portray an attractive, even compelling future that motivates the members to work together to achieve it. The great visionaries of history (Moses, Jesus Christ, Mohammed, Buddha, Lincoln, Gandhi, King) were able to inspire people with their vision of a better world. Many people, of lesser stature perhaps but no less noble purpose, are trying to do the same thing today.

But one does not have be a grand historical leader to have a vision, to be a visionary, or to change the part of the world over which they have some influence. Truck drivers can pursue their craft with the same zeal for safety, dependability and customer service that Moses had leading the Hebrews from Egypt. Each is pursuing their vision of a better world; each is creating change in themselves and in the people who know them.

Create the future

The follow-on to vision is the effort it takes to organize and mobilize resources to achieve that vision. In some cases, those actions seem to leap into existence. More ordinary mortals must plan, persuade and scavenge to get the resources to achieve their vision. Preparing to work to achieve a vision is called strategic planning. Unfortunately, most strategic planning isn't strategic; it is incremental, such as some per cent increase over time. True strategic planning is transformational. It identifies the long-term goals and strategies that will move the individual or the organization toward their vision. It also kicks off near-term initiatives that start to implement those strategies. The purpose is to create a long-term transformation that creates a better future.

The final step in creating that future is implementation, often called change management because it is fundamentally the creation of change. The objective is to change the world. In order to do that effectively, most individuals and organizations usually have to begin by changing themselves. Their strategic goals and the implementation of their long-term strategies usually require them to be different than they were in the past. Change management is first of all building the capacity to change and to bring about change – first in oneself, then in others and finally in the world. It is a wrenching process because it involves uprooting old beliefs and habits in order to make way for new attitudes and abilities. But without it, the individual and the organization will simply be unable to move forward toward the vision. As the famous philosopher once said, "If you keep doin' what you been doin', you'll keep gettin' what you been gettin'."

THE TRICKS OF FORESIGHT

Every field – accounting, law, medicine, engineering, and so on – has its tricks. Experienced practitioners learn the tricks and produce better results than those without their experience. Foresight has two tricks that stand out as most useful. The extent to which one practices those tricks and encourages others to do the same, the better prepared one will be and the more the future will match one's aspirations.

Telling stories

Stories are an ancient form of communication. Story-telling might even be hard-wired into people's evolutionary mechanism. The story has meaning and carries a message using details that may not be true. Novels, movies, even some music contain stories about fictional characters. The events are not true, but the message is. A scenario is a story about the future. The details of the scenario may not be true; in fact, they probably are not. But the message may be true – the essence of a plausible future that should be considered and perhaps prepared for. The extent to which

Elements of a good story [scenario]	
Storybook	more than just a description
Specific	facts, events, names, dates
Plausible	it could happen
Relevant	it would change the future
Dramatic	conflict, suspense, unresolved issues
Balanced	bad things have good consequences good things have bad consequences
Personal	putting individual in the future
Integrated	cohesive; plot hangs together

one tells stories every day, the more prepared one will be for a surprising future.

Pursuing visions

A vision is the story of an ideal state which, if one works hard and is lucky, one just might achieve. It's this side of a dream or wish; it's not magic. But it is bold and ambitious. "Could we?" "Might we?" Those are the initial reactions to visions. When the answer is "Yes we can," that's when the race begins. Pursuing a vision is what a full life is about – it motivates, energizes and empowers one to do extraordinary things. Even though the vision itself may be elusive, chasing it sets one off strongly in the right direction.

People and organizations not afraid to consider the future in all its uncertainty and complexity and not afraid to pursue a vision that is almost beyond expectation are the people and organizations that are not only prepared for the future but also those who will be a major force in shaping it. Management guru Peter Drucker once said, "The best way to predict the future is to create it." While that is not entirely true, the more influence one exerts on the future, the better the odds of having a better future.

THE BENEFITS OF FORESIGHT

An analysis of our last book, *Thinking about the Future* (2007), which culled the collective wisdom of three dozen professional futurists globally, identified 316 benefit statements from applying foresight. Table I.1 shows how these are sorted into the Thinking about the Future framework, which comprises six categories: framing, scanning, forecasting,

Table I.1 Benefits of foresight

Activity	Benefits
Framing (22%) *Scoping the project.*	1. Thinking more diverse, open, balanced and non-biased (9%) 2. Focusing on the right questions and problems more clearly (7%) 3. Being aware of, and influencing, assumptions and mental models (6%)
Scanning (16%) *Collecting information.*	4. Understanding the context, in all its complexity, through establishing frameworks (5%) 5. Anticipating change and avoiding surprise (11%)
Forecasting (22%) *Considering a range of future possibilities.*	6. Producing more creative, broader, and deeper insights (17%) 7. Identifying a wider range of opportunities and options (5%)
Visioning (10%) *Choosing a preferred future.*	8. Prioritizing and making better and more robust decisions (10%)
Planning (7%) *Organizing to achieve the vision.*	9. Constructing pathways from the present to the future that enable rehearsing for the future (7%)
Acting (23%) *Implementing the plan.*	10. Catalyzing action and change (7%) 11. Building alignment, commitment and confidence (14%) 12. Building a learning organization (2%)

Source: Hines, A. (2007).

visioning, planning and acting (covered in greater detail in Chapter 1). (Note: The number in parenthesis shows each item as a percentage of overall benefits. Thus, 22% of the benefits statements related to framing, 9% of which related to "Thinking more diverse ..." and so on.)

What stands out in Table I.1 is the high percentage of benefits attributed to the "bookends" of the foresight framework: framing and acting. Futurists have recognized the importance of being as clear as possible about what the problem to be studied really is, and that the problem as presented is not always the "real" problem. Also, futurists have recognized the importance of being more action-oriented, of not studying for the sake of studying but being oriented to spurring action.

The table suggests less emphasis on visioning and planning than might have been expected. But, on reflection, these activities were reengineered, or drastically reduced, in the 1980s and early 1990s. So foresight repositioned itself accordingly to meet the needs of today's organizations. This "repositioning" is amply demonstrated by the single highest scored benefit: "more creative, broader, deeper insights." Organizations today see foresight as a useful means to stretch their thinking about consumer behavior, new product and service development, or where technology is headed – in short, helping them to identify what they need to do today to thrive tomorrow.

STRUCTURE OF THE BOOK

So, how do you teach people about the futures? At the highest level, one needs to understand how to think about the future conceptually, then one needs to be able to map the future, or craft descriptions of what the future might look like, and finally, one needs to know how to influence the future. These three over-arching categories – understanding, mapping and influencing – are used as organizing principles in forming the three parts in this book.

Part I, Understanding, contains the conceptual backdrop to thinking about the future. In our curriculum, three courses deal primarily with this topic: Introduction to Foresight, Systems Thinking, and Social Change (syllabi appended). The four chapters in this section lay out the theoretical underpinnings and mindset of future studies. They explore how futurists think about the future. "Models," "Systems," and "Perspectives" provide frameworks through which to view the future. "Social Change" provides a framework for how change happens on a large scale. It is impossible to cleanly separate theory, method and application in most fields and that is no different in foresight. So there will be some overlap.

- Chapter 1. Models of Change
- Chapter 2. Systems Thinking
- Chapter 3. Perspectives on the Future
- Chapter 4. Social Change

Part II, Mapping, describes how to construct forecasts of potential future outcomes or alternative futures. In our curriculum, two courses deal directly with this topic: Futures Research and World Futures (syllabi appended). The three chapters cover how to forecast baseline and futures: the baseline is the most likely future that emerges *if* present trends continue (they rarely do) and then there are the alternatives to that. The raw material for these alternative futures comes from research and scanning.

Futurists often refer to this as inbound change – the change that happens to people. It comes at people from the "outside" world.

- Chapter 5. Research
- Chapter 6. Scanning
- Chapter 7. Forecasting

Part III, Influencing, explores how to take action to shape the future. In our curriculum two courses cover this topic: Advanced Strategies and Professional Seminar in Foresight (syllabi appended). The four chapters in this section address the "so what" question of foresight. We study the future in order to influence it to help create a better future. Futurists often refer to the changes here as outbound change: the change that people bring about and effect on the world.

- Chapter 8. Leadership
- Chapter 9. Visioning
- Chapter 10. Planning
- Chapter 11. Change Management

Each chapter has a common structure for reading and reference:

- *Introduction*
- *History*: background of the topic
- *Generalization*: chapters are based on courses, or parts of courses, with descriptions that highlight the key ideas and learnings to be covered
- *Approach*: describes how the topic is taught and applied in practice
- *Conclusion*
- *Resources*: briefly annotated items for digging deeper into the topic.

History

Futurists recognize the value of history in illuminating the present and thus providing important guidance to understanding the future. The relevant background history of each topic is thus highlighted.

Generalization

Each course begins with a course generalization, a single statement that embodies the essential learning in that course. It guides the selection and development of the modules in the course, with each module elaborating and reinforcing the generalization.

Approach

The chapters cover a mix of how the topic is taught and how it is applied in practice, with the emphasis on the latter. The approach to teaching is consistent across topics and thus need not be fully repeated in each chapter. Our basic approach to learning consists of the following elements:

- *Instruction*: reading, lecture, discussion
- *Demonstration*: exercises, simulation
- *Activity*: practice, feedback
- *Assessment*: tests, products.

These elements are part of every good instructional design.

The emphasis on applications in practice reflects the curriculum's intent to prepare students to become professional practitioners in foresight. The applied emphasis does not mean that theory is neglected; simply that practice is primary with theory providing the supporting role. Not every student has this aim, but they do appreciate the practical orientation of the curriculum as they typically seek to apply their futures learning in their original career or setting or as new professional futurists.

Part I
Understanding

The chapters in this part lay out the conceptual underpinnings of the curriculum. They emphasize the mindset of future studies. They explore how futurists think about the future. The first three chapters provide frameworks through which to view and think about the future. Chapter 4, Social Change, gathers together and describes leading theories on how large-scale change actually happens. It is impossible to cleanly separate theory, method, and application in most fields and that is no different in foresight; as a consequence there will be some overlap.

- Chapter 1. Models of Change: explores the key concern of foresight, the study of change, in its various dimensions, as well as other key concepts such as eras, assumptions and alternative futures, and provides an overview of methods.
- Chapter 2. Systems Thinking: covers the fundamental skill of seeing how different aspects of the world relate and connect to one another.
- Chapter 3. Perspectives on the Future: introduces additional aspects of thinking about the future, including creativity and the role of values and newer aspects of futures thinking, including Causal Layered Analysis and Integral Futures.
- Chapter 4. Social Change: describes the various theories about how large-scale change takes place in and across societies and highlights the critical assumptions of each theory.

1
Models of Change

INTRODUCTION

This chapter introduces some of the key concepts underlying foresight, and provides a brief overview on methods. These concepts and methods permeate the curriculum and will reappear throughout the text. They are important enough to merit a separate treatment.

The prime foundational concept of foresight is that the discipline is about change. As a result, a good deal of attention is paid to exploring change in its various dimensions. The discipline starts with a basic description of change and how much change there is. From there, the various dimensions of change are explored: What types? Where does it come from? How broad does it spread? What speed? In other words, a synthesis of how change works.

A second key concept is that of alternative futures, which is used to understand how change could play out in the future. Futurists seek to identify a plausible range of potential future outcomes, rather than trying to predict the future. For reasons that are explained, it is viewed as impossible to get the future right on any sort of regular basis, but that a series of possibilities can be laid out in a way that enables planning and preparation.

Several related concepts are introduced as well. The role of uncertainty – as well as certainty – is explored and explained. Assumptions are central to dealing with uncertainty as it relates to the future. It is widely accepted that most forecasts of the future go awry based on faulty or hidden assumptions, thus the curriculum devotes significant time to identifying them.

Finally, a third major concept describes the two major divisions of foresight: (1) mapping the changes in the world; (2) influencing those changes toward a more preferable future. Futurists often refer to mapping as *inbound change*, the change happens to people. Forecasting is the approach used to anticipate and describe this form of change. Futurists often refer to influencing as *outbound change*, the change people produce themselves. Outbound change is the change people bring about through planning and subsequent action.

The two forms are interrelated. Forecasting helps one understand the future and discover options about how to best navigate it, and planning helps one identify one's preferred future option, develop plans for realizing it, and bringing it about through action. People's future and the future of organizations and societies is always a combination of what the world does and what people do about it. It is never just one or the other. People are not pure victims of the world; they always have some discretion. At the same time, people cannot have any future they want; the world limits their influence by what it does or does not allow.

The methods module shows the link between methods and concepts. The conceptual framework used to categorize methods builds upon the concept of inbound and outbound change. The framework sorts methods into six categories. The first three – framing, scanning and forecasting – relate to identifying and describing inbound change with the outcome of describing that change in the form of alternative futures. The second three – visioning, planning, and action – relate to outbound change by working toward creating one's preferred future, with context provided by the alternative futures produced by the first three steps.

UNDERSTANDING CHANGE

The world is changing at an apparently dizzying pace. The 20th Century produced upheavals that changed lives through changes in population, technology, the economy, the environment, governance, values, and so on – all on a global scale. These changes tore down traditions and shifted world views and structures by promoting a truly global economy, creating new forms of communication and changing fashion, lifestyles, parenting, politics, crime, climate, and an untold number of other things. And that was just the 20th Century! The 21st Century has already brought more astounding changes – the attacks on the World Trade Center, ubiquitous hand-held wireless devices, the greatest recession in 80 years, unprecedented political change in the Middle-East, and novel biological forms and treatments.

Each of these changes comes with weighty practical and ethical implications. For instance, British scientists have just created artificial sperm from human embryonic stem cells. Will babies now be born artificially? Will long-deceased fathers fertilize their widows? Will science make men unnecessary? Faced with this level of change, it is no wonder people are asking themselves how they should deal with change. How will it impact their life, their business, their relationships, and their future?

So understanding change is crucial for navigating the world. Several questions relating to change are explored below:

- What is change?
- How much change is there?
- What are the dimensions of change? (Where does it come from? How broad does it spread? How long does it take? And how fast does it occur?)
- In other words, how does change work?

What is change?

The Merriam-Webster online dictionary says that change means to make different in some particular way, to make radically different; to transform; to give a different position, course, or direction to. The very fact that the word can be found in seconds without even opening a book or going to the library is an example of change in our time. The printed dictionary (1604), the printing press (1450 in Europe), or even writing in the first place (4th millennium BC) represent profound changes over longer periods of time. Each of these events is a change according to the dictionary, but they differ in timing and scope.

How much change is there?

The expression "X has changed everything" is tossed about rather freely, but is it ever really true? Probably not. Big changes do bring noticeable change: Losing a job or a loved one, a serious injury, being promoted, moving to another country, winning the lottery – these are all significant changes in a person's life, but not everything changes as a result. The people affected are still who they are. Though they are different, much remains the same.

And the same can be said about organizations and even whole societies. New presidents, for instance, can produce profound change in their governments and countries, but even they cannot change everything.

The people in the government or the country are still the same, and many of the characteristics of the organization or country will outlast even the most powerful rulers.

Of course, an individual's death or a group's dissolution is the ultimate change, but only for that individual or group. Others may be affected by the change; but they go on, remaining the same in many ways.

So the first principle of understanding change is to recognize how much is actually changing, that some things remain the same even in the course of the most profound change. Change occurs in the midst of constants – what is changing and what is staying the same? The point is not to become so preoccupied with change that what is staying the same gets neglected.

However, people seem bound to focus on change more than on constants, perhaps for very good reason. The mind and even the primary senses automatically respond to change – the movement out of the corner of the eye, the bump in the night, the touch of a loved one. People are wired to pay attention to change.

On a social level, the media uses that tendency to bombard people with what is changing (the "news") hour by hour or even minute by minute. Most of these changes are unimportant or even trivial, but people pay attention to them anyway. By the same token, the media rarely reports the constants, even when they are important – the good, like the millions of people who are born, graduate from school, get married, go to work, do a good job each day, or the deplorable, like persistent malnutrition, disease, poverty and oppression around the world. Once in a while, perhaps, but it has to be news, and constants are not news.

The tendencies to overemphasize change can be countered by asking the question – what is changing and what is staying the same? That way, neither the change nor the constants are ignored.

The four dimensions of change

The next step in understanding change is cataloguing the various types of change. Early naturalists catalogued the various plants and animals in the meadow and thereby established the disciplines of biology and ecology, as did early astronomers, chemists, anatomists, and even sociologists in their own fields. Making distinctions is the beginning of making theory, so explaining a phenomenon begins with seeing its different manifestations.

Change occurs along four dimensions that combine to create many different types and varieties of change. The first dimension is categorical, meaning that the change is either of one type or another. It is where change comes from – its source. The other three are continual, meaning that they can take on any value between two extremes. The four dimensions of change are:

1. Sources and levels (from where?)
2. Time horizons (how long?)
3. Rates of change (how fast?)
4. Forms of change (which shape?)

1   Sources and levels (from where?)

Change comes from two sources: the world and ourselves. As discussed, change from the world is called inbound because it comes at individuals. Change that individuals produce themselves is called outbound because it influences what happens in the world.

These two sources of change (along with the constants) combine to create our future. Every difference in the future (change) is a combination of what the world does and what individuals do, or do not do, over time. So individuals cannot control the future because the world has a role, but they are not completely powerless either because they can influence the future. It is encouraging to realize that individuals can actually influence the future, but this knowledge also makes one careful because the world is changing at the same time. Just as it is prudent to look both ways before crossing the street, so one should watch how the world is changing (inbound) before acting to influence the future (outbound). Together the world's and the individual's actions create the future.

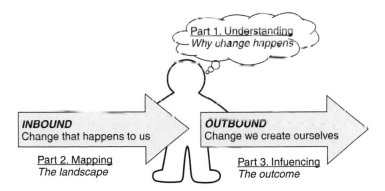

Figure 1.1   Sources of change....as covered in text

Long before the futures movement became mainstream, the famous sociologist C. Wright Mills described the relation between the immediate and the global environment in his book *The Sociological Imagination*.

Nowadays people often feel that their private lives are a series of traps. They sense that within their everyday worlds, they cannot overcome their troubles, and in this feeling, they are often quite correct. What ordinary people are directly aware of and what they try to do are bounded by the private orbits in which they live; their visions and their powers are limited to the close-up scenes of job, family, neighborhood; in other milieu, they move vicariously and remain spectators. And the more aware they become, however vaguely, of ambitions and of threats which transcend their immediate locales, the more trapped they seem to feel....

The well-being they enjoy, they do not usually impute to the big ups and downs of the societies in which they live. Seldom aware of the intricate connection between the patterns of their own lives and the course of world history, ordinary people do not usually know what this connection means for the kinds of people they are becoming and for the kinds of history-making in which they might take part.

As Mills says, understanding change in the immediate environment requires understanding change in the global environment. Individuals are each a part of history, their own history and the history of their times. And just as people in past times were part of a larger tapestry of change, so we are part of that historical tapestry as well. The significant difference is that today we have a perspective on the world that few had in the past.

In the study of history, one can abstract from the daily details of the world at the time and see what was going on in a larger sense. People today are no longer condemned to remain ignorant of that larger sense in their own time. Even though they cannot have the benefit of the long-term perspective that future generations will have, they do not have to focus only on their immediate environment either. They can connect their world and its future with the larger world. They can see their world as a microcosm of the larger world. And, most importantly, they can see change coming over the horizon, even before it affects them directly. That is the futures perspective, and it comes by paying attention to what is going on in the global environment and imagining how it might affect their immediate environment.

Mills continues:

What [people] need, and what they feel they need, is a quality of mind that will help them to use information and to develop reason in order to achieve lucid summations of what is going on in the world and of what may be happening within themselves. It is this quality, I am going to contend, that journalists and scholars, artists and publics, scientists and editors are coming to expect of what may be called the sociological imagination.... The first fruit of this imagination – and the first lesson of the social science that embodies it – is the idea that the individual can understand her own experience and gauge her own fate only by locating herself within her period, that she can know her own chances in life only by becoming aware of those of all individuals in her circumstances. In many ways it is a terrible lesson; in many ways a magnificent one.

This book is not teaching sociology; it is teaching about the future. But the sociological imagination, as described here by Mills, is also the futures perspective. For people to comprehend what might happen to them in the future, a broad understanding of what is going on in the world is necessary. So futurists focus on the global environment, not because it is more important but because it is often invisible, to most people at least. Futurists pay attention to the global environment just as everyone else is paying attention to their immediate environment.

Once in a while, however, every individual and group should look past the immediate environment and see what is coming in the global environment. They do not have to be futurists, but they should listen to them and to others who are monitoring change at that level. And, fortunately, people are not powerless in the face of those forces either. They cannot control the future, but they can influence it, most easily in their immediate environment but, in some cases, in the global environment as well.

The future changes at three levels: the organization, the organization's immediate environment, and the global environment. The global environment is often categorized into large sectors to help make sense of the massive amount of change going on there. One popular framework among futurists is called STEEP, which is an acronym for Social, Technological, Economic, Environmental, and Political aspects of society. Many include other sub-categories, such as demographic,

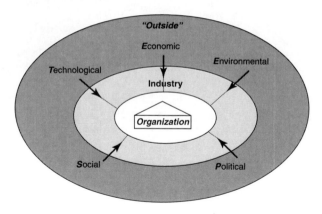

Figure 1.2   Levels of change

legal, military, informational and cultural, though few of those produce pronounceable acronyms! Each of the subdivisions of the STEEP environment is itself changing, and each one is affecting the others, too. So technology affects economy which affects the demography which affects the culture and on and on. It is impossible to know all of these changes, but knowing some of the more important ones is absolutely essential for anticipating the long-term future.

Organizations and individuals tend to be most interested in themselves! They live in an environment consisting of two levels – the immediate environment and the global environment. The immediate environment consists of those individuals, groups or parts of the physical environment that the individual or group interacts with on a regular basis. So for individuals, the immediate environment consists of family and friends, business or school acquaintances, the neighborhood, one's job or school.

The different levels in the ocean are a good illustration of the levels of change in society. The surface wind whips up the waves but only on the surface. When the wind stops, the waves stop. These are the daily changes that count as news. Beneath the waves, the tide moves the water in and out against the shore, but the surface wind does not affect the tide much at all. Those are the changes in the immediate environment. And then the deep ocean currents move huge amounts of water, but they move slowly and silently around the world. The surface winds and the tides have no impact on the deep currents. These are the deep changes going on in the global environment.

The distinction between the immediate and global environment is not very precise, nor does it have to be. Is the mayor of the town or the police officer in the neighborhood part of the immediate or the global environment? It depends. If the individual or group is involved in city politics, then the mayor would be part of that individual's immediate environment. Otherwise, probably not. By the same token, a flood in one's neighborhood is an event in one's immediate environment, but sea level rise is part of the global environment, unless one's neighborhood is on the coast.

The important thing about the levels of change is that inbound change comes to organizations and individuals from both environments. One's immediate environment affects the organization, for sure. But changes in the immediate environment rarely start there. More often, they are themselves affected by changes in the global environment. So people get and lose jobs (immediate environment) on the basis of the overall economy (global environment). They get sick from the air pollution in the city (immediate environment), or they lose a loved one in war or in traffic accidents (immediate environment) ultimately because of changes elsewhere (global environment).

Understanding long-term change requires a broad vision of what is going on in the world so people can understand what may happen to them in the future. Futurists focus on that global environment, not because it is more important, but because it is often ignored by most people. Futurists pay attention to the global environment while most everyone else is paying attention to their immediate environments.

2 Time horizons (how long?)

The physical horizon is the farthest one can see. In a valley, it is quite short; in a meadow or a desert much farther, and on top of a mountain or in an airplane, farther still. In the same way, the time horizon is that part of the future one chooses to focus on. Unlike the physical horizon, which is fixed, the time horizon is variable. One can focus on short-, medium- or long-term change.

The time horizon is usually expressed as a number of years, like next year or the next five years, or as an exact year, like 2020 or 2050. That sounds very precise and scientific, but the numbers should not be taken too seriously. No one really knows exactly what life will be like in 2020 or 2050 as opposed to 2019 or 2051. Rather those years simply indicate roughly how much change is expected to occur.

The time horizon also varies with the domain, which is the area of the future being focused on. Climate change, for instance, has a long time-horizon; it will take a long time for significant effects to occur. Political change, on the other hand, has a very short time-horizon, often equal to election cycles. Even though significant change can occur in a short time in any domain, like the fall of the Berlin Wall or the attacks of 9–11, they usually do not. So constants generally dominate the short term, and change and difference become more visible at longer time horizons.

Futurists focus on longer time horizons than most other professionals. They focus on long term because change in the global environment takes longer to affect people than change in their immediate environment does. The global environment will not affect most people for a while, but will impact eventually. It is common therefore for futurists to be talking about 2020 or 2030 these days, ten to twenty years into the future.

Some would argue that ten to twenty years is too long, that it is a waste of time to think that far into the future. Most strategic plans, for instance, only focus on three to five years, even though that is still a stretch for many people. The futurist response is that it is important to anticipate the future that far out because many of the decisions being made today have consequences for that time. Choosing a mate or a major, building a facility or a company, making an investment or buying a home – many of these will be successful or not depending on how the future turns out ten to twenty years from now.

Even more importantly, it takes that long for most people to influence the future in any significant way. Most individuals have little power to change the global environment; it's not in their sphere of influence. But exerting the power they do have, over long periods of time, toward a consistent goal, can produce marvelous results. Think of those historical figures who accomplished great things in government, or science, or art. In most cases, their greatest achievements came only after decades of work, exerting themselves toward the same goals over all that time. If one aspires to do great things – and who doesn't at some point in life? – then one must also be patient about how long it will take.

Futurists often refer to the 200-year present, a concept coined by sociologist Elise Boulding (1996). It suggests an appropriate timeframe for consideration of an issue that includes the lifespan of the oldest and the youngest individual alive at any given time. It provides a past, a present, and a future perspective. The purpose is to encourage a long-term thinking that also acknowledges the important role of the past in shaping the present and the future.

3   Rates of change (how fast?)

The rate of change, how fast things change, varies across a continuum from continuous, long periods of gradual change, to discontinuous, short periods of intense change. Most change is continuous, such as getting older, growing the economy, or warming the planet. As a result, people are pretty good at anticipating continuous change since they have experience with it and they have time to adapt. They can even predict the future of continuous change if it goes on long enough, sometimes using very sophisticated mathematical models and simulations.

The opposite is true of discontinuous change. It happens rarely so that people have little experience dealing with it. It happens so suddenly that there is little time to adapt. And it is generally unpredictable so one never knows when or how it will occur. It is the discontinuity, the sudden event that makes the future problematic. If the future were all a continuous path into the future, like a road or a river, it would not be nearly as difficult to deal with.

The past is full of discontinuous changes:

- In technology, the invention of the printing press, the steam engine, the electric light, the transistor, the birth control pill
- In the economy, the invention of currency, the establishment of the joint stock company, repeated crashes of the stock markets, and more recently the appearance of financial derivatives that contributed to the recent recession
- In governance (politics), various wars and revolutions, including the American Revolution, the assassination of political leaders, the passage of important legislation, like the Civil Rights Act or Medicare.

In fact, most of the study of history involves discontinuities. Historians are just as fascinated with sudden change as the news media is. It is curious therefore that people's overall image of the future, rather than being filled with events, is fundamentally "more of the same" – more people, more computers, more money, more problems. People do not see a future that is populated by discontinuous events, only by continuous changes.

The reason is that the future of continuous change can be predicted, but discontinuous change cannot. Since discontinuous events cannot be predicted, people fail to recognize that these events will be just as or even more important than the continuous changes that can be predicted. So the paradox remains: people see the past as full of interesting and important events, but they see the future as one long, continuous stretch, generally uninterrupted by events.

Futurists focus on potential future events and generally surprising developments since everyone else is focusing on continuous changes.

Not that they want to make people uncomfortable, but someone has to do the work that no one else is doing. Futurists do not know what discontinuous events lie in the future any more than anyone else does, but they guarantee that they are out there. So the futurist acts like the sailor on watch, aware that there might be rocks or reefs under the water, unseen yet there nevertheless.

So in sum, futurists are focusing on those aspects of change that most of the rest of society does not focus on – the global environment, the long-term horizon, and the potential discontinuous changes.

4   Forms of change (which shape?)

The last dimension relates to how change occurs over time. The forms of change are represented below as four graphs of continuous change and one of discontinuous change.

A. Linear. This is the most commonly known and simplest form of change. It's typically studied in algebra – the famous equation is $y = mx + b$ – and in statistics. When graphed, linear change forms a line. Unfortunately, straight lines never occur in nature or in change over time. Einstein, in fact, showed that even space itself is curved.

In fact, thinking linearly can get one into trouble when trying to create change (outbound). People mistakenly assume that the impact of their effort is proportional to the amount of effort that is put in. (How many times have students who received a lower grade than they expected said that they "worked very hard during the course"?) So if one expends twice as much effort, they should get twice as much change in return? Alas, life rarely works out that way. In many cases, one can expend enormous effort and get little or no return; in other

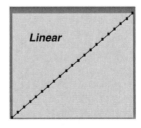

Figure 1.3   Linear change

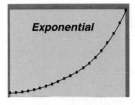

Figure 1.4   Exponential change

cases, even a minor effort can produce a tremendous change, such as when a butterfly in the Amazon can create a hurricane in the Atlantic Ocean (for more on this, see Chapter 2 on Systems Thinking). Most change is not proportional to the effort expended, and thinking so can be quite misleading.

B. Nonlinear (exponential). People make investments for compound interest; not equal amounts in equal times (simple interest), but equal per cents in equal times. So one buys a $1,000 Certificate of Deposit at 5% annual interest and gets $50 at the end of the year. If that gets reinvested, one now has $1,050 in the Certificate which returns $52.50 at the end of the second year. And so on.

The mathematics of exponential growth can be misleading. There is the famous story of the Maharaja who was so grateful to the Wise Man that he told the Wise Man to name his price. The Wise Man said that all he wanted was for the Maharaja to place one grain of rice on the first square of a chess board and double it for each square after that. So, two on the second, four on the third, eight on the fourth, and so on. The Maharaja readily agreed because he thought he was getting off cheap. Actually he went bankrupt because, before he got to the 64th square, he already had to spend all the grains of rice that had ever been grown in the history of human civilization! So beware of exponential growth!

Exponential growth – or decline – is probably the most common form of continuous social change. It describes the growth of populations (both human and non-human), technologies (such as the Internet), economies, or political power. But nothing goes on forever, even exponential growth. Just as the Maharaja could not possibly pay the price he agreed to, so the planet will never contain the 100 billion people that would result if current growth were to continue for the next 180 or so years. Something will happen to stop or reverse that change before it gets out of control. So exponential change goes on for a while, but not forever, and the end often surprises people.

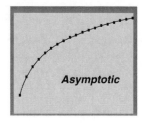

Figure 1.5 Asymptotic change

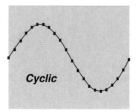

Figure 1.6 Cyclic change

C. Nonlinear (asymptotic). Another common form of change is one that approaches a limit. World records in sports are an example of asymptotic change, also called logarithmic or the law of diminishing returns. Swimmers break the world record by thousandths of a second. They rarely if ever leap ahead by a whole second. Even though they are much better trained than swimmers were ten or twenty years ago, they can only swim so fast until they approach the limit of human capacity. They can spend years getting ready for the Olympics, and they are grateful if they shave a half-second off their time.

As with the other forms, the law of diminishing returns can also fool people. Take a sales meeting discussing a product that is experiencing increasing sales but the rate of increase of sales is decreasing – classic asymptotic change. One side looks at the absolute increase and judges that the product is doing fine; the other side looks at the relative decrease and believes that the product is nearing the end of its life cycle. Both are correct. They are just using different measures to judge the health of the product.

D. Nonlinear (cyclic). The last type of change to be considered is cyclic change. Cyclic change oscillates between a maximum and minimum. It is not as regular as the classic sine wave depicted here, but it does increase for a while, then decrease, then increase, over and over again.

As with the other forms of change, cyclic change can be deceptive because for short periods of time it looks like a trend, increasing or decreasing. Then people are surprised when it reverses. They expected it to continue in that same direction.

Political power tends to behave in a cyclic fashion. One political persuasion or party (liberal or conservative, for instance) gains support and power, but after a while it loses favor and the other party gains power. The tendency for companies to centralize and decentralize seems to follow a cyclic pattern as well.

E. Discontinuous (S-curve). The four shapes above involve continuous change. Discontinuous change is captured by the shape of an S-curve. S-curves are not covered in ordinary math or stat classes even though they are a common and useful way of describing change.

The S-curve (called that because it looks like an elongated S) has three distinct phases:

1. The old era that most people expect to continue (along the bottom of the graph)
2. The transition period that follows a discontinuous event (the little explosion)
3. The new era that eventually emerges from the transition (along the top of the graph).

The S-curve actually fools people in two ways. The first is that people expect the existing era to continue for a long time, if not forever. They do not realize that the era has the potential for tremendous change, rather quickly, following a discontinuous event. The second way is that, once in the transition period people expect that to go on for a long time as well. So in the 1950 people thought the automobile and airplane era would result in flying cars. In the 1970s, some oil companies

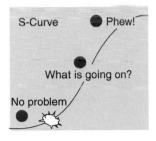

Figure 1.7 S-curve

thought that the price of oil would reach $100 a barrel, but it barely got above $40. Today some people believe that brains will be downloaded into computers someday. Is that extension of the transition period going too far?

The reason for reviewing these shapes of change is to not be fooled by how things are changing, but the important lessons are:

- There is no linear change, so do not use that one
- Exponential change can speed up unexpectedly, but it also does not go on forever
- Asymptotic change is still increasing, but the change is actually coming to an end
- Cyclic change looks like a trend until it reverses
- And finally and most importantly, discontinuous events begin the transition from one system to another, but that transition does not go on forever either.

A model of change: Punctuated equilibrium

Most people believe that their lives and society are relatively stable, and they are usually right. Stuff gets done. And when things get a little out of whack, usually something comes along to put things back on a steady course. So one might have to get the car fixed, but that's what savings are for. Or one might experience a higher return on one's investments and so buy a new car. That's the description of equilibrium: some change, but nothing too great, and whatever change does occur tends to die off after a while. But that's not the whole story.

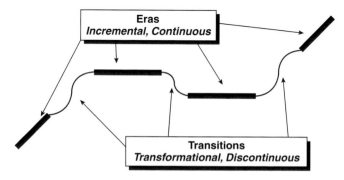

Figure 1.8   Punctuated equilibrium

Punctuated equilibrium

Equilibrium is the product of continuous change and the minor adjustments one makes to move forward. Once in a while, however, one encounters a discontinuous change, something that really upsets the equilibrium – a lost job, illness or, on the positive side, a promotion, marriage, or birth of a child. No equilibrium there. This is really different!

This type of change is called punctuated equilibrium, a term proposed by Niles Eldredge and Stephen Jay Gould to describe the episodic character of biological evolution. Punctuated equilibrium is a different model of change from incrementalism or gradualism, as proposed by Darwin. As brilliant as he was in articulating the theory of natural selection, Darwin assumed that evolutionary change was continuous. In fact, he used Leibniz's famous phrase *Natura non facit saltum* – Nature does not jump. But when biologists dug up the fossil record from the bottom of the ocean, they found that it did. They found long periods of relative stability among species interspersed with brief periods of significant change. That record led Niles Eldredge and Stephen Jay Gould to coin the term "punctuated equilibrium" in their famous article in 1972. That term applies to changes in society as well.

Eras

So it is equilibrium most of the time interrupted, or punctuated, by a few sudden changes. And each punctuation changes the equilibrium substantially. The equilibrium periods are called "eras," a term borrowed from history. Historians will speak about the Napoleonic or the Victorian era. The Renaissance, the Depression and the Cold War were

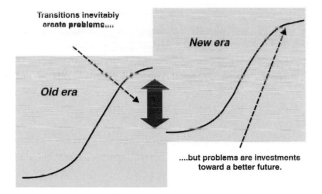

Figure 1.9 Transitions between eras

eras as well. Eras are periods of relative stability and coherence, they have a distinct identity, and they begin and end with a discontinuity. So the era of the Depression, in the United States at least, began with the crash of the stock market in October 1929 and ended with the attack on Pearl Harbor in December 1941. The Cold War began when the Soviets exploded their first nuclear weapon in August 1949 and ended when the Berlin Wall fell in August 1989, almost 40 years to the day later.

Transitions are troubled periods of confusion and conflict. Few people like the transition period because the familiar is passing and the unknown is approaching. Joseph Schumpeter, the Austrian economist, called these transitions "waves of creative destruction," where spurts of innovation destroyed established organizations and yielded new ones. The better descriptive would perhaps be "waves of destructive creativity" because the destruction happens before the creativity.

The good news about the transition is that transitions do not last forever. A new equilibrium eventually emerges into a new era. The bad news is not knowing where one is on the transition curve and therefore how long before the new era emerges. More important than the timing, however, is what the characteristics of the new era will be. How will it be different from the old era?

The answer to that question is not easy. As this book was being written the transition to mobile computing was underway. The iPhone and the whole bevy of other hand-held, wireless devices were changing the way people communicate. It is clear that almost everyone will have one of these devices in the future. And some of their new uses, such as paying bills and navigating through cities, are already apparent. Other uses are not as clear. For instance, will people get ads every time they pass by a store? Will people need to use their devices while driving? Will people be able to steal my identity from this device? Those who get a sense of the characteristics of the new era before others do have an obvious advantage. And that is part of what anticipating change is all about. While the characteristics of the new era cannot be predicted with any certainty, one can imagine and prepare for some of them nevertheless.

But the old era does not go away quietly. People are comfortable with the era that they know and understand. Change grows uncomfortable, if not downright dangerous. Imagine how a person from the past would feel if they were suddenly thrust into the current era – the era of cell phones and email, the threat of global terrorism, of stress, of financial crisis; they would quickly seek refuge back in their own time. Yet also imagine a person of the 21st Century trying to live in an age without telephones, automobiles, air travel, penicillin, or the Internet; they would be miserable as well. Future children will be happy in the world in which they live, even though people in the present might not want to live there themselves.

And if not everything changes at once, what will change and what will not? Which elements of the old era will remain and which will change? Most people's reaction to the benefits of the new era is, "Yes... but." Yes, it will be great, but it also means some things will have to change. Sorting through what remains and what needs to change is one of the most difficult and tricky parts of navigating the transition from one era to the next.

So granted that punctuated equilibrium is the correct model of long-term change, why are there punctuations in the first place? Why is change not simply continuous, getting better all the time, as Darwin thought? The reason is that the era matures and settles into a successful way of being. Change in the new era takes time to get going, to get things right. But once right, the era tends to level off into relatively modest continuous change. The era becomes subject to the law of diminishing returns; more change is harder and harder to achieve even with increasing effort. So one can push and sweat and spend more money and time, but the more mature the system in that era, the less good it will do. One cannot make the system do much more than it is currently doing. In other words, it has reached its inherent capacity for performance.

Figure 1.10 provides a simple example showing different modes of transportation. It's clear that one can ride a bicycle faster than one

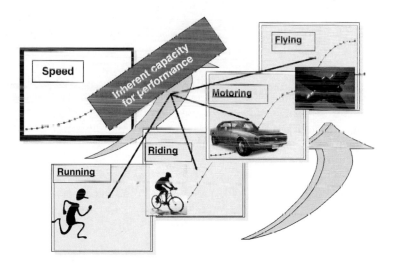

Figure 1.10 Successive eras

can run, but not faster than a car. Even Lance Armstrong will never go as fast as a car. The bicycle has an inherent capacity for performance (speed) that even the most high-tech bicycle ridden by the most highly trained athlete cannot exceed. But the same is true for any mature system, such as a business or an education system or a military system. The longer the era goes on, the closer it gets to its inherent capacity for performance, and the more difficult it is to create significant improvement (breakthrough performance). At that point, the only way to create significant change is to radically alter the system, in fact to create a new era.

That sounds simple enough, but it's not as easy as it seems. The old era is comfortable to most people; they know how to be successful there. While they admit it's not perfect, they are afraid of changing it too much. And the process of change is not going to be easy. Figure 1.10 illustrates how the new era doesn't just pick up where the old era leaves off. Rather there is a short-term decline in performance, a gap, between the mature phase of the old era and the beginning of the new. For instance, if one wants a new kitchen or a new road, the old kitchen or the old road must be torn up first. If one wants a new healthcare or education system, one has to first dismantle some parts of the old system to make way for the new. In general, getting from a lower mountaintop to a higher mountaintop begins first by climbing down before climbing up. But nobody wants to climb down!

Deciding which parts to dismantle and which to keep is not easy. Nor is it easy to get people to give up the old parts while trying to maintain enough performance to prevent the system from failing altogether. The old parts work; they are still working. "Why give them up?" they say. What is more, the new era is new, and learning something new always takes time. The gap always involves costly mistakes and a level of disorganization that is uncomfortable. And there is no guarantee that abandoning the old era will result in the breakthrough performance promised in the new era anyway. One might destroy something that is okay and not get the glorious future after all. What a bummer!

So people resist discontinuous change for good reason. Nevertheless, changing from one era to another is necessary sooner or later. The only choice is when to make the change. Most people prefer to delay the inevitable, hoping that the change will not be necessary or at least not during their time. But waiting too long can be fatal, too. The longer one waits, the more chance there is that the world will come in and say, "Game over," and shut the system down. That is what happened to the Soviet Union. They waited too long, and the system ultimately collapsed. The Chinese, on the other hand, began changing before the system had become totally useless – a much more successful approach.

While futurists cannot tell when the present era will end, they monitor the global environment for signs of change and imagine how it might end. Even if they "get it wrong," people still have to come to terms with the fact that the current era will end eventually. Should they take on board the input of the futurist projection, they will be more prepared to make the change when it actually comes, because they do not mistakenly assume that the present will go on indefinitely. The longer the current era goes on, the easier it is to confuse it with "reality" – simply the way things are and the way they will always be. Foresight guards against that misconception. Even "reality" is temporary in the futures perspective!

ALTERNATIVE FUTURES

Futurists use the concept of alternative futures to understand how change might play out in the future. It provides a means for dealing with what can be known about the future, including the role of prediction and certainty. It also relies on assumptions, with each alternative future having different assumptions at their core. The concepts come together in the cone of plausibility, a visual tool for clarifying alternative futures, which shall be revisited later in the chapter.

"What can we know about the future?"

The old phrase "Look before you leap" suggests it's a good idea to know about the future before trying to change it. That doesn't mean one has to study the future before deciding what to do; however, it does mean that one needs to study the future before finalizing plans and definitely before initiating actions to change it.

That sounds obvious, but few people or organizations do it that way. The beginning of a typical planning session begins with, "OK, what do we want to accomplish?" And then "OK, now that we've decided that, how are we going to do it?" People rarely stop to look out the window, so to speak, to see what the weather (the world) might be doing. That works a lot of the time or else there would not be so many successful people and organizations. But it's risky. It assumes that they know how the world works and that it will work that way throughout the time period of the plan.

The assumption that they know how the world works is a pretty good one if the people in the organization have talked about the world and have come to an agreement about how it works. Most organizations haven't done that nearly enough. Therefore, different people probably have different ideas about how it works. Everybody thinks they are talking about the same thing, but they are not. They are using different mental models. Some of those models are pretty good; some not so. The point is that the lack of a general discussion about how the world works will make it doubly difficult to change it.

The assumption that the world won't change before the planning period is over is also pretty good if the plan is short term or if the organization's environment is fairly static. The assumption is not very good, however, for plans with longer time horizons in more turbulent environments. In those cases, the world is bound to change in significant ways – ways that could upset the plan altogether. What is more, significant change can occur suddenly even in apparently benign environments.

(Not) predicting the future

When most people are asked to describe the future, the first thing they do is predict what is going to happen. Prediction is a well-known, scientific process. It is taught in school, mostly in science class. It has worked for centuries in everything from stars to sub-atomic particles; from rocks to species.

The problem comes when people are thrown into the mix. Just like the physical sciences, the social sciences (sociology, anthropology, political science, economics and the rest) try to base their conclusions on observations (evidence). The big difference, however, is that the social sciences have no single unified theory of how the world works. Instead, they have many theories, too many perhaps, in a modern day Tower of Babel. So they do not agree on the fundamental influences on human behavior (free will or external conditions), on the motivations for action (selfishness or altruism), or even on the fundamental unit of analysis (the individual or the group). They even disagree about whether such an overall theory is possible (modernism versus postmodernism).

The role of observation in this cacophony of theories is frankly a minor one because different observers will draw different conclusions from the same observations depending on their fundamental theory. And not only will they offer different explanations for the same phenomena, more importantly for our purpose, they will make different predictions of how that phenomena will develop over time. No doubt that social science has made tremendous contributions to the understanding of human behavior, but it is lousy at predictions.

Nevertheless, most social scientists believe that someday they will have such a theory; that they will be able to predict human behavior as well as the behavior of a planet or the ideal gas can be predicted. That belief was illustrated dramatically in Isaac Asimov's classic *Foundation* trilogy many years ago. Hari Seldon, a mathematics professor, develops psychohistory, allowing him to predict the future in probabilistic terms, but of course that was fiction. Others disagree, and that debate will continue until such a theory is developed or until people give up trying because they find out why they can't.

For the time being, therefore, the fact remains that the future cannot be predicted with any degree of accuracy. Everyone knows this, but few know what to do with it. They acknowledge the fallibility of their predictions, but they go right on making them anyway. For the most part, they ignore even the grossest uncertainties, hoping that the uncertainties will not upset their predictions.

Futurists approach the future with a completely different attitude. First of all, they acknowledge that the future does emerge as the result of a causal chain of events, just as other social scientists do. Thus, if one knew the causal chain, one could predict what would happen fairly accurately. They differ, however, in that they believe that those forces are not well enough known to use scientific prediction as a guide to the future. The uncertainties involved in the long-term future are simply too overwhelming to disregard. In other words, they believe that what is not known about the long-term future is larger and more important than what is known.

Social scientists, meanwhile, continue to focus on prediction even when the uncertainties are part of the natural world. They believe, "We'll figure this out someday if we keep trying." Maybe. But that assumption treats uncertainty as something to be overcome rather than as a reality to be dealt with. The result is to continue to predict the future no matter how flawed the knowledge usually is. "We'll figure this out someday." The futurist's alternative is to focus on how much is not known and learn to deal with that rather than waiting for the day when prediction becomes useful. The future might be predictable some day, but for right now, it isn't, and that's the world people live in. Deal with it!

If one accepts the fact that uncertainty about the long-term future is larger and more important than what is known about it, what then? What does one do with that uncertainty? The sticking point is that uncertainty in science is either something to be measured, as in statistical uncertainty, or overcome, as in mysteries and puzzles to be solved.

But in order to deal with uncertainty, another fundamental assumption about the future has to be overturned – namely, how many futures are there? That seems like a silly question. The answer, of course, is one. All the uncertainties will be resolved when the future finally arrives; all the possibilities will collapse to one present.

But that was not the real question. How many futures are there *before* it becomes the present? How many *possible* futures are there? That's a different story – very many, perhaps even an infinite number. Most people know that, too. Nevertheless, they believe that anticipating the future begins with discovering the *real* future, the one that will eventually become the present, and rejecting all the rest. Then the question becomes: is that a useful strategy? In other words, is there one real future, one that can be known today before it happens? The futurist answer is a definite "no." There might be a real future in some abstract, philosophical sense, but practically there is no way of knowing what it is before it occurs. Figure 1.11 notes there are four types of futures that futurists consider. The widest possible set is those futures that are at least mathematically possible. A smaller set is those futures that are plausible, that is, the "story" of that future hangs together in a reasonable and coherent way. Smaller still are the probable futures, which could emerge from present trends (discussed in depth in Chapter 7), and finally the preferable futures that one hopes will happen and builds visions around (discussed in depth in Chapter 8).

In other words, it is impossible to predict the future. So looking for the one future that will become the present is a futile and useless exercise. "Don't waste your time," the futurist says. "There is a better way."

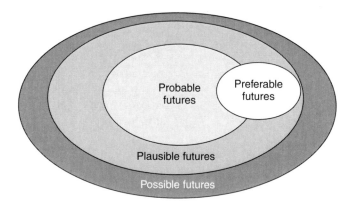

Figure 1.11   Four types of futures

They recommend instead that one accepts that the future one can know is really plural – that is, the future(s) – the set of all possible futures. That is a big assumption to accept, but once done, it offers enormous benefit. And it's been done before, by very smart people. The founders of quantum mechanics (Bohr, Heisenberg, Schrödinger) had to come to accept that matter at the tiniest level was inherently unpredictable, that one could not know the position and velocity of a particle without observing and hence disturbing it. That fundamental assumption was so revolutionary that even Einstein could not accept it. He said, "God does not roll dice with the universe." Despite his resistance, almost all physicists today accept that probability and uncertainty are inherent characteristics of the universe.

Some have tried to draw a link between quantum uncertainty and the uncertainty in the macro world. There may well be such a link, but one doesn't have to depend on it to know that prediction is impossible and that uncertainty dominates knowledge of the future, particularly in the long run. One simply has to admit that one doesn't know how to predict the future today, which in turn frees one from the tyranny of having to predict the future in order to know it. One is free to know *all* the futures as possibilities rather than having to argue over which one will become the present. One is free to examine them on how probable they may be, on what their implications would be, and on which one prefers.

In fact, grammarians distinguish between the language of fact (certainty) and the language of possibility (uncertainty) in the "mood" of the verb. "I will go to the city" is indicative mood; "I might go to the city" is the subjunctive. Notice the difference. One is strong, certain, factual; the other appears weak, uncertain, tentative. The indicative represents a strong commitment to do something, but the subjunctive might be truer, particularly about things that take a long time to occur and over which one has no control, such as the long-term future!

The etymology of these two words is also instructive. "Indicative" comes from the Latin word *dicare*, to proclaim. "Subjunctive" comes

Indicative	Subjunctive
~~Will~~	May
~~Must~~	Might
~~Should~~	Could

Figure 1.12 Language of plausibility

from *sub*, beneath, and *jungere*, to join. Taken together, it means to join beneath – in other words, to subordinate or "to treat as of less value or importance" (Merriam-Webster). Could anything be clearer? The indicative mood – "The war will end in two months, and the economy will recover" – is a proclamation for all to hear. The subjunctive form – "The war might end in two months, and the economy might recover" – is subordinated, treated as of lesser value. So the stronger language of fact is preferred, even about the future, to the weaker language of possibility. Bertrand de Jouvenel (1967) in *The Art of Conjecture* said, "There are no future facts." Pretty obvious, even though most people speak about the future (using the indicative mood) as if there were and even when the "facts" (predictions) they proclaim are more often wrong than right.

"OK," someone says, "I admit that there are many possible futures. But aren't some more probable than others? And can't we take the most probable future as our prediction and reject the less probable ones?" Yes, that is, in fact, what most people do, but they shouldn't. That strategy is called "the best estimate" or the "most likely future." It is usually true that one of the many possible futures is more probable than any of the others, but should the focus be on just that one?

A more familiar future is represented by rolling dice. (Thanks, Einstein, for bringing it up!) A pair of dice produces eleven possible outcomes, from two to twelve. One of those (7) is the most probable, more probable than any of the others. The dice can produce a 7 in three  ways (6–1, 5–2, 4–3) and the other numbers in only one or two ways. But the actual chance of rolling a 7 is exactly one in six, which is more than any of the others, but it is *un*likely in an absolute sense. Over the long run, a person will roll approximately one 7 in every six rolls. Would you therefore predict that a 7 will come up each and every time? Yes, because it will be right more often than any other number, even though it will still be *wrong* five times of out six!

The problem is that people think they should pick just one outcome, one future from among all the possibilities. Dice are simple enough in that there are multiple outcomes, some more probable than others. It would be foolish to predict just one of those outcomes each time because it would be wrong many times more than it would be right. But isn't that what is done in asking for a single prediction of the future?

People who use forecasts, such as decision-makers and policy-makers, routinely ask, "What is your best estimate?" "What is most likely to occur?" "Just tell me what you think is *really* going to happen?" They would not ask for a single prediction at the dice table or the roulette wheel, but they make that mistake every day in business and government. If the probability of a simple 7 is only one in six, how less likely are the most likely outcomes in the marketplace, in the voting booth, even in our own families? So the futurist will say that it is better to know the many futures rather than just the most likely one because that one isn't very likely at all.

A more scientific discipline than foresight came to the same conclusion many years ago. In the 1950s, way back in the age of black and white television, TV weather forecasters predicted the weather over the next few days. "It's going to rain" or "It's not going to rain." They were usually right, but often wrong – wrong enough that they lost the respect of their audience. People complained how little the forecaster knew about the weather. But then the profession came up with an ideal solution. It's called "the 20% chance of rain." Rather than predict rain or shine, they gave a probability of rain with an implied probability of shine. They forecast alternative futures; and given the precision of their discipline, they could even put a probability on it. And the complaints stopped because they could no longer be accused of being "wrong." Presumably they were keeping track so that it did rain 20% of the time when they said it would, but the public didn't know one way or the other.

The purpose of this story is not that the weather forecasters silenced the complaints, though that's a nice thing, too. The point is that they were giving the public a more accurate description of the real future than just a single prediction, a description that included a set of futures (two in this case). They do the same for hurricane predictions. The expanding cone of the hurricane's track on the weather map provides a picture of the alternative futures of the hurricane's landfall.

Certainty

If people should not predict the future, then what should they do? The advice is to deal with the future as a set of alternatives, but how to do that? There is a trick, as there is with most skills, and this trick is to focus on what is *not* known about the future in addition to what is known. Unfortunately, focusing on what is not known is surprisingly difficult in

> "Doubt is an unpleasant state, but certainty is a ridiculous one" – Voltaire (*Jeuer*, 1999)

society because people are taught to talk only about what they do know. "If you do not know, keep your mouth shut!" In other words, don't appear foolish by admitting ignorance.

On the flip side, being clear and precise is a good way to persuade people that one is right; it's the way to win arguments, get people to listen, or to assert power in a group. The language of certainty trumps the language of possibility in most cultures – even though those who are the most certain about things are also the ones who are most often wrong.

The rule about being certain is first learned in school and carried over to work. Students are usually encouraged to ask questions in school. When they do, they are admitting that they do not know something. But when the teacher answers, they often get the feeling that should have known it, that it was a *stupid* question because the teacher always knows the answer (or at least appears to). Does the teacher ever not know? Of course not. "Good teaching means that you know everything, right? Is that true or does it just appear that way?" Does the teacher – even a really good one – know everything about the subject? Probably not. But do they ever model what it's like to *not* know something, to not be sure, to be confused, or even to be wrong. Hardly ever. So if good teachers are their model, students grow up with the belief that they must know everything (or at least appear to) to be successful.

The rule about certainty becomes even more important at work. When was the last time someone influential and well respected said, "I don't know that." The reason they are influential and well respected is that they seem to know everything. But is that possible? Or are they like the teacher, who knows a lot, but who puts up a good front when they don't?

No one is being accused of doing anything wrong here. All the people in this discussion are good people. They are not consciously deceiving anyone. Rather they are playing the role that society asks them to play. Everyone plays roles: parent–child, teacher–student, boss–employee, friend, spouse, customer, and so on.

Part of the role of being successful in society then is to know for sure what is going to happen in the future. Even though knowing (predicting) the future is impossible, it's still part of the role, so it is done anyway. There is no deception involved. Usually one is not even aware that they are playing a role. They are just "being themselves." They do not know that they are appearing to do something that is impossible. They really believe that one can know what is going to happen in the future.

They are sure of that knowledge because a part of the process of coming to that knowledge is hidden. Knowledge of the future is always a conclusion (an inference) that is made based on experience and other knowledge that one has (evidence). The future cannot be observed directly, just as one cannot observe the inside of the sun, the behavior of an electron, or the lifestyle of a pre-historic tribe. In all those cases, things that can be observed (data) are used to help understand things that cannot be observed.

But there is a catch. No piece of data, no observation automatically leads to one and only one conclusion. There are always alternatives. Those alternatives are basis for novels and short stories "with a twist." The twist is that things are not always as they appear, that the "obvious" conclusion turns out to be wrong. The guy with the gun in his hand is obviously the shooter. Well, maybe or maybe not. (Notice the subjunctive mood coming back!)

The skill of evaluating the evidence for a conclusion is called critical thinking. More is said about that in Chapter 3, Perspectives, and Chapter 7, Forecasting. For now it needs to be pointed out that the hidden part of drawing conclusions – the reason that observations always support at least two conclusions and the reason that two people can draw different conclusions from the same observations – are the assumptions one must make in order to draw the conclusion in the first place.

Assumptions

An assumption is a belief, usually about how the world works. It is not a fact, and it cannot be proven or disproven. Therefore, one is not forced to accept one assumption over another. Rather one is allowed to choose certain assumptions as true and others as false. So, for instance, one chooses to believe that people are fundamentally good or not. One chooses to believe that people are free and mostly responsible for their actions or they are constrained and conditioned by their environment. One chooses to believe a democratic government generally does good for a society or does not. And so on. Of course, reasonable (and good) people will disagree about these assumptions since they cannot be proven or disproven.

The problem is not the choosing of these assumptions. The problem is choosing them unconsciously. One does not usually know one's assumptions nor has one evaluated them in light of one's alternatives to see which ones might be more reasonable. And that's too bad because assumptions play a crucial role in what is known about the world and its future.

It turns out that when the assumptions are wrong, the conclusions are wrong. It's usually the assumptions that are at fault. "I told the kids to turn off the water, and now the tub has overflowed!" Assumption: Kids do what they are told. Well, not always, even though they usually do. So the assumption is usually true, but not always. And not enough to be certain that it is true each and every time.

Assumptions get a bad reputation since they are often wrong. As a result some recommend that one should never make an assumption. In the early 20th Century, a whole philosophical school, called Logical Positivism, was built on just that recommendation – that scientists make no assumptions – that they stick only to the facts (observations). Sounds good. But the problem is that if they do not make any assumptions, they could not draw any conclusions either. So the Positivists could say what they observed very accurately, but they had to stop there. They could not say what it meant or what else they knew as a result. Pretty boring. So that philosophy failed!

Anything that one says about the future is necessarily a conclusion since the future cannot be observed directly. There are no future facts. And drawing a conclusion necessarily requires making assumptions. Therefore, one has to make assumptions to say anything about the future. But that's where the trouble starts. Since assumptions are beliefs, not facts or well-supported conclusions, they are highly uncertain. That does not mean they are wrong, but they can be, much more often than those who make predictions claim. And since they are also hidden from others and often from the one making the prediction, they are the source of considerable and unrecognized uncertainty about the future.

Let's examine a prediction to see how this works. In June 2008, the US Census Bureau projected that the world's population would reach 9 billion people in 2040.[1] The Census Bureau forecasters are very good at what they do, and they would be the last ones to claim that population will be exactly that number at exactly that year. They have been wrong before, and they will probably be wrong again. In fact, since the 1950s all the projections for the size of the world's population in the future have been too high, up to 7% too high for a forecast made in 1968. And forecasting the population of specific countries is even less accurate.

---

[1] See http://www.census.gov/ipc/www/idb/worldpop.html) and for a discussion of the role of assumptions, see http://www.census.gov/ipc/www/idb/estandproj.html#ASSUMP.

The Census Bureau missed the actual size of the populations of specific countries in the year 2000 by an average of more than 10% when it made projections in 1987, just 13 years before the forecast horizon.[2] And demographic forecasts are among the most accurate in futures studies.

But what is the reason for the consistent overestimate of the world's population? Assumptions! The forecasters in the 1970s predicted that the world's population would grow more slowly in the future than it had since World War II, and they were right. The reason for the slower growth was that countries were getting richer, and richer countries had slower growth. So they projected where population in rich countries would be in 2000, and reduced the growth rate by that much. So far so good, except that they did not reduce it enough.

Another assumption was that the only influence on the growth rate was how rich a country was, but that assumption was wrong. As it turned out, an equally important influence on population growth is the education of women. If woman are educated, they have more say in the decision to have children or not, and they tend to want fewer children than men do. After all, they are the ones bearing and taking care of them!

The errors in these forecasts were not large, and no harm was done because they were too high, but they are an excellent example of how important assumptions are even in population forecasting, one of the most sophisticated forecasting topics.

Types of futures: The cone of plausibility

Table 1.1 shows how three forces of change that combine to create the future are often depicted as an image of a cone expanding through time (Figure 1.13). The baseline future is the center-line of the cone; the plausible futures are all the other regions of the cone, and the preferred future is one area of the cone selected as the vision or goal for an individual or a group. The purpose of traditional predictive forecasting is to establish the center of the cone; the purpose of scenario forecasting is to explore the other major regions of the cone – other plausible futures; the purpose of visioning and goal setting is to select a region to use as the guide for decision and action.

The cone has limits, however. It does not include all *possible* futures. That would be too much to handle. Rather it includes plausible futures,

---

[2] Thanks to the contributors J. Bongaarts, & R. Bulatao, (eds) (2000) *Beyond Six Billion: Forecasting the World's Population*. Panel on Population Projections, Committee on Population, National Research Council.

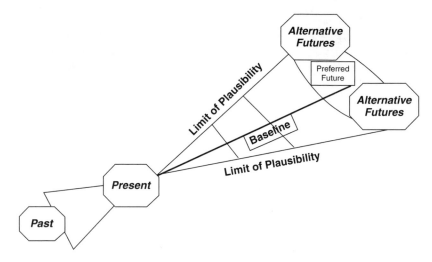

Figure 1.13   Cone of plausibility
Source: Based on Charles Taylor, Army War College.

those with a probability of occurrence somewhat larger than zero. The distinction is purely subjective, but the operational definition of a plausible future is that someone could tell a story about how it comes about and reasonable people would admit that they could see it occurring. The story does not contain any fantastical leaps of imagination or violations of the known rules of science. There are plenty of plausible futures to consider without getting into all the possible ones, too.

People can move toward their preferred future in two ways:

- outside-in, scanning and understanding their future and then deciding how to proceed through it
- inside-out, establishing a vision or a goal and taking the best path to it.

Each approach uses the same sets of tools, but in different order. The inside-out approach begins with research and forecasting, then goes to visioning and goal setting and finally ends with planning and action. The outside-in approach begins with visioning and goal setting, then assesses the future environment through research and forecasting, and finally ends with planning and action.

The processes are iterative because the future is always changing, requiring continuous scanning and learning which, in turn, may lead to

Table 1.1 Types of futures

These forces of change....	lead to these types of futures...	Characterized by this type of thinking.....	and best understood by these techniques
Trend. Continuous change of some variable over time, often described by a mathematical function, such as the aging of society.	*Probable.* Trends lead to the probable future (aka baseline future). It is expected and relatively predictable assuming nothing surprising happens.	Logical, scientific, and quantitative.	Historical analogy; trend extrapolation; trend analysis.
Event (discontinuities). A sudden change in some condition, usually closing one era and opening a new one, such as the collapse of the Soviet Union.	*Plausible.* Events lead to plausible futures (aka alternative futures) that could happen instead of the baseline.	Speculative and imaginative.	Scenarios; simulations.
Choice. Decisions and the actions to implement those decisions, such as Roosevelt's decision to create Social Security	*Preferable.* Choices lead to the preferred future. Individuals and groups strive for their preferred future.	Visionary and empowered.	Visioning and planning.

different strategies and plans. By the same token, acting strongly on the future changes that future, requiring a re-analysis of implications and consequences. The future is therefore the result of a dynamic balance among trends, events, and choices.

Each category of action contains a set of tools for working that category. Some important tools for research and forecasting are systems thinking, information retrieval, environmental scanning, Delphi surveys, stakeholder analysis (including competitive intelligence), trend extrapolation (including sensitivity analysis), scenario development and critical thinking. Important tools for visioning and goal setting are appreciative inquiry, shared visioning, decision analysis, and strategy development. For planning and acting, there are organization modeling, strategic planning, leadership, and change management.

FUTURES METHODS

A course is an environment designed to assist in acquiring knowledge and skills. The skills in this course are some of those required of a professional futurist in forecasting the future. The curriculum contains the methods that all professional forecasters use in describing the future (typically aimed at the baseline future), as well as those techniques that are unique to professional futurists, such as scenario development.

The multitude of futures methods makes it impossible to provide a "how to" in each one of them. Rather, the approach is to introduce and practice with a handful of most commonly used methods, and to survey the rest. The demonstration of these skills is the key criterion for students to do well. The skills and demonstrations are described in written form and judged according to an explicit set of criteria.

There are several excellent compilations of methods.[3] Shaping Tomorrow has a nice wiki-based list.[4] Jerry Glenn and Ted Gordon have been updating their CD-Rom of methods, currently in its third edition.[5] Wendell Bell's well-regarded *Foundations of Foresight, Vol. 1*[6] has a nice chapter on methods. Finally, Richard Slaughter's *Knowledge Base of*

---

[3] Thanks to the contributors to an APF listserv discussion on the topic: Mike Jackson, Ruben Nelson, Andrew Curry, Bob Hawkins, Joe Voros, and Kate Delaney.

[4] See http://practicalforesight.wetpaint.com/page/Futuring+Methods.

[5] See http://www.millennium-project.org/millennium/FRM-V3.html.

[6] See http://www.amazon.com/Foundations-Futures-Studies-Purposes-Knowledge/dp/0765805391.

Foresight CD[7] also has an excellent compilation of methods. And there are many more!

There, as yet, is no agreed-upon framework for methods in foresight. The consultancies and academic programs each tend to have their own unique frameworks and approach that share common elements. Therefore, before describing the approach used in this work, it would be useful to define some terms.

Some definitions around methods

There is confusion in foresight, as well as many other disciplines, around just what a method is. The terms method, technique and tool are often used interchangeably in the literature and in practice. There are subtle but useful differences in the terms, described below (Bishop, Hines & Collins, 2007, 6):

- *Project*. A foresight or foresight project is the largest unit of professional work. It includes the sum total of the objectives, the team, the resources and the methods employed in anticipating and influencing the future. Projects may be simple, involving just one product and method, or complex, involving many steps, each of which produces one or more products and uses one or more methods. And projects may go on for a long time, such as an ongoing scanning project that may go on for a year or years (ongoing projects are sometimes referred to as *programs*). An example of a project would be Shell's scenario planning – their latest project is captured in a publication, *Signals and Signposts*, available on the web.
- *Approach*. The process that one employs in conducting a project is the approach. The approach consists of an ordered series of steps to accomplish the objectives of the project. Every project has an approach, whether or not it is explicitly articulated at the beginning. Some approaches are widely practiced, such as the approach to develop a strategic plan. Most professional futurists and consultants use a favorite approach that they have honed over time. Each approach produces one or more products or deliverables that satisfy the objectives of the project. The product is the final result of the work done in the approach – as a report, a database of trends, scenarios in various forms, a strategic plan, and many more. Usually

---

[7] See http://www.foresightinternational.com.au/catalogue/product_info.php?products_id=34.

each step in the approach generates a product and together they form the deliverable from the project. For example, at the University of Houston, we use the framework published in *Thinking about the Future* as our basic approach. It breaks foresight into six activities: framing, scanning, forecasting, visioning, planning, and acting.

- *Method.* This is the systematic means or specific steps used to generate a work product. Method and technique are used rather interchangeably in the literature. Method involves the specific steps for carrying out a project, where technique relates to the style or manner of carrying out the steps. For example, scenario planning is perhaps the most popular method used by futurists.
- *Technique.* This relates to the particular style or manner in which a method is carried out; it can be thought of as variations of a particular method that relate more to style than substance. For example, Bishop, Hines & Collins (2007) note that there are more than two dozen techniques for carrying out the scenario planning method.
- *Tool.* A tool is a (physical or software) device that provides a mechanical or mental advantage in accomplishing a task, such as video projectors, questionnaires, worksheets, and software programs. For example, our Systems Thinking course uses the Vensim tool for doing systems modeling.

That said, it is suggested that one recognizes the reality that the terms are used interchangeably, and not get too hung up on the distinctions.

Thinking about the Future framework

The UH curriculum uses the framework set out in *Thinking about the Future* (2007) for organizing how foresight is approached and thus the framework is useful for categorizing methods as well. One additional tricky definitional item is distinguishing methods and perspectives. As noted above, a method outlines specific steps for carrying out a project. A perspective is much broader in that it is a way of thinking about the future as a whole or ontologically (the nature or reality itself). More will be said about perspectives in foresight in Chapter 3. For now, it's sufficient to note that the newer perspectives in foresight, critical and integral, are envisioned by some as sources of new methodologies, creating a fuzzy boundary – is it a method or perspective, or both?

The curriculum organizes methods by six types of activities, described in detail in the book, which was based upon work carried out in tandem with three dozen contributors as well as drawing upon work done with the Association of Professional Futurists' Professional Development

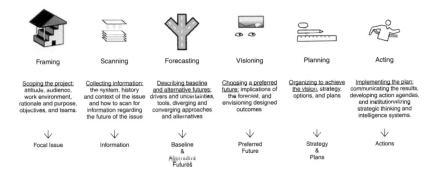

Framing	Scanning	Forecasting	Visioning	Planning	Acting
Scoping the project: attitude, audience, work environment, rationale and purpose, objectives, and teams.	Collecting information: the system, history and context of the issue and how to scan for information regarding the future of the issue	Describing baseline and alternative futures: drivers and uncertainties, tools, diverging and converging approaches and alternatives	Choosing a preferred future: implications of the forecast, and envisioning designed outcomes	Organizing to achieve the vision: strategy, options, and plans	Implementing the plan: communicating the results, developing action agendas, and institutionalizing strategic thinking and intelligence systems.
↓	↓	↓	↓	↓	↓
Focal Issue	Information	Baseline & Alternative Futures	Preferred Future	Strategy & Plans	Actions

Figure 1.14 Thinking about the Future framework

group. The framework activities are each treated in more depth as individual book chapters (with the exception of Framing, which one might argue is covered by the first two chapters, and "Change Management" and "Leadership" serving as the surrogate for Acting).

These activities are arranged in the order most commonly encountered when doing a strategic foresight project. It is not a rigid, step-by-step chronological order. For instance, some projects start with Visioning after the Framing, instead of after Forecasting as presented here.

To put this framework into context regarding change, the first three activities – framing, scanning, and forecasting – relate to describing inbound change (that is, the change coming at one from the external world). The second three activities – visioning, planning, and acting – relate to outbound change (that is, the change that one seeks to effect upon the world, as the result of understanding the outbound change). So the first three activities, and the methods within them, describe what the futures will most probably look like, and the second three include methods aimed at realizing a preferred future given those possibilities.

Methods can and often do fall under more than one of the six activities. For convenience's sake, they are placed where they are judged to have their most effective impact. Also, methods that are not specific to futures are excluded, such as project management.

Framing: Identifying and solving the right problems

Framing helps to scope, situate, and bound a futures project. Investing the time to clearly frame the objective and how to address it pays big dividends in later phases of the project. Far too many foresight activities – and business analyses in general – end

Table 1.2 Thinking about the Future approach and methods

Activity	Description	Methods	Product
Framing	*Scoping the project*: methods concern attitude, audience, work environment, rationale and purpose, objectives, and teams.	Causal layered analysis, integral futures, stakeholder analysis, issue analysis, team-building methods.	Project plan.
Scanning	*Collecting information*: methods concern the system, history, and context of the issue and how to scan for information regarding the future of the issue.	Environmental/horizon scanning, content analysis, leading/lagging indicators, text mining, trend tracking, secondary research.	Information (such as scan hits, trends, drivers).
Forecasting	*Describing baseline and alternative futures*: methods concern using the information from Scanning and outlines guidelines regarding drivers and uncertainties, tools, diverging and converging approaches, and alternatives.	Bellwether analysis, critical thinking methods, cross impact analysis, Delphi, emerging issue analysis, framework forecasting, gaming/simulation, historical analogy/pattern recognition, morphological box/predictive markets, scenario techniques, statistical modeling (time series), systems analysis, technology forecasting (roadmapping, patent analysis, etc.), trend analysis.	Baseline and alternative futures (typically scenarios).

Visioning	*Choosing a preferred future*: methods concern thinking through the implications of the forecast and envisioning designed outcomes for the organization; envisioning the best outcomes, goal-setting, performance measures.	Futures wheel, implications analysis, appreciative inquiry, backcasting, creative imagery, visualization.	Preferred future (vision, goals).
Planning	*Organizing the resources*: methods concern developing strategy and options for carrying out the vision.	Decision modeling, risk analysis, strategic planning, technology assessment.	Strategic plan (strategies).
Acting	*Implementing the plan*: methods concern communicating the results, developing action agendas, and institutionalizing strategic thinking and intelligence systems.	Action research, change management, coaching, consulting, issues management	Action plan (initiatives).

up addressing and solving the wrong problem. The methods here are aimed at helping to identify and clarify just what the project should be about. They center on critiquing and questioning basic assumptions (Hines, 2006, 19).

Scanning: Mapping the landscape

Once the challenge is framed, the next step or set of activities is scanning the internal and external environment for information and trends relating to the challenge.  This includes researching the past and present of the issue as well as identifying the signals of change (scanning hits in our parlance). The goal is to come up with a mix of basic or fundamental driving forces that suggest the most likely future. The environmental-scanning process will also reveal potential change-drivers that may lead to alternative future outcomes. The methods here involve designing and executing searches and crafting the resulting trends, and evaluating what is found. In effect these methods help create the raw material for forecasting (Hines, 2006, 19).

Forecasting: Generating a range of future possibilities

Forecasting takes what was generated in Scanning and uses it as the basis for creating both the baseline future (present trends continued) as well as alternative futures.  The goal is to reduce the likelihood and magnitude of any future surprises, as well as influencing mental models about what may happen, thus helping navigation through whatever future does emerge. The methods here center on generating alternative futures – a term often equated with scenarios. In a separate piece (Bishop, Hines & Collins, 2007), the authors developed a taxonomy of scenario methods that identified more than two dozen separate techniques organized into eight categories (Hines, 2006, 20).

Visioning: Imagining the preferred future

The goal of strategic foresight is to make better, more-informed decisions in the present. 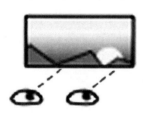 Forecasting lays out a range of potential futures to consider so that the organization can act effectively now. The visioning phase focuses attention back on the present, because now one must ask, "So what?" Given the future possibilities outlined, what does the organization want (or need) to do? What is the *preferred* future? Because this question now arises in an atmosphere well grounded in the reality constructed throughout the foresight process, it is not mere wishful thinking (Hines, 2006, 21).

Planning: Linking the future to the present

Planning is the bridge between the vision and action, the "strategy" portion of the strategic-planning team's work. The specific sets of tactics and strategies that are outlined will be tailored to the individual organization. The goal of the planning phase is to help 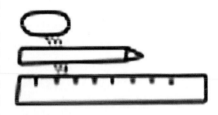 the organization translate the vision and alternative future possibilities into strategy, and just as there are alternative futures, there are alternative ways of achieving them. By developing strategic options and multiple contingency plans, the organization will be equipped to manage the uncertainty of the future (Hines, 2006, 21).

Acting: Translating into action...on an ongoing basis

Organizations reluctant to devote precious resources today to a sometimes uncertain future payoff must be able to see their goals clearly. The acting phase thus is largely about communication, making the abstract progressively more concrete: What is to be done, who will do it, how, and when? An ongoing capability can become an important asset for the organization. Strategic  foresight can become a fundamental part of a learning organization, which is essential to success in today's fast-changing environment (Hines, 2006, 21).

An approach to mapping futures methods, developed by Bishop and Pero Micic, highlights a common division of methods into forecasting and planning. The forecasting methods on the right (to deal with inbound change) help one map and understand the future, and the planning methods on the left (to create outbound change) help one to influence the future.

CONCLUSION

The key concepts of the program center on the study of change. As the saying goes, they are simple, but not easy to apply. They are introduced early, and reinforced often as different aspects of the futures discipline are covered. They are also linked with the approaches and methods for carrying out actual futures work. The curriculum has an explicit goal of preparing students for professional practice, thus a strong link between theory and application is replete throughout the coursework.

A second key concept is that of alternative futures, the identification of a range of plausible futures. To support this central concept the role of uncertainty and assumptions are given extensive treatment.

Finally, foresight at the highest level can be divided into two major activities: forecasting to describe what the future might look like, and planning for devising what to do about it.

Graduates of the program commonly cite how they leave the program with a different mindset than when they came in. While that is a goal of any graduate program, foresight is in a unique position to influence decisions that one makes on a daily basis. People think about the future all the time, and after going through the program, they think about it differently.

RESOURCES

Overviews

Bell, W. (1996) *Foundations of Foresight: Human Science for a New Era: History, Purposes, and Knowledge, Vols I and II* (Piscataway, NJ: Transaction).

- A well-regarded and much-referenced description of all the aspects of foresight. Volume I covers forecasting and Volume II is about values.

Cornish, E. (2004) *Futuring: The Exploration of the Future* (Bethesda, MD: World Future Society).

- An update of his 1977 *Study of the Future* that long served as the classic introduction to foresight.

Slaughter, R. (2005) *The Knowledge Base of Foresight: Professional Edition.* (Indooroopily, Australia: Foresight International) [CD-ROM].

- An international overview of foresight and applied foresight that is the best compilation of the core material of the field. It is organized into four volumes: (1) historical and conceptual lineage, futures concepts, literature, epistemologies and methods; (2) futures organizations, practices and products; (3) considers how the meaning and action we construct today impacts future generations; (4) one hundred "views of futurists."

Change

Eldredge, N. & Gould, S. J. (1972) "Punctuated Equilibria: An Alternative to Phyletic Gradualism" in T. J. M. Schopf (ed.) *Models in Paleobiology* (San Francisco, CA: Cooper), 82–115. Reprinted in N. Eldredge (1985) *Time Frames* (Princeton, NJ: Princeton U Press).

- Describes how evolution proceeds episodically, rather than continuously. Long periods of equilibrium are punctuated by brief bursts of evolutionary change. This concept has been adapted to describe social change by futurists.

Lombardo, T. (2006) *Contemporary Futurist Thought* (Bloomington, IN: AuthorHouse), 251–81.

- An excellent summary of various writers and theories about change.

Prediction

Asimov, I. (1951) *Foundation* (Gnome Press); (1952) *Foundation and Empire* (Gnome Press); (1953) *Second Foundation* (London, England: Panther paperback).

- A series of science fiction novels based on the premise that a math genius Hari Seldon developed psychohistory, a method to predict the long-term future.

Assumptions

Coates, J. (1999) "Getting at Assumptions Is Troublesome," *Technological Forecasting & Social Change*, 62, 97–9.

- Provides 15 reasons why it is difficult for futurists and other analysts to clearly identify and articulate their assumptions when discussing the future.

Alternative futures

Taylor, C. (1990, October) *Creating Strategic Visions* (Carlisle Barracks, PA: Army War College, Strategic Studies Institute).

- Introduces the concept of the cone of plausibility to help constrain the number of alternative futures to consider by focusing attention on those that are plausible (the story "hangs together" reasonably well) rather than all possible alternatives.

Methods

Glenn, J. & Gordon, T. (eds) (2009) *Futures Research Methodology, V3.0*, CD (Washington, DC: Millennium Project).

- The best single compilation of futures research methods.

Hines, A. & Bishop, P. (2007) *Thinking about the Future: Guidelines for Strategic Foresight* (Washington, DC: Social Technologies).

- Culls the wisdom of three dozen leading futurists from around the globe in the form of guidelines for doing strategic foresight, organized into the six principal activities: framing, scanning, forecasting, visioning, planning, and acting.

2
Systems Thinking

INTRODUCTION

Systems thinking is a fundamental perspective of future studies. Even calling it a "perspective" underestimates its importance. Some claim that it is *the* paradigm of foresight. It is the lens through which futurists view the world. It embodies some of the foundational principles of foresight, such as:

- Every entity (thing) is a system that consists of parts (subsystems) and which is also a part of larger systems – a "holon" to use Arthur Koestler's term popularized by Ken Wilber (2001, 27)
- Every system and every part of a system are connected to every other system, at least indirectly
- Systems and parts of a system interact in ways that can produce surprising and counter-intuitive results
- The tendency to produce unexpected results makes predicting the outcome of systems' interaction difficult, if not impossible.

As a result, it is critical that futurists introduce students and others to these principles if they are to approach the future in a sophisticated and systematic fashion.

Unfortunately, teaching systems thinking is easier said than done. The subject is so fundamental that it is obvious to those who understand it and opaque to those who do not. While even those who don't *get it* might agree with these principles, they still may not *see* the world that way. And those who do see the world that way cannot understand why everyone does not. Teaching systems therefore requires a communication across a deep paradigmatic boundary in a language that is quite foreign to the listener. That is very hard to do.

Chris Dede, now at Harvard, created the Systems Thinking course at the University of Houston-Clear Lake in 1975. Chris is an outstanding educational futurist and a brilliant teacher, and the course became a tradition. He said that it was the hardest course he ever taught – and the authors agree!

HISTORY

While the principles of systems thinking are embedded in most ancient philosophies, the theory of systems thinking was first articulated in the early 1930s by the biologist Ludwig von Bertalanffy. Since then a library of literature has developed around the subject. Other notable contributors were Jay Forrester (*Industrial Dynamics*, 1961), Russell Ackoff (*On Purposeful Systems*, 1972), Karl Weick (*The Social Psychology of Organizing*, 1979), C. West Churchman (*The Systems Approach*, 1984), Peter Senge (*The Fifth Discipline*, 1990), Ken Wilber (*A Theory of Everything*, 2001), and finally Donella Meadows (*Thinking in Systems*, 2008).

The practical application of systems theory began during World War II in the work of two eminent scientists – Norbert Weiner at MIT and John von Neumann at Princeton. Weiner is credited with articulating the fundamentals of control theory, also called cybernetics, in which negative feedback is applied to changes in a system to keep it stable within certain limits. The household thermostat is the most obvious example. Control theory was the basis for the development of much more complicated systems in the Post-War world – from intercontinental ballistic missiles and nuclear submarines to computers and the Internet. Systems engineering has since emerged as a separate discipline with a deep mathematical basis and universal application to all machines.

Jay Forrester, also of MIT, was the first to apply control theory to social systems. Forrester also invented the formal language of causal models (also called influence diagrams) and systems dynamics, which allowed the simulation of first-order differential equations using simple difference equations. Forrester used these tools to describe the development of cities in his 1961 book *Industrial Dynamics*. Dennis and Donella Meadows and Jorgen Randers used systems dynamics in their famous *Limits to Growth* in 1972. Forrester and his colleagues offered system dynamics to the public in the Apple IIe program called *Dynamo*, which Barry Richmond turned into *Stella* and *iThink* for the MacIntosh and Ventana Systems turned into *Vensim* for Windows. Today, even high

---

Limits to Growth: Three strikes!

The original *Limits to Growth* (1972) study used systems dynamics modeling to conclude that "if the present growth trends in world population, industrialization, pollution, food product, and resource depletion continue unchanged, the limits to growth on this planet will be reached sometime within the next 100 years." Twenty years later, they revisited their findings with *Beyond the Limits* (1993), and then ten years after that took another look with *Limits to Growth: The 30-Year Update* (2004). Despite heavy criticism in some quarters, in particular about a perceived under-estimating of the role of technology in providing solutions, their adjusted and refined model suggests that the original forecasts are largely on track. In fact, they estimate that perhaps the planet is 20% above the limit of sustainable carrying capacity. In each book, the authors conclude that there is time left to address the limits, but they are getting increasingly worried.

---

school students (and probably some elementary students) can simulate quite sophisticated systems using these simple tools. Forrester's tradition continues at MIT as the inspiration for Peter Senge's groundbreaking book *The Fifth Discipline* in 1991 and the continuing influence of John Sterman and others at the MIT Systems Dynamics Group. Finally, the Systems Dynamics Society is a well-known and prestigious society of researchers who use these theories and tools today.

John von Neumann, Weiner's contemporary, was also credited with establishing a different branch of systems theory called cellular automata (CA). As opposed to cybernetic systems, in which variables are the components, von Neumann's systems consisted of independent agents (the CAs) whose actions depend on the conditions in their immediate environment and on the actions of other CAs close to them. What is now called complexity theory or agent-based modeling took longer to develop since complex systems cannot be modeled using differential equations the way control systems can. Rather they must be simulated in a step-by-step fashion, and the computers required to do any meaningful simulation did not become available until the 1980s. Before that, John Conway invented the famous *Game of Life*, a two-dimensional array of agents operating on very simple rules that produced surprising and beautiful patterns. Stephen Wolfram used a one-dimensional CA to investigate the various states that an agent-based system could take in a famous article in 1982, which he later turned into his book *A New Kind of Science* (2002). The Santa Fe Institute was founded in 1984 to study complex adaptive systems after powerful graphical workstations from Sun Microsystems were available. They also pioneered the development of network theory which is now a staple of many scientific and engineering disciplines.

So the abstract (and somewhat arcane) systems theory of the 1950s has come to define the world and to influence the many technologies created within it. Earth scientists use systems theory to describe the operation of the inanimate parts of the planet – the oceans, the atmosphere, the land, and the energy that flows among them. Biologists use systems theory to describe living systems – organisms and the ecologies they live in. Psychotherapists use systems theory to describe the interactions among family members or small work groups. Futurists use systems theory to describe larger human systems – communities, organizations, regions, nations, and indeed the whole of human society itself. Systems theory, then, is essential for understanding the world and how it might develop and change in the future.

> A system's behavior is a function of its structure

GENERALIZATION

The generalizations for many of the courses in the curriculum are obvious and somewhat simplistic, but no generalization is as important as the one for this Systems Thinking. Or, as Peter Senge (1994, 40) put it, "Structure influences behavior." That simple statement contains the essence of systems thinking, but first some definitions:

Table 2.1   Systems definitions

Term	Definition
System	a set of parts that interacts to produce observable effects (behaviors) outside the system
Behavior	a change in (or the stability of) an externally observable or measurable unit or quantity associated with (or produced by) the system over time
Structure	the relationship of the system's parts (subsystems, variables or entities) interacting with each other according to fixed rules

In other words, a system's behavior is a function of the relation and interaction of its parts – its structure. As such, the generalization seems pretty obvious and therefore not too impressive, except for the fact that it is not the most common explanation of phenomena in the world. In fact, two other explanations are more commonly advanced for why things (human systems, in particular) behave the way they do: the personal explanation and the external explanation.

The personal explanation claims that systems behave the way they do because of the people in them. According to this theory, people (such as leaders, managers, workers, suppliers, regulators, or customers) account for the system's behavior. Change the people in the system (by re-training, supervising or replacing them), and that changes the behavior of the system. "If we could only get rid of.... If the boss would only think.... If the employees would only behave like.... If only *they* would do something, then everything would be all right." People think that greedy politicians, selfish employees, threatened managers or our own inadequacies are the source of their problems and the reason that things don't change or that things go wrong. Systems thinkers claim otherwise. Most importantly, they hold that changing the people in a system rarely changes the behavior of the system.

The US Congress, to take just one example, an institution not held in particularly high regard by the American people, has been around for more than two centuries. Tens of thousands of people have served over that time, yet the institution still seems to behave the same. Is it the people? Clearly not. And one could say the same for businesses, schools, churches, families. Indeed the people in a system cannot explain the behavior of that system when that behavior persists long after the people are gone.

The second popular explanation for a system's behavior is that forces external to and beyond the control of the system cause it to behave the way it does. Laws, regulations, the market, the physical world are all used as reasons why the system behaves as it does. That of course does not explain how some systems operating in those same environments behave differently. So some businesses succeed in a heavily regulated environment and others do not. The same can be said of almost any type of environment. Blaming external events for trouble is common, but again systems thinkers do not take that easy way out either.

People do make a difference and the environment does influence behavior, but not nearly as often as most people believe. The situation is illustrated in Figure 2.1. While people might acknowledge that a system's structure does influence its behavior, they rarely use the structure to explain the behavior because it is "underwater" – invisible and hard to see. People in the empirical West prefer to explain things

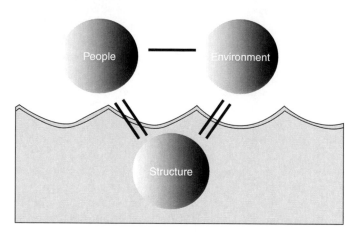

Figure 2.1   Understanding system behavior

using tangible evidence (people and events) rather than the apparently ethereal and largely invisible *structure of the system* (whatever that is!). Systems thinking, however, "drains the water from the pond" in order to see the structure and allow it to play its proper role in explaining the system's behavior.

A course in systems thinking thus provides the understanding and the tools to reveal the structure of a system and its effects on the system's behavior. The course achieves this mission by reading what others have said about systems, by reviewing cases of structural explanations of system behavior and by modeling and simulating systems themselves. The ultimate objective is always to explain a system's behavior in terms of its structure.

The first item on the agenda is to understand what a system is. The definition on page 66 gives the essential pieces – a set of interacting parts. The concept of system is so big, however, it is hard to think of something that is not a system. Some examples of living systems are cells, organs, organisms, ecologies, families, organizations, communities, societies – even the global society is a system. On the inorganic level, systems are atoms, molecules, crystals, oceans, atmospheres, solar systems, galaxies, along with machines, circuits, utilities (water, electricity, telephone), and, of course, the Internet.

Each of these entities has a number of things in common:

- Each is made of parts
- The parts interact with each other

- The interaction of the parts produces behavior at an observable level. (The patterned interaction of the parts is the structure.)

So from one of the smallest system examples, the cell, the interaction of proteins (its structure) consumes oxygen, stores energy, and excretes hormones. At the largest level, the seven billion people on the planet emit carbon dioxide, release CFCs and alter the earth's atmosphere. All of these are examples of system structures that produce behaviors – observable changes outside themselves.

Understanding a system and its behavior begins with constructing a model or representation of the system. Models come in various types – physical, graphical, mathematical, verbal and so on. Each has its own use, and most systems can be modeled using many of these types. The model focuses on certain aspects of the system to explain the system's behavior. The model is always a simplified representation of the actual system because its simplicity demonstrates how the system operates. So an ecological model of a lake would include the species but not the chemical bonds of the water molecules because those are not required to explain the system behavior.

What to include and not include in a system is called the system boundary. What is left out is the system environment – that part of the rest of the universe that interacts with the system and influences its behavior to some extent. In the long run, everything is connected to everything else so boundaries are arbitrary in some sense. Therefore, the boundary of a system is an analytical concept, meaning that it is not part of reality. Rather it is a device created by the analyst to improve understanding.

Establishing boundaries is arbitrary because there is no single way to define a system's boundary. Nevertheless, there are useful boundaries and useless ones. For example, Texarkana is one of the few towns in the United States that has a state boundary (Texas and Arkansas) running through it. That boundary is as arbitrary as any other boundary. It is useful when considering matters of state law and taxes that apply to its citizens. It would be harmful, however, to consider the two parts of the town as separate communities since they act as one system in every other way.

The rule for deciding a system's boundary optimizes two principles:

- *completeness*: include all the parts in the model necessary to explain the system behavior
- *parsimony*: do not include any more parts in the model than are absolutely necessary.

The first rule is obvious. If one leaves out an essential part of the system, some of the behavior will not be explained. But if one includes too many parts, then the model becomes too complicated to understand. Since the purpose of a model is to aid understanding, if it is too complicated, it is not achieving its purpose.

System behaviors

Why does the world act the way it does? That is the central question of systems thinking, applied to one system at a time. The world is a complicated place, and people do not understand the half of why things are the way they are. Here are some examples of complicated systems that don't seem to work which a class came up with one year:

- The US healthcare system, though the most technologically advanced in the world, does not take care of everyone, and as expensive as it is, it does not produce any better outcomes than many others
- People don't accept alternative medical treatments despite their proven successes
- Welfare does not help those who need it the most
- Although schools spend more money than they used to, students are exhibiting no higher skill levels than they used to
- Slash-and-burn agriculture continues
- Arabs and Israelis cannot resolve their differences
- NASA has spent a fortune on organizational consultants, but the culture remains the same
- Politicians often do not fulfill their campaign promises.

Not everyone would agree that all these statements are true, but to the extent that they are, they represent a list of curious behaviors of the systems in our world. Systems that are designed to do one thing (healthcare, education) seem to end up doing something else and, as a result, do their intended mission poorly. Healthcare is really not taking care of healthy people, but rather treating sick people; it should be called sickcare. Roads are built, but traffic jams increase. Security is paramount, but terrorism continues. How do such things happen?

Take the experience of dieting. Most people believe that if they eat less, they will lose weight. Simple: A (reduce eating) leads to B (lose weight). But then why are the people who diet the most also the heaviest? They should be the lightest. Does anyone understand why this happens?

The most common explanation for the fact that heavier people usually don't benefit from dieting is that they lack will-power – an explanation rooted in the people themselves. If they would only eat less, then they would lose weight. Some people might indeed eat less, but most don't. Are those that don't eat less therefore to blame for their overweight condition? Most people believe so.

The people themselves, however, have a different explanation. They believe that something outside them forces them to eat, usually identified as stress. Children, spouses, jobs, homes – whatever – all force them to head to the refrigerator. That represents the second most popular explanation for a system's behavior – something outside the system is responsible. So businesses blame regulators, regulators blame legislators, legislators blame lobbyists, lobbyists blame regulators, and on and on. Everyone has some external explanation for their behavior. Good try, but still usually not adequate.

The final type of explanation is somewhat more accurate, but still not sophisticated. It is the simple cause or linear explanation. Einstein once said, "To all the complicated problems in the world, there is a simple solution, but it is always wrong." He appreciated how complex and subtle the world is. Simple explanations fail to capture complex reality. So obesity is caused by an eating disorder – nice and simple, but hardly adequate. Corruption is caused by greed; pornography by moral decline; poor educational performance by a lack of family values. All nice and simple, but hardly explanations to count on.

A systems explanation of why dieting does not work very often is based on human metabolism – a system. People on a diet consume fewer calories. In the early days of the human species, when metabolism was developing, people consumed fewer calories, not by choice but because food was scarce. So the body developed mechanisms for using calories more efficiently and storing excess calories as fat. But the body does not know right away when a person ends their diet, which they inevitably do. The scarcity regime is still in place so the new calories are not burned, as they would be in normal times. Rather they are stored as fat. The result is that people put on just as much weight as they lost, or even more. It's the metabolic system not their will-power or external circumstances that made them fat.

Take another seemingly simple solution of raising taxes to reduce the government deficit. Government deficit is the result of revenue that is less than expenditures. One way to solve the problem of deficits is to raise the tax rate to produce revenue to equal the expenditures – nice, simple, straightforward. But as many political leaders have found out,

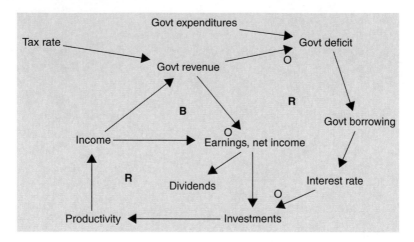

Figure 2.2   Attacking the deficit

that solution may not work. They raise the tax rate and the revenues go down. They raise the tax rate again and the revenue goes down again! How to understand this system behavior?

Understanding begins by listing the parts of the system that produce the behavior:

- Revenues
- Expenditures
- Deficit
- Tax rate
- Gross profit (pre-tax)
- Net earnings (after-tax)
- Dividends
- Retained earnings
- Adjusted gross income (pre-tax)
- Net income (after-tax)
- Living expenses
- Savings
- Investments
- Productivity
- Growth

Tax rates apply to adjusted gross income for individuals and profits for businesses (income less deductions). The higher the tax rate and the taxes paid, the lower the savings that would be used to buy stocks and bonds or make business investments. Lower investments lead to lower productivity which in turns leads to lower growth. Lower growth means lower profits for business and lower incomes for individuals resulting in lower revenues for the government. As a result, a higher tax rate may actually lead to lower government revenues – just the opposite that one would expect.

The paragraph above is a verbal model of the government revenue system designed to explain the unusual result that higher tax rates may lead to lower revenues. That model would also explain that under certain circumstances, lower tax rates might even lead to higher revenues. That actually happened in the Kennedy administration in 1963. The Reagan administration tried the same thing in 1982, but it did not lead to lower deficits because the tax rate was already low. In any case, the verbal model shows how it might happen. Most importantly, the explanation is:

- not due to any person or group of people involved in the system
- not due to forces outside the system
- not a simple explanation from just one cause.

Rather the explanation is based on the structure of the system – the interaction of its constituent parts. Not to say that people and external influences don't shape behaviors – they do. But more things happen because of the structure of the system than is usually admitted. Therein lies the power of systems thinking – understanding and forecasting system behaviors that are poorly understood using a better mode of explanation.

APPROACH

So if the objective is to learn the course generalization and be able to apply it to explain system behaviors, how is that done?

The first overriding consideration is to distinguish between the two types of system structures – cybernetic and complex. As described above, cybernetic system theories and models are based on control theory; complex system theories and models are based on agents. Cybernetic models are macro, top-down, that describe the system as a whole; complex models are micro, bottom-up, that describe the actions of individual agents. Each of these paradigms will be described in turn, as it is done in the course.

Cybernetic systems

The best introduction to systems thinking is contained in two short books by Draper Kauffman entitled (cleverly) *Systems I* (1980) and *Systems II* (1981). *Systems I* contains the theory and *Systems II* contains illustrations of the theory. Kauffman's books are deceptively simple. They might seem beneath a university course, but they contain all the important elements of systems theory in an engaging and easily understood manner. Who says that learning can't be fun, too?

The classic text in systems thinking is, of course, Peter Senge's (1994) *Fifth Discipline*. Senge not only introduces Forrester's insights about causal modeling, but he provides the rationale for studying systems on the very first page. From a very early age, kids are taught to break apart problems, to fragment the world. This apparently makes complex tasks and subjects more manageable, but it contains a hidden, enormous price. People can no longer see the consequences of their actions; they lose their intrinsic sense of connection to a larger whole.

Part of that socialization is a model of how the world works, something cognitive psychologists call a "schema" and futurists (and others) call a mental model. People have mental models for everything – how to meet someone, how to eat dinner, or how to teach a class. Futurists point out that people also have mental models for the larger systems in the world – why sales go up or down, why crime occurs in certain neighborhoods, or why wars erupt. Some of those mental models are well supported by scientific evidence, such as the operation of the economy; others are little more than common sense and traditional wisdom handed down over time.

But not everyone has the same mental model for the same phenomena. People from different cultures dress, eat, and greet each other differently. People learn those mental models while they are growing up. In fact, they learn them so well that they don't even realize that they are learned and that other people might have a different way of doing things. It is only when they interact with people from different cultures or lifestyles that they realize that the world is made of all kinds of mental models, some apparently quite bizarre.

People also have different mental models for how the large systems in the world operate – the physical, biological, and human systems of the planet. For instance, some will disagree on whether nature is there just for humans to use as they wish or whether it has independent status and value that must be respected. That mental model will guide decisions and actions toward nature, such as how people vote, what teachers teach, or what philanthropists donate.

Part of systems thinking, then, is revealing the mental models that people use to understand and explain the world. The behaviors in that world are apparent, but the structures that produced those behaviors are not. So a tool is needed, an X-ray machine of sorts, to expose those structures. Once exposed, they can be examined, tested, and discussed. They help to understand how the world works in a conscious and explicit way. Once people see the mental models that others use, perhaps they can agree on a model of how the world works or at least develop an under standing of the different models that different people use to make sense of the world. One cannot discuss what one cannot say or show. Systems thinking provides the means to identify people's deepest assumptions about the world so people can choose which ones they want to use.

Demonstration of cybernetic systems theory

One of the most memorable parts of this course is the participation in an actual demonstration of the course generalization – showing that a system's behavior *really* is a function of its structure.

The two most famous simulations are *The Beer Game* and *Fish Banks*:

- *The Beer Game* is written up in Senge's *The Fifth Discipline* It simulates a four-station supply chain in which retailers, distributors, wholesalers, and manufacturers order and receive (or produce) shipments of beer based on their expected demand. Not to give away the plot, but the behavior at every station is almost always shortage followed by a huge oversupply because of the built-in delays in the system. They still exhibit the same behavior even when participants have heard or read about *The Beer Game* before they play. The behavior is a function of the structure, not of the participants or their knowledge.
- *Fish Banks* is now distributed through the Sustainability Institute, a successor to the Institute for Policy and Social Science Research at the University of New Hampshire – the same people who produced the *Limits to Growth*. The simulation consists of teams fishing in the

same water, and it produces the same behavior as *Limits* – overshoot and collapse.

Nothing is more powerful than demonstrating the power of the course generalization, particularly when the students themselves participate in the system and produce the behavior themselves. Several demonstration tools are listed in "Resources" at the end of the chapter.

Modeling cybernetic systems

Systems thinking is primarily a skill, not just an intellectual pursuit. One could teach a course just about the theory, and there are many fine ways to do so. But a professional program should be focused on skills – not just *knowing* something, but also *doing* something. In systems thinking, the "doing" is constructing models.

A model is a representation of reality in some form. There are several types of models:

- Physical (scale) models
- Mathematical models (equations)
- Computer models (programs)
- Geographical models (maps)
- Process models (steps).

As a representation, a model is like the reality, but it is not the reality. In the same way, the map is not the territory and the picture is not the person. A model necessarily extracts only a limited number of parts of the reality for representation, and that is its value. The model focuses on those few parts for a better understanding of the whole and, in dynamic models, better manipulation in ways that cannot be done with the real system for practical or ethical reasons. So maps that include only the locations of towns and roads give direction even though the map leaves out almost everything else in the territory. Likewise, pharmaceutical researchers use disease models in animals that they believe are similar to the disease mechanisms in humans so they can experiment and treat them in ways that would not be ethical in humans.

The systems thinking course distinguishes four types of models:

1. Verbal
2. Formal
3. Simulated
4. Validated.

1. Verbal models use ordinary language to explain the system's behavior using the system's structure. People really don't need any instruction on how to explain behaviors using language because they do it all the time. Language is highly flexible, but flexibility comes with a price. Language is also ambiguous. Different people can understand different things even when using the exact same words. So language is not a perfect way to articulate a mental model. In fact, there is no perfect way. Different types of models are useful for different purposes.

2. Formal models solve that problem, to some extent, because they use a formal language to describe the system structure in a precise and unambiguous way. Mathematics is a formal language, and it is used to model most systems in science and engineering. In social systems, however, the language needs to be somewhat more flexible and forgiving, hence the use of Forrester's causal models, also called influence diagrams by some. Causal models are composed of three types of entities:

- *Variables*: any quantity that can vary
- *Links*: the association of one variable with another
- *Loops*: circular sets of variables and links.

Figure 2.3 shows a simple reinforcing or positive feedback loop that describes wage-based inflation as a function of the structure of the manufacturing system.

Figure 2.4 shows a simple balancing or negative feedback loop that describes adjustments to the price of gasoline as a function of the structure of the market. In each of the relationships between the variables, an increase in one leads to a decrease in the other and vice versa. For example, more driving reduces the amount of gas available. Less gas available leads to an increase in the price. An increase in the price leads to a decrease in the amount of driving.

The purpose here is not to teach causal modeling, but rather to show that a formal language is a way of describing mental models and systems structures more precisely than verbal language. Causal models also take the individuals and the events out of the explanation. Any person in these systems is assumed to act in the same way. That is not exactly true, of course. Some manufacturers might not increase their wages to meet the cost of living, or they might move their factories overseas to prevent wage increases. So formal models do not ignore the possibility that people and events do influence system behaviors, but they do focus on the system structure as the explanation since it is so rarely identified as such.

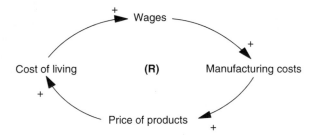

Figure 2.3   Reinforcing (positive feedback) loop

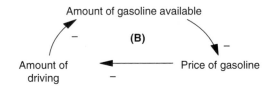

Figure 2.4   Balancing (negative feedback) loop

Formal models solve the problem of the ambiguity of language, but they do not directly link the system behavior and its structure. Causal models are pictures, static pictures. It can be said that, "When A goes up, B goes up," but the picture does not do that itself. The next level of modeling actually produces behaviors as output.

3. Simulated models produce behaviors using a computer program. Any programming language can be used to simulate a system since they all produce output (values of a variable over time), and most depict those values in graphical form as well. The structure of a system can be modeled using the relationships of variables, and the behavior of the system is the numerical or graphical output of one or more of those variables. So a specific behavior is to be explained, the behavior of a system as manifested in the changes of a variable over time, usually depicted in graphical form. The model of a system explains why a particular variable acts the way it does, and that action is shown as a graph of the value of that variable over time.

The second reason for depicting the behavior of a system as the graph of a variable over time is to be able to perform an experiment. First, identify the behavior of the system to be explained (in the form of a graph), model the system structure, simulate its operation over time using a computer program, produce the output of the variable to be explained in graphical form, and compare the first graph with the second. If they do not match, the system has not been modeled correctly. If they do match, that is evidence that one *might* have modeled the system correctly.

One cannot know for sure if the system model is exactly correct because many models can produce the same behavior. One can never be sure that it is *the* one that produced the behavior in the world. That is an assumption, and a pretty good one, barring evidence that another model is better, but it will always remain an assumption. Since the structure of the system is fundamentally unobservable, one can never know for sure that it is the right model. But one or more models that produce the targeted behavior is better than none.

Jay Forrester developed another formal language, called stock-flow or systems dynamics, for simulating systems. Stock-flow models contain three types of variables:

- *Stocks*: variables that retain their value over time. They are like tanks that hold water
- *Flows*: variables that adjust the value of stocks, either increasing (inflows) or decreasing (outflows) them. They are like the faucets and drains connected to the tank
- *Auxiliaries*: variables that hold parameters or perform calculations during the simulation.

Figure 2.5 contains a classic stock-flow model of population change (absent immigration).

In this model, the number of individuals in the Population is the stock; it persists over time. Individuals enter the population by Birth and leave the population by Death (the flows). The rates of those flows are held in the Birth and Death Rates (the auxiliaries). The actual number of Births and Deaths in any time period is the size of the Population times the respective rate.

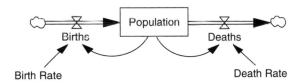

Figure 2.5 Stock-flow model

This model can exhibit three different behaviors depending on the relative size of the Birth and Death Rates. The Population is stable (constant) when the rates are equal; the Population increases when the Birth Rate is higher than the Death Rate, and it declines when the Birth Rate is lower. Figure 2.6 shows the graph of Population increase from 1,000 to about 1,800 when the Birth Rate is 40 per 1000 and the Death Rate is 10 per 1000, as exists in many developing countries.

Again the purpose here is not to teach systems dynamics or stock-flow models. Rather simply to show that simulated models are useful in understanding systems thinking. While one can verbally explain how a systems structure explains a behavior using ordinary language and one can even draw that structure using a causal model, there is no substitute for actually producing that behavior with a modeling program and comparing the output to the expectation. That is the real test of systems thinking.

At the same time, modeling is no easy task. Aside from getting the structure correct, it also involves finding the right form for the equations and the right value for the parameters contained in the Auxiliaries to produce a behavior that looks like the system's behavior in the world. So some knowledge of how variables in different equations behave and a lot of fiddling with parameters is necessary to get the behavior one

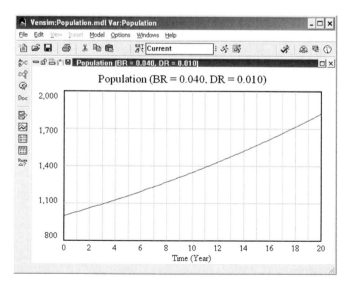

Figure 2.6 Modeling population increase

wants. Nevertheless, the reason for introducing simulation into an introductory course in systems thinking is:

*   to demonstrate how simulated models work
*   to examine the assumptions necessary in modeling
*   to show how the structure (the model) actually produces the behavior (the graph).

The purpose of simulation is to produce the *shape* of the system behavior, not the actual values. While real values are the output of the model, they are not necessarily the values that the variable would have in the world. Shapes are usually enough to understand and explain the behavior of a system. But for prediction, one needs to know not only the shape but also the actual values of those variables. For that, there is the final level of system modeling.

4. Validated or calibrated models produce not just the shape of the behavior but also the values themselves. These models are "validated" because they are fitted to some historical time series to be sure that the structure, the parameters, and the initial conditions of the model explain the past before extrapolating the model into the future. Validated models go well beyond an introductory course in systems thinking, but they are used extensively in physical science (such as modeling the effects of CO_2 and the other greenhouse bases in the global atmosphere) and economics (such as forecasting the growth of the economy over the next year).

The most famous validated systems model in foresight was called World3 in the *Limits to Growth* (Meadows et al., 1972). Published just months before the OPEC oil embargo in 1973, the model predicted long-term scenarios of overshoot and collapse for the world's economy.

The systems thinking course includes a collection of examples gathered over the years from various sources. A final exercise is to send them out on the Internet to look for feedback themselves. The ability to recognize feedback in a real world system is as important as being able to model it in a system presented to them.

Complex adaptive systems

Complex adaptive systems (CAS), the term now used for von Neumann's approach to system structure, are based on cellular automata and independent agents. CAS was in its infancy in the 1970s when the UH-Clear Lake Systems course was established. It took the development of more powerful computers before any meaningful agent-based models could be simulated. Even today, the materials, the demonstrations, and the tools available to most people are many years behind what they are in cybernetic systems. CAS is basically where cybernetic systems modeling was in the 1970s before *Stella/Vensim, The Fifth Discipline*, and *The Road Map*. Nevertheless, a compact treatment of CAS was introduced to the systems course in the late 1990s. Today, about a third of the course is devoted to CAS, but it is nevertheless essential to understanding that a system's behavior is a function of its structure.

Theory

A starting point is to clear up the confusion surrounding recently developed terms associated with the notion of complex adaptive systems. Regrettably, all have connotations in ordinary language that have little or no relation to their actual meaning in systems thinking. As a result, they are often thought to be other than what they are. And coincidentally all of which begin with "C."

1. Chaos
2. Catastrophe
3. Criticality
4. Complexity.

1. Chaos is the first and most widely used term associated with CAS. It often appears with complexity, as in "chaos and complexity," just like "ham and eggs" or "peanut butter and jelly." It is similar to complexity since (1) it does begin with "C," (2) it was discovered after World War II, and (3) it is a type of system behavior that is unpredictable in the medium term. But that is where the similarity ends.

   Chaos is one of three types of behaviors that a system can exhibit:

- *Fixed*: a static equilibrium state (the bottom of the ocean)
- *Periodic*: oscillations between two or more fixed states (the ocean tides)
- *Chaotic*: movement from one state to another, but never returning to any previous state (the surf crashing on rocks).

Chaotic phenomena were first identified by Henri Poincare in trying to explain the orbit of Neptune around the turn of the 20th Century. Though considered the "father" of chaos theory, Poincare never did explain the behavior orbit of Neptune because it was chaotic. (Any mutual attraction of three or more bodies exhibits chaotic behavior.)

The practical application of chaos theory was developed by meteorologist Edward Lorenz in 1963. Lorenz was running a weather simulation that he had run before, but this time he interrupted the simulation for some unrelated reason, and restarted it using the last numbers on the printout. He noticed, to his surprise, that the simulation produced entirely different results after the first few time periods compared to the first run. He thought he had entered one of the numbers incorrectly, but he had not. It turned out that he had re-entered the numbers using the first six digits that the computer was printing out, but the computer was actually calculating the numbers using ten digits internally. So the numbers on the restarted run were too small by less than 0.0001%; yet that incredibly small difference produced a significant difference in a relatively short time.

Before this discovery, there were thought to be only two types of systems: deterministic and stochastic. First developed by Galileo, Kepler, and Renaissance scientists and later perfected by Newton, deterministic systems acted according to fixed laws, expressed as mathematical equations. They could be used to predict the future state of the system within a fairly narrow range, leading Enlightenment philosophers to believe that one could know the future.

In the 16th and 17th Centuries, European mathematicians identified probability theory in the study of games of chance. Their work provided insight into the analysis of random phenomenon. Stochastic systems, as they came to be called, are systems whose values are independent of each other. They form a distribution of possible outcomes, each with its own probability, but no single outcome could be predicted from the previous data or from the overall distribution. So deterministic systems were predictable; stochastic systems were not.

All very neat, until Lorenz discovered this third type of behavior, a deterministic system (a computer program) that was unpredictable (after the first few time periods). The characteristic of a system that displays chaotic behavior is "sensitivity to initial conditions." In other words, the system is sensitive to the incredibly small difference in the initial conditions like the ones Lorenz entered when he restarted his program. Those differences rapidly build up to create large differences in output before long.

Given the same initial conditions in a computer simulation, the system will behave exactly the same way for as long as the simulation is run. In the real world, however, it is impossible to measure the initial conditions with infinite precision. There is always some measurement "error," some difference between the measure and the reality. It is that difference that builds up to produce a measurably different behavior after a short time.

Chaotic behavior is often confused with stochastic behavior because they are both unpredictable. People think that, like its everyday connotation, chaotic behavior is disordered and random, when things get out of control, when nothing makes sense. "All chaos breaks out!" But chaos is not disordered or random; it is deterministic. One can predict the very next state with mathematical precision. One could even predict all future states if one knew the initial conditions exactly, but that is not possible. Those quite minor differences in the initial conditions produce measurable differences after a short while.

And, unlike stochastic systems, no system is inherently chaotic. The weather is the best example of a system that displays chaotic behavior. Predicting the weather from one hour to the next is not very hard, more difficult for the next day, and just about impossible for the next week or two. Just three well-known equations describe the behavior of a weather system using only three well-understood variables: temperature, pressure, and humidity. Weather in the world is chaotic (deterministic but unpredictable), but the "weather" in a building could be stable or oscillating. So there are no inherently chaotic systems. There are only systems that have the potential of exhibiting chaotic behavior.

These three types of system behaviors (fixed, periodic, and chaotic) can be produced in the same system depending on the choice of parameters. Chris Langton[1] at the Santa Fe Institute depicted these states in his "American football" image.

Certain human systems are thought to have chaotic behaviors. For instance, markets of all types – especially stock and commodity markets – are thought to be chaotic, but it is not known for sure since the equations that move the markets from one moment to the next are not known – as they are with the weather.

The occurrence of chaos (in the mathematical sense) is an important part of systems thinking because it gives us reason to distrust predictions of future system behavior. Some of those predictions might come about, but it cannot be known which ones. If human systems are predominantly chaotic, then the results of intervening in those systems are inherently unpredictable. That does not mean that people should not act on those systems. Rather it means that when they do act, they should do so with caution and prudence lest they produce unintended and harmful effects.

---

[1] Langton coined the term "artificial life" in the late 1980s and organized several influential conferences and publications on the topic.

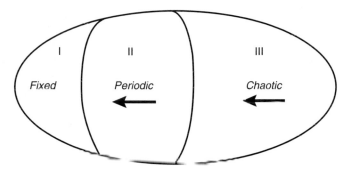

Figure 2.7 Three types of systems

Before complexity, however, the star of the show, there are catastrophe and criticality, which describe a different type of behavior from the ones considered so far.

Catastrophe and criticality are behaviors that shift suddenly from one stable state to another. Continuous behavior is smooth; it does not jump; all the points lie along a line. Discontinuities exist, however, in mathematics and in nature, and catastrophe theory and criticality describe those behaviors.

A simple example of discontinuity is a bottle that is stable sitting on its bottom. One can even push the top gently to one side and the bottle will return to an upright position, as long as it is not pushed too far. That range of variation in the vertical orientation of the bottle is called a basin of attraction. The image is that of a marble rolling around on a surface consisting of a number of bowls or depressions. If the surface is tilted, the marble rolls around in its bowl and returns to the bottom when the tilting stops. But if the surface is tilted too much, the marble leaves the first bowl by going over a ridge and enters another in which it will stay. That is a discontinuous change.

2. *Catastrophe* theory was developed by Rene Thom to describe certain types of discontinuous change. The mathematics is quite complicated and the applications quite narrow so few people actually learn and use the theory today.

3. *Criticality*, on the other hand, is a common way of describing discontinuous behavior. The image here is "the straw that broke the camel's back." One piece of straw cannot do that, but when added one piece at a time, sooner or later the camel's back will fail, due

to the addition of one piece of straw. The more common analogy is adding sand to a sand pile, one grain at a time. A sand pile is a cone whose sides form an angle that depends on the sand's viscosity (stickiness). Adding one grain of sand at a time allows the pile to grow beyond its natural angle, but only for a while. Sooner or later, one more grain will cause the pile to collapse in a little avalanche and return to the natural angle.

While neither of these models is worth covering in-depth in a course in systems thinking, it is worth mentioning because not all system behavior is continuous. Tipping points do exist, after which the system behavior changes dramatically. Examples of discontinuous change abound in physics, chemistry, biology, and in all of the social sciences:

- Anthropology: societal collapse
- Psychology: conversion
- Economics: asset bubbles bursting
- Political science: revolution
- Sociology: white flight.

All of these terms are examples of a broader category of behaviors called nonlinear dynamics. A system is linear when its output (behavior) is proportional to its input. The classic linear equation is $y = kx$, a straight line on a graph. One application is the relation of the force pulling on a spring to the distance the spring travels. "k" is the spring constant – larger for looser springs, smaller for tighter ones. The point is that doubling the force will double the distance; halving the force will halve the distance. The output is proportional to the input.

A nonlinear system then is any in which the output is not proportional to the input. Technically, any curved line is nonlinear. Compound interest, which grows exponentially, is not linear because one year's interest late in the series returns more than one year's interest earlier in the series.

The importance of recognizing nonlinear behavior in systems thinking is that people are often surprised at nonlinear behavior, even though they can calculate the future of many of those systems exactly. Linear behavior seems somehow built-in and easy to imagine. When asked to draw a trend, most people will draw a line – equal amounts of change in equal time periods. On the other hand, exponential increase, diminishing returns, oscillation, and overshoot and collapse all seem harder to imagine and therefore more surprising when they do occur. And discontinuous change, the fundamental shift from one state to another, seems even harder.

It is strange that nonlinear behavior is hard to imagine and expect because some would say that all change is nonlinear. In other words, change does not happen in a linear way. That point was made by Story Musgrave, a famous NASA astronaut in the Shuttle era, when he said that all the straight lines he could see on the Earth from space were man-made – contrails, ship wakes, roads, pipelines. Even the famous border between Israel and the Sinai desert is a straight line – green to the East and brown to the West. So with change. All systems behaviors are nonlinear. So getting used to that fact is one of the most important skills in systems thinking.

4. *Complex* systems consist of agents acting independently according to often simple rules based only on information from their local environment. Given that definition, complex systems are quite different from the cybernetic systems in classical systems thinking.

Stephen Wolfram's one-dimensional CAS models also produced a fourth type of behavior, interesting, even engaging, patterns that lasted for only a short time. They are not mathematically equivalent to the first three because they are only reproducible in CAS simulations. He labeled these behaviors "complex." Complex behaviors lie in a shadowy region between the periodic and the chaotic. Chris Langton called that region the "edge of chaos," another unfortunate Madison Avenue label. That region, however, does contain some unique properties, most importantly a balance between order and disorder – enough order to keep the system together, and enough disorder to allow change and adaptation. For that reason, most believe that that behavior describes living systems, including social systems, very well.

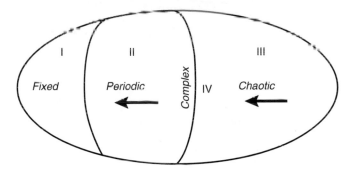

Figure 2.8   Four types of systems

Dave Snowden (2000) has created a similar typology of four types of systems:

- *Simple*: can be understood with little effort, such as the springs described above or compound interest in a saving account
- *Complicated*: have lots of parts and relationships requiring some tool, like causal modeling or systems dynamics, to understand them
- *Complex*: even more parts such that the system can produce novel and surprising behaviors
- *Chaotic*: a deterministic system, as described above, that is so sensitive to initial conditions that it is unpredictable in the medium term.

The big distinction here is between complicated and complex. Complicated can be mapped and simulated given enough time and effort. Complex systems cannot. They can produce new behaviors quite suddenly that are impossible to predict.

The essential differences between cybernetic and complex systems are listed in Table 2.2.

The biggest single difference is that the complex perspective takes the ground-level view of the individual agent while the cybernetic perspective takes the global view of the whole system. At the same time, global patterns do emerge from local interactions. These patterns are called emergent because they emerge from the untold number of interactions that agents have with each other. But there is no master control, no blueprint, no overall rule book to create these behaviors. Each agent acts according to its own rule book, yet macro order and patterns emerge nevertheless.

The clearest examples of complex systems are biological organisms. Each cell is an agent acting on information in its local environment. Some cells, like axons, are long so they transmit electrical impulses

Table 2.2 Cybernetic and complex systems

Cybernetics (top-down)	Automata (bottom-up)
Macro behavior	**Micro behavior**
Rational and intelligible	Unintelligible, unpredictable
Direct causal relations	No direct causality
Direct feedback	Reciprocal feedback
Explanation and prediction	Explanation but not prediction
Possibility of control	Surprising, creative, innovative
Model of mechanical systems	Model of living ecologies

for relatively long distances, but all the inputs and the outputs, even of axons, are just local to that cell. Some organs send information to distant cells by releasing hormones or enzymes, but the distant cell only receives that information in its local environment. People think of their bodies as a machine, designed and organized for life. But they can think of them just as readily as a colony of agents cooperating to perform that same function. The latter seems even more miraculous than the former.

So order arises even though there is no overall blueprint and no master control. Koestler (1990) noted how wondrous it was that every person in Manhattan ate everyday even though the system that delivered that food (to all the homes, stores, restaurants, and carts) was not planned or designed by anyone. It was an emergent property of the millions of interactions that constituted the food system of that city.

Most, though not all, complex systems exhibit emergence. And the emergent patterns cannot be explained or predicted from knowledge of the agents and their rules. So not only are future emergent patterns unpredictable, they can even be creative, generating new patterns that persist over time. So the development of consciousness, the appearance of different species, and even life itself constituted an unpredictable emergent pattern based on the interaction of independent agents. Emergence is another reason to be humble and cautious when trying to understand, much less predict, the future of complex adaptive systems.

Modeling CAS

Modeling programs for CAS have also existed for a long time. They are called event modeling programs because they program a series of events, like cars arriving at an intersection or products moving down a manufacturing line. The most highly developed agent-based modeling language for teaching systems thinking is NetLogo from the Center for Connected Learning (CCL) at Northwestern University.[2] NetLogo, like StarLogo offered previously by MIT,[3] is a modeling language based on Logo, a programming language developed by Seymour Papert in the 1960s. (Papert played the same role in the development of agent-based modeling that Forrester played in cybernetic modeling.) Logo is a language that controls a "turtle" that can move and draw lines on a screen. Sounds simple, if not simplistic, but it is actually a rich and exciting programming environment.

---

[2] See http://ccl.northwestern.edu/netlogo/.
[3] See http://education.mit.edu/starlogo.

StarLogo and NetLogo use the turtle concept, but rather than the program controlling one turtle, it controls many – each turtle being an agent in the simulation. Rather than programming the agents and their environment, MIT and Northwestern offer ready-to-use simulations that illustrate most of the important system behaviors and structures that one would like to investigate in a course like this. One can run some of these simulations right from a browser or download the NetLogo program and associated files and run them locally.[4]

The CCL also has developed two variations of agent-based modeling, called Participatory Simulations, and Integrated Simulation and Modeling Environment respectively. Both are server-based applications running the HubNet version of NetLogo.[5]

Participatory Simulations allow students to interact with each other and with computer-controlled agents using computers or TI graphing calculators. One of the simulations lets students control the traffic lights in a city grid to see how they can increase the flow of traffic in the grid.

The Integrated Simulation and Modeling Environment is another project that uses the HubNet application. The project's premise is very much the same as this course – that there are two paradigms of systems modeling today, cybernetic (or what they call aggregate) and agent-based.

These two forms of reasoning are very powerful ways of making sense of complexity in the world – yet, the communities who practice them and the literature describing them are largely separate and distinct. The aggregate and agent-based modeling tools themselves are deployed by different communities – each community focused on its tool and attendant form of reasoning. The time has come for a synthesis of these two approaches at both the cognitive level and the tool level. Thus, the course explores how the two forms of reasoning complement each other in making sense of complexity and change.

CONCLUSION

So that is Systems Thinking as taught at the University of Houston. As described at the outset, the course generalization is fundamental: *A system's behavior is a function of its structure.*

The meaning of these, system, behavior and structure, is explored, the behavior described in the form of graphs of key variables over time, and

---

[4] See http://ccl.northwestern.edu/netlogo/models/ and http://ccl.northwestern.edu/netlogo/download.shtml.
[5] See http://ccl.northwestern.edu/netlogo/hubnet.html.

the structure is modeled using the cybernetic and CAS paradigms. The course objective is primarily to teach systems *thinking* not just systems theory so that demonstration and practice, supported by instruction, is the primary instructional strategy in the course.

The course is challenging and requires very hard work for most. As one graduate put it, "It's hard to remember that I used to think like the people I work with," that is, in simple, linear cause–effect sequences. But many of those who came to the course with a more linear perspective actually remember when these key ideas hit them:

- Every thing is a system consisting of parts that is itself part of larger systems
- Every system and every part is connected to every other system, at least indirectly
- Systems and parts of a system interact in ways that can produce surprising and counter-intuitive results
- The tendency to produce unexpected results makes predicting the outcome of systems' interaction difficult, if not impossible.

And once one sees the world that way, one cannot see it any other way. The process of acquiring a systems perspective is irreversible. Once done, it's that way forever.

RESOURCES

Systems thinking

Anderson, V. & Johnson, L. (1997) *Systems Thinking Basics: From Concepts to Causal Loops* (Cambridge, UK: Pegasus).

- The primary text for teaching causal modeling. The publisher, Pegasus Communications, is also an excellent source for other materials on causal modeling.

Kauffman, D. (1980) *Systems One: An Introduction to Systems Thinking* (Houston, TX: Future Systems).

- The best introduction to systems thinking is contained in two short books by Draper Kauffman entitled *Systems I* and *Systems II*. *Systems I* contains the theory, and *Systems II* contains illustrations of the theory in three broad domains.

Senge, P., Kleiner, A., Roberts, C., Ross, R., & Smith, B. (eds) (1994) *The Fifth Discipline Fieldbook: Strategies and Tools for Building a Learning Organization* (NY: Currency Doubleday).

- Tools and resources for building a learning organization that builds heavily from systems thinking principles.

Systems dynamics

Meadows, D., Meadows, D., Randers, J. & Behrens, William W. (1972) *Limits to Growth: A Report for the Club of Rome's Project on the Predicament of Mankind* (NY: Universe Books).

- Classic projection of exceeding planetary capacity derived from a systems model. This work and the two subsequent revisions (*Beyond the Limits* and *Limits to Growth: The 30-year Update*) make fascinating reading, but students in this course can get the essence from a small pamphlet entitled *A Synopsis: The Limits to Growth* at http://www.sustainer.org/tools_resources/games.html.

Meadows, D. & Randers, J. & Meadows, D. (2004) *Limits to Growth: The 30-Year Update* (White River Junction, VT: Chelsea Green).

- Second update of the original 1972 study concluding that the planet is still approaching the limits of its resources unless suggested corrective measures are taken.

Meadows, D. (2008) *Thinking in Systems: A Primer* (White River Junction, VT: Chelsea Green).

Radzicki, M. & Taylor R. (1997) *Introduction to System Dynamics: A Systems Approach to Understanding Complex Policy Issues* (US Department of Energy, Office of Policy and International Affairs, Office of Science & Technology Policy and Cooperation), http://www.albany.edu/cpr/sds/DL-IntroSysDyn/inside.htm.

- The excellent discursive introduction was produced for the Department of Energy.

Sterman, J. (2000) *Business Dynamics: Systems Thinking and Modeling for a Complex World* (NY: McGraw Hill).

- The definitive text for systems dynamics, but it is expensive.

Demonstration Tools

The Beer Game

- Written up in Senge's *The Fifth Discipline*. It simulates a four-station supply chain in which retailers, distributors, wholesalers, and manufacturers order and receive (or produce) shipments of beer based on their expected demand. The Systems Dynamics Society sells the materials for the board game (http://www.albany.edu/cpr/sds/Beer. htm). MIT (http://beergame.mit.edu/) and MA System (http://www. masystem.com/beergame) offer online versions, and MIT also offers a simulator that plays the game automatically based on input parameters (http://web.mit.edu/jsterman/www/SDG/MFS/simplebeer.html).

Fish Banks

- Now distributed through the Sustainability Institute, a successor to the Institute for Policy and Social Science Research at the University of New Hampshire – the same people who produced the *Limits to Growth* (http://www.sustainer.org/tools_resources/games.html).

The Road Map

Jay Forrester's group produced this excellent set of tutorials, available at http://sysdyn.clexchange.org/road-maps/rm-toc.html.

Stella

- a modeling program for the Apple Macintosh, but also runs on Windows, http://www.iseesystems.com/softwares/Education/ StellaSoftware.aspx.

Systems Thinking Playbook

- Many other activities and simulations in this, http://www.sustainer. org/tools_resources/games.html.

Vensim

- Most use this package from Ventana Systems because it is free for educators and students, http://www.vensim.com/download.html.

World3

- From the *Limits to Growth* series by Dennis and Donella Meadows and Jorgen Randers.

Catastrophe

Thom

- For a good description of Thom's catastrophe theory, http:// en.wikipedia.org/wiki/Catastrophe_theory.

Criticality

Bak, P. (1996) *How Nature Works: The Science of Self-Organized Criticality* (NY: Copernicus Press).

• The best book on criticality. Bak and his co-authors introduced the concept in a 1988 article – "Self-organized criticality," Physical Review. A 38, 364–74, http://prola.aps.org/abstract/PRA/v38/i1/p364_1.

Chaos

Gasmann, Fritz. *The Waterwheel Lab*

• An animation of the chaotic behavior that results from a constant supply of water to a waterwheel is produced by the Paul Scherrer Institute in Switzerland, http://people.web.psi.ch/gassmann/ waterwheel/WaterwheelLab.html.

Rucker, R. *The Chaos Game*

• For chaotic behavior, the most complete set of computer simulations is from Rudy Rucker called The Chaos Game. It runs a number of chaos and fractal routines that are quite amazing. The Chaos Game with the magnets is also an interesting visual representation of chaotic behavior, http://www.cs.sjsu.edu/faculty/rucker/chaos.htm.

Thijssen, Jos. *The Sand Pile Model and Self Organised Criticality*

• Thijssen, a professor of computational physics at Delft University of Technology in the Netherlands, provides a simulation of self-organized criticality at http://www.tn.tudelft.nl/tn/People/Staff/ Thijssen/sandexpl.html.

Complexity/CAS

Hundreds of programs demonstrate CAS behaviors. Two long lists are at Major Complex Systems Software from the Swarm Development Group (http://oasis-edu.com/Oasis/synergie/accueil/soft.htm) and the Artificial Life Section of the DMOZ Open Directory Project (http://www. dmoz.org/Computers/Artificial_Life/). Some favorites are:

• Boids by Craig Reynolds (http://www.red3d.com/cwr/boids/)
• Microants by Stephen Wright (http://www.calresco.org/sos/mants21. zip)
• Stephen Prata's *Artificial Life Playhouse* can be purchased second hand (http://www.alibris.com/search/books/qwork/440419/used/

Artificial%20Life%20Playhouse:%20Evolution%20at%20Your%20
Fingertips). It contains a number of genetic algorithms, including WordEvol (http://www.jmu.edu/geology/evolutionarysystems/
programs/wordevolexp.pdf).

Axelrod, R. & Cohen, M. (2000) *Harnessing Complexity: Organizational
Implications of a Scientific Frontier* (NY: Free Press).

• This is the course text used to investigate agent-based systems.

Conway, J. *Game of Life*

• This is the most famous CAS demo. It is a two-dimensional grid of
cells, each of which can assume two states – on or off – in successive
generations. Cells turn on if three of its eight neighboring states are
on, and they stay on if two or three of its eight neighbors are on.
Otherwise, they turn off. Simple rules, but complex patterns emerge.
Some of those patterns and a list of the more popular programs can
be found at http://en.wikipedia.org/wiki/Conway's_Game_of_Life.

Holland, J. (1992) *Adaptation in Natural and Artificial Systems, Emergence,
and Hidden Order* (Cambridge, MA: MIT Press).

• Holland is probably the best known theoretician of complex adaptive systems, genetic algorithms and artificial life so any of his books
are always excellent, including this and his relatively non-technical
introductions: *Emergence* and *Hidden Order*.

Lewin, R. (1992) *Complexity: Life at the Edge of Chaos* (Chicago, IL: U of
Chicago Press).

Waldrop, M. (1992) *Complexity: The Emerging Science at the Edge of Order
and Chaos* (NY: Simon & Schuster).

Levy, S. (1993) *Artificial Life: A Report from the Frontier Where Computers
Meet Biology* (NY: Vintage).

• These histories of the development of complexity science cover the
same ground, but all have their own interesting stories and anecdotes
about the characters that developed this field.

Mirek, W. *Cellular Automata*

• An amazing gallery of all types of cellular automata at Mirek's
Celebration, http://www.mirekw.com/ca/index.html.

Swarm Development Group, Major Complex Systems Software (http://oasis-edu.com/Oasis/synergie/accueil/soft.htm) and DMOZ Open Directory Project, Artificial Life Section (http://www.dmoz. org/Computers/Artificial_Life/).

Center for Connected Learning (CCL), NetLogo

* The most highly developed agent-based modeling language for teaching systems thinking is comes from CCL at Northwestern University (http://ccl.northwestern.edu/netlogo/). NetLogo, like StarLogo offered previously by MIT (http://education.mit.edu/ starlogo), is a modeling language based on Logo, a programming language developed by Seymour Papert in the 1960s.

3
Perspectives on the Future

INTRODUCTION

This chapter covers material for a proposed new course. As the foresight field grows and evolves, it becomes more difficult to fit new material into existing courses. Eventually a new course becomes necessary, presenting a challenge to an already full core-curriculum. Thus, the material here will likely find its home as an elective, and fills a role of holding tank for some of the newer perspectives, skills, and content that has emerged.

Figure 3.1 shows the five levels of the curriculum. The core of the curriculum includes theory, methods, and content, kicked off by an overview introductory course and capped with a professional seminar course and a Master's option that includes a project, thesis, or internship. The emphasis on theory is typical of any academic program. The theory is tied to methods and approaches (groups of methods). Causal Layered Analysis (CLA) and Integral Futures are two of the newer ideas to foresight that sit on the boundary between theory and methodology. They provide foundational concepts for thinking about the future. Yet they are also emerging as important methodologies. CLA is more developed as a methodology at this point, but the great interest and enthusiasm for Integral Futures suggest that it will generate methodological applications as well. For example, the well-respected journal *Futures* commissioned a special issue on Integral Futures methodologies in 2008 (Hayward, Slaughter & Voros, 2008).

Theory and methods are emphasized to a greater extent in the curriculum than specific domain knowledge. The idea is to teach people how to fish, rather than catch the fish for them. However, some domain knowledge is important. The course "World Futures" is the only explicit

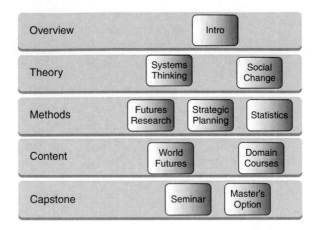

Figure 3.1　Five levels of the curriculum

content course in the core curriculum (some highlights are appended). Electives are typically used to fill out the content piece. Students have three electives to build specific domain knowledge, whether it be in marketing, planning, technology, or whatever their interest is. There are also content modules sprinkled throughout the curriculum.

This chapter emphasizes these newer theories and methods. It begins by putting them into a larger context of foresight traditions.

HISTORY

Futurist and educator Richard Slaughter (2004, Ch. 11) has developed a framework for describing the evolution of foresight. He suggests three traditions based on theoretical perspectives of foresight work.

The foundational empirical and cultural traditions emerged separately but more or less at the same time after World War II. The roots of the empirical tradition are in the US and the cultural in Europe. The critical emerged later out of those perspectives – principally the cultural – and the integral has emerged from the critical most recently. Of course, each of the traditions is in operation today and they are not mutually exclusive but complementary.

Empirical and cultural

The US roots in foresight emerged after World War II in the military policy context, from the work of systems thinker and strategist Herman

Kahn at the RAND Corporation. Kahn (1962) used scenario planning to "think the unthinkable" about the potential outcomes of nuclear conflict. His successful use of scenario planning in the military context attracted interest in the corporate sector and foresight expanded its reach. The empirical focus is on mapping or forecasting changes in the external world. It rests upon an objective view of reality. The goal is to discover and describe the key trends and systems connections and develop accurate forecasts of the future. Scenario planning became and has remained a popular qualitative forecasting tool for doing so. Alongside it, a variety of quantitative forecasting techniques emerged, such as trend extrapolation, systems modeling, and growth curves (Martino, 1972). The most popular was the Delphi method, which gathered expert input using an iterative approach that was very successful in identifying expert consensus. Quantitative forecasting has become less used by futurists over time as it became clear that the world is simply too complex to simply plug formulas into models and get the right answer. Nonetheless, systems thinking and newer related ideas, such as chaos and complexity, have developed – along with simulations and gaming – and remain important tools in the futurist tool kit.

Alongside the US approach, a European tradition, based principally in France and including the former USSR, took a more culturally based approach to exploring the future. Where the empirical approach favored an objective or value-free mapping or description of potential futures, the European tradition was more subjective and emphasized the search for preferred futures. It embraced the influence of culture and relied on a more rational and intuitive approach. Gaston Berger established the International Center for Prospective (foresight) in the 1950s, which influenced French national planning and inspired a generation of French futurists. In the sixties, Bertrand de Jouvenal (1967) established the influential Futuribles project and published his foresight classic *The Art of Conjecture* (Cornish, 2004, 189–93).

They are grouped together in that they are highly complementary. The empirical seeks to describe the future in order to influence decision-makers to act in a way that leads toward preferred futures. Similarly, the cultural emphasizes the preferred future, but first requires a description of the futures landscape. They have similar goals but different emphases and approaches. The empirical and rational traditions came together in the 1970s in a very public way when French scenario planner Pierre Wack drew upon Kahn's work and used scenario planning successfully with Royal Dutch Shell to anticipate the Arab Oil Embargo, and enabled the company to prepare and improve its position in the industry dramatically as a result. His rational intuitive approach – backed with significant empirical research – led scenario planning to its great popularity.

Critical

The European tradition was picked up by many nations, especially Australia, and many US futurists as well, and eventually formed the basis for the critical tradition. In fact, Berger had talked about how looking at the future "disturbed it" (Godet, 2006, 2). The critical tradition's goal is to broaden and deepen the nature of futures inquiry – to probe beneath the surface. It raises fundamental questions about "the given," and looks for insights from challenging basic assumptions. In contrast to a "pure" empirical approach that attempts to describe the future in an unbiased way, the critical tradition seeks to "problematize" the future, challenging the basic notions of "the good." It would ask, for instance, good for whom? Who wins and who loses? Who participates and who is left out? It gains insight into the future by asking these types of probing questions and exploring how the future might turn out differently if current arrangements or conventional wisdom does not turn out as expected. A new health care proposal, for example, may be deemed "good" by the current system, but leave out many constituents, and those left out may come back to challenge the system and create an unexpected alternative future.

The critical tradition suggests that reality is not best understood in objective (favored by the empirical tradition) or subjective (favored by the cultural tradition) terms, but rather as a social construction, that is, it is what "we" agree it is (Berger & Luckman, 1967). Reality is open to interpretation and thus open to question – critical futures raises those questions. It therefore emphasizes that multiple perspectives and interpretations are not only valid, but necessary in making sense of the future (as well as the past and present). The emblematic methodology of this approach is CLA, developed and popularized by futurist Sohail Inayatullah (1998).

Integral

This emerging third phase builds upon the critical tradition by incorporating the work of Integral philosopher Ken Wilber and colleagues. Slaughter introduced the notion of Integral Futures to the foresight community as a new approach to combat what he termed a flatland approach that emphasized the measurable at the expensive of the interpretive. He noted that in catering to client demands for hard data, futurists were missing insights from the "soft" or interpretive realm. He suggested a need to rebalance approaches to incorporate insights from both (Slaughter, 1998).

The key insight driving Integral Futures is that the future is best understood from multiple perspectives and viewpoints. It draws up different ways of understanding and knowing, with the goal of developing broader, wider and deeper views of the future.

GENERALIZATION

A perspective, according to the Cambridge Dictionary, is "a particular way of considering something." The goal of this course is to introduce alternatives to the empirical and cultural perspectives upon which the field is founded and grew up around. These perspectives are represented throughout the curriculum and this text. The reset of this chapter focuses on the newer critical and integral perspectives.

The critical perspective is currently represented in a module on critical thinking. It introduces the theory and provides a specific process to analyze assumptions and evidence about the future. There is also currently a module on CLA.

A key emphasis of these modules is to challenge assumptions and "the given." What people take for granted is challenged to see if perhaps there are changes underway, or at least possible, that would in turn have ripple effects throughout the future. Insights arising from these challenges can thus be very powerful, particularly when a foundational assumption is found to be open to challenge. For instance, before 9/11, it was largely assumed in the US that the terrorist threat was "abroad." Efforts were chiefly aimed at tracking terrorists down "over there," thus little preparation was done to ready for an attack on the home front. After the attack, of course, a Department of Homeland Security was established. Hindsight is 20-20, but the idea is that challenging key assumptions enables the possibility to consider threats – or opportunities – that escape conventional analysis.

Integral Futures is an exciting new development in foresight that has been increasingly represented in the curriculum. In addition to being a module in the curriculum, it has been the subject of independent studies and a Master's project by enthusiastic students. While the jury is still out on how best to use it or how useful it is, it has stimulated discussion, debate, and some controversy. It highlights a key point of this course: that the perspective one employs in analyzing a topic or problem has a tremendous influence on the nature of the results. Thus, having access to a wide range of perspectives increases the range of potential results.

APPROACH

The proposed course would bring together CLA and Integral Futures as "alternative perspectives," that is, an alternative to the empirical and cultural perspectives.

Causal Layered Analysis

Causal Layered Analysis (CLA) is a relatively new tool, developed by futurist Sohail Inayatullah (2003, 2), emerging out of the critical perspective. CLA is "offered as a new research theory and method. As a theory it seeks to integrate empiricist, interpretive, critical, and action learning modes of knowing. As a method, its utility is not in predicting the future but in creating transformative spaces for the creation of alternative futures. It is also likely to be of use in developing more effective – deeper, inclusive, longer-term – policy."

As a theory it provides a perspective that can inform any approach or method. The concept of thinking in layers was introduced by Richard Slaughter (1985). He used an architectural metaphor to distinguish surface structures and the underlying foundation. It influenced Inayatullah's thinking, as did the ideas of Galtung, Foucault, and Sarkar.

Time Scale of Change		The "Litany" – "observations"
Continuous	**Problems**	observational: events, diagnosed problems, media spin, opinions, policy; visible and audible; unconnected (scanning)
Years	**Driving Forces**	**Trend Analysis** Trends, start connecting; systems analysis, feedback interconnections, technical explanations, social analysis, policy analysis (systems)
Decades	**Worldviews**	**Breadth & Depth Analysis** culture, values, language, postmodernisms, spiral dynamics memes (alternatives)
Societal/Civilizational	**Archetypes**	**Myth/Metaphor Analysis** Jungian archetypes, ancient bedrock stories, gut level responses, emotional responses, visual images – may not be words for it(visioning)

Figure 3.2   The layers of Causal Layered Analysis
Source: Derived from Inayatullah (2003), Slaughter (2003), List (2003) & Schultz (2004).

Inayatullah's CLA, in addition to its theoretical perspective, provides a technique for drilling down into the layers of driving forces, belief systems, worldviews, and fundamental myths and metaphors to better understand a problem and explore the context around it.

The first level, problems, is often exaggerated and used for political purposes and usually presented by the news media. The events, issues, and trends at this level are not connected and appear disconnected. The problem level is the most visible and obvious, requiring little analytic capabilities. Assumptions are rarely questioned. It is useful to think of this level in terms of disconnected events and news headlines, sometimes referred to as observations when they are related to a particular issue or topic being monitored.

The second level, driving forces, is concerned with causes and explanations, including economic, cultural, political, and historical factors that produce the problems above. Interpretation is given to quantitative data. This type of analysis is usually articulated by policy institutes and published as articles or editorial pieces in newspapers or in non-mainstream journals. The role of the state and other actors and interests is often explored at this level. It is useful to think of this layer in terms of the trends and systems underneath or driving what shows up in the headlines.

The third level, worldviews, is concerned with structure and worldview that supports or legitimizes a problem or issue. The task is to find deeper social, linguistic, cultural structures that are actor-invariant (not dependent on who the actors are). Discerning the deeper assumptions behind a problem or issue is crucial as are efforts to develop an alternative vision or interpretation. The way that problems are presented and described is questioned at this level.

The fourth and bottom level, archetypes, explores fundamental metaphors or myths. These are the deep stories – the unconscious and often emotive dimensions of the problem or the paradox. This level provides a gut/emotional level experience to the worldview under inquiry. The language used is more concerned with evoking visual images, with touching the heart instead of teaching the head. This level includes very powerful influences, and they can be difficult to identify since they operate at the sub-conscious. It takes us to the civilizational level of identity. The "American Dream" and Gaia concept of the Earth as a fragile, living organism are examples of myths.

The table below gives an example of how an issue can be analyzed using Causal Layered Analysis.

There are several ways for applying the layers to a problem or issue being explored. It is common to use CLA in conjunction with another

Table 3.1 Using CLA to analyze boomer retirement

Level	Description
Problems ("The Headlines")	The essence of the headlines fall into two camps: (1) Boomers won't be able to retire, due to economic necessity; (2) If Boomers do retire, there won't be enough people to take their place. Both are bad! Not much is said about Boomers wanting to keep working.
Driving Forces (Trends)	But several trends suggest that Baby Boomers will continue to work, often switching from jobs they "had" to do for economic reasons to jobs that want to do because they are fulfilling.
	• *Age Bending.* Age "inappropriate" behavior increasingly common.
	• *Death of the schedule.* People in general are less inclined to follow schedules, especially schedules that are imposed upon them by others.
	• *Life-long learning.* People are learning when they need to learn, at whatever life stage that need emerges.
	• *Wellness and beyond.* Boomers are expecting to live longer.
	• *Virtual work enables flexibility.* Telecommuting, flexi-time, and greater reliance on virtual technologies will provide the flexibility that will make it easier for Boomers to continue working.
	• *Project-based work.* Facilitates contracting, temporary, part-time, and flexible work, which is well suited to Boomers.
	• *Talent shortage.* There is no shortage of work – rather there is a shortage of people willing and capable of doing certain work for what they feel is appropriate compensation.
Worldviews	• *Those with traditional values/worldviews* are most likely to follow the conventional route. They would prefer to continue with patterns and plans that have worked before – they follow the script and plan. They will form the bulk of those who completely retire.
	• *Those with modern values/worldviews* will tend to take a market-based approach to retirement. Is it in their interest to retire? More and more of them will tend to answer no. They will bristle at being forced to retire. They will feel like they have plenty left to contribute, and won't want some bureaucrat or policy telling them what they have to do. They want to continue achieving, even if that energy is directed differently.
	• *Those with postmodern values/worldview* will feel a sense of duty to continue to share their talents with their colleagues and communities. They will be the most likely to shift to cause-related kinds of work. Perhaps they will donate their time to improving their community.

Table 3.1 Continued

Level	Description
	• *Those with integral values/worldview* will take a strategic view of retirement. They are least likely to be on a conventional path in the first place. They will have some sense of long-term direction, with little consideration of retirement, but will simply proceed along a path that makes most sense for what they want to do.
Archetypes (the Story)	The current archetype or story about retirement is that it is a reward for a lifetime of hard work. Historically speaking, it's a fairly new story. In Britain it can be pegged to the Old Age Pensions Act introduced in 1908 and in the US to the Social Security Act of 1935. Before that, stopping work at some fixed point was simply not an option. People kept working as long as they could on the farm. Industrialization brought a different model: with a greater emphasis on efficiency it eased those judged less productive, that is, "older" workers, out of the workforce. Although initially resisted, it eventually came to be seen as a desirable thing, and then an entitlement.

Source: Derived from Hines (2010).

method. It provides a means to ensure that the problem is approached from a variety of angles and perspectives and does not fall victim to being led astray by hidden or unquestioned assumptions. It will often lead to a reframing of the original topic or issue, as it may identify that what the team originally thought was the problem is actually not the real problem at all.

Integral Futures

The key concept underlying Integral Theory is to include as many perspectives, styles, and methodologies as possible when exploring a topic. Integral Theory suggests there are four irreducible perspectives (subjective, inter-subjective, objective, and inter-objective) that should be consulted when attempting to fully understand any issue or aspect of reality.

These four perspectives (within a perspective) are represented in a four-quadrant model. Incorporated in quotes are examples of how the issue of sustainability might be viewed from each of the quadrants. Below is a summary of the four perspectives embodied in each quadrant in Figure 3.3.

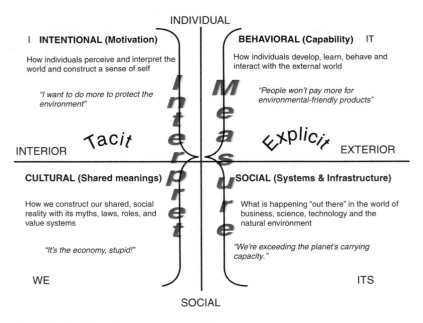

Figure 3.3   Wilber's four quadrant model
Source: Hines, based on Slaughter (1999).

The upper left: Intentional (subjective) is the individual's interior world, which can only be accessed via interpretation. The concerns are individual motivation, changes in people's values, perceptions and goals, and the meaning of life. Regarding sustainability, in this case individuals have a value of environmental protection.

The upper right: Behavioral (objective) is the individual's exterior world, in which individual behavior can be observed. The concerns are changes in the ways people act externally, for example, voting patterns, consumer behavior, or reproductive practices. Regarding sustainability, in this case individuals often behave at odds with their values; they profess environmental values but purchase the less environmentally friendly product because it is cheaper.

The lower right: Social (inter-objective) is the collective exterior world, often referred to as the physical world, or world of systems and infrastructure. The concerns are objectively measurable changes in natural and constructed external environments. Regarding sustainability, in this case evidence is increasingly pointing to ecological systems being overloaded.

The lower left: Cultural (inter-subjective) is the collective interior world of the shared meaning of groups, as expressed in the culture. The concerns are shared collective structures, such as changes in languages, cultures, and institutions. Regarding sustainability, in this case the culture often values the economy over the environment.

There are many different perspectives within each quadrant – which is the point. The goal of Integral Futures is to explore these different perspectives from a holistic vantage point and evaluate their interactions in forecasting the future.

While there is much, much more to Integral Theory, the four-quadrant model is at its core. What distinguishes the Integral approach is that it considers the subjective experience and integrates it along with the objective, inter-subjective, and the inter-objective. Effects in one quadrant influence the others. The theory suggests that solutions which include a balanced consideration of all four quadrants will typically lead to outcomes that are more successful for individuals and groups.

The primary benefit of Integral Futures so far has been to provide a perspective or framework upon which to compare various futures theories. Applying the integral model to futures thinking helps to encourage a holistic approach that incorporates multiple points of view. A second benefit is as a source of methodological innovation for practitioners. There is currently debate on whether its strength is as a perspective or a methodology. Some suggest it may not be method at all. Futurist Peter Hayward says, "The integral approach is, at its essence, perspectival rather than methodological. That is to say that method alone will not evoke the integral perspective but rather that integrality in methods is enabled by taking integral perspectives" (Hayward, 2008, 109).

These potential benefits and debate are at the core of the diffusion of Integral Futures. Its diffusion is captured in three phases (Collins & Hines, 2010, 6–13):

There is evidence, albeit anecdotal, that Integral Futures has value as a perspective that can lead to broader and deeper futures thinking, and that it can improve the practice of individual futurists. The extent of its impact on methodology, particular the development of new methods, is less clear at present. There is evidence of a positive impact on revitalizing existing tools. But the support is still quite thin for the development of new methods and applications. It is probably unreasonable to expect much more at such an early stage of diffusion, so it would be inappropriate to draw firm conclusions at this point.

Table 3.2   Phases of Integral Futures

Phase	Focus
1. Perspective (1998–2004)	The focus was mostly on the theory and initial attempts at applications; it involved introducing Integral Theory to futurists and exploring ideas for how it might be applied to foresight.
2. Methods (2005–2008)	Attempts to apply Integral Theory to futures practice in the form of methods; incorporated discussion of ideas around methodological application, including for organizational development, strategic change, deeper and richer scenarios, uncovering worldviews, awakening individual capacities, development of paradigms for inquiry, and assessing existing foresight tools.
3. Sense-Making (2009-present)	Debate and some controversy; an Integral Futures "Special Issue" in *Futures* generated several responses that were captured in a follow-up special issue. The articles took on Integral Theory and its proponents, some in a casual tone, some more strident, and others in a more serious academic style.

CONCLUSION

The UH Futures program has its roots in the empirical tradition with an influence of European cultural stream. Empirical methods are surveyed in the Futures Research course. The course on Systems Thinking, which has evolved to include more recent developments on complexity and agent-based modeling, provides a conceptual framework for this tradition. The cultural tradition gets its most focused attention in the course on Social Change.

As mentioned above, as concepts and methods have arisen from the newer Critical and now Integral tradition, they have been inserted into the core curriculum on a piecemeal basis. The proposed new course – and this chapter – calls out some of these important new pieces to give them the more focused attention they deserve.

The proposed course on perspectives would bring together several different perspectives for thinking about the future under one umbrella. Having access to a wide range of thinking and ideas for conceptualizing the future is an obvious benefit to students. The curriculum does not take a position on the "right" one. The goal is to provide students with as many options as possible and enable them to put together their own viewpoint.

While the course has a theoretic orientation, it also provides access to practical tools and methods. A critical thinking guide provides a useful process and template that can be applied to evaluating works related to the future. Ideally, it becomes embedded in one thinking process, such that it becomes almost impossible to critically evaluate information. Similarly, the creativity module provides a generic process guide and tools useful to any creative problem-solving agenda that in turn can be applied to any futures project.

The curriculum continues to evolve alongside developments in the field. Thus Causal Layered Analysis and Integral Futures are highlighted as leading examples of new perspectives for thinking about the future, as well as for providing new methodological approaches.

RESOURCES

De Jouvenel, B. (1967) *The Art of Conjecture* (NY: Basic Books).

• Representative work of the European cultural tradition in futures thinking. Explores the fundamental concept of how ideas about what may happen in the future can be a means of deciding what actions to take in the present.

Slaughter, R. (2004) *Futures Beyond Dystopia: Creating Social Foresight* (NY: Routledge/Falmer).

• Chapter 11 has a nice summary of the epistemological origins and evolutions of foresight.

Critical thinking

Toulmin, S. (1972) *Human Understanding: The Collective Use and Evolution of Concepts* (Princeton, NJ: Princeton U Press).

• The critical thinking process used in the curriculum was adapted from the Toulmin Model of Argumentation, which contains six interrelated components used for analyzing arguments.

Creativity

Buzan, T. with Buzan, B. (1996) *The Mind Map Book* (NY: Penguin).

• A thorough overview of the principles and techniques for doing mind-mapping from the pioneer.

De Bono, E. (1993) *Serious Creativity* (Des Moines, IA: Advanced Practical Thinking Training).

- The best of de Bono's dozens of books on creativity.

Hermann, N. (1989) *The Creative Brain* (Lake Lure, NC: The Ned Hermann Group).

- Went beyond right brain–left brain by adding the upper and lower hemisphere. The four quadrants included investigation, creation, evaluation, and activation. While later research found this anatomically inaccurate, it remains a useful metaphor for characterizing different thinking styles.

Weisberg, R. (1993) *Creativity: Beyond the Myth of Genius* (NY: W. H. Freeman).

- Investigates how some great creative thinkers came up with their key insights, dispelling the myth that they simply came out of nowhere. Rather, they emerged after years of prior research and thought.

Causal Layered Analysis

Inayatullah, S. (1998, October) "Causal Layered Analysis: Post-Structuralism as Method," *Futures*, 30 (8), 815–29.

- The article that introduced CLA to the futures field.

Inayatullah, S. (2004) *The Causal Layered Analysis (CLA) Reader: Theory and Case Studies of an Integrative and Transformative Methodology* (Taipei, Taiwan: Tamkang University).

- Substantial collection of essays, case studies and resources about CLA.

Integral Futures

Esbjorn-Hargens, S. (2009) *An Overview of Integral Theory: An All-Inclusive Framework for the 21st Century*, Integral Institute, Resource Paper No. 1, March.

- Outstanding overview of Integral Theory – goes beyond the work of pioneer Wilber to survey the wider landscape of Integral Theory.

Slaughter, R. (ed.) (2008) "Special Issue: Integral Futures," *Futures*, 40.

- The special issue is a landmark development serving as "take notice" alert to the field. Slaughter coordinated the issue and suggested why Integral Futures is relevant to Futures inquiry and application.

Wilber, K. (1991) *Sex, Ecology, Spirituality: The Spirit of Evolution* (Boston, MA: Shambhala).

* The groundbreaking work on Integral Theory that was subsequently applied to foresight.

Wilber, K. (2001) *A Theory of Everything: An Integral Vision for Business, Politics, Science and* Spirituality (Boston, MA: Shambhala).

* The "pop" version of Integral Theory.

4
Social Change

INTRODUCTION

Social change is a fact of our time, perhaps even a fact of all times. There are those who believe that change is *the* fundamental reality. The ancient Greek philosopher Heraclitus famously said, "You cannot step into the same river twice." The river is different, and people are different, moment to moment. So everything in the world is in continual motion, no doubt.

At another level, however, it seems that some things do stay the same, or at least people think of them as the same thing, moment to moment. It is the same river in many ways. It has the same name, the same course, the same banks, the same springs, year after year, perhaps for centuries. People also say, "I stepped in the river yesterday." And who is the "I" unless they think of themselves as the same person day to day? Different to some extent, yes, because people are changed by all experience, but also the same in many ways. Everything does not change at each instant.

HISTORY

A French intellectual in the second half of the 19th Century, Auguste Comte, used these observations to define the new social science of sociology. Sociology is the study of humans in groups – families, work groups, communities, and societies. Comte proposed that sociology be divided into two main branches – social statics and social dynamics. Social statics would study the persistent characteristics of groups and societies, those things that lasted for some time. Social dynamics would study how those characteristics changed over time. He observed that change in societies was the same as change in people and rivers. Societies have persistent qualities even when the people in them are replaced with completely different people. The United States is fundamentally the *same* country, in many ways, as it was 100 years ago, even though almost everyone who lived in the country at that time is now gone. At the same time, no one doubts that the United States is a very *different* country from what it was 100 years ago as well.

So one would think that sociologists would divide their time more or less evenly between these two branches of their discipline – asking the questions (1) how societies maintain their identity and stability over long periods of time and yet (2) how they still change over time as well. But modern sociology does not divide its time evenly. Almost all sociological research is about social statics, the modern term for which is social structure, and almost none is about social dynamics, what we now call social change. Just look at the table of contents of Giddens et al.'s (2009) *Introduction to Sociology* – the introductory text that came up first on a search in both Barnes & Noble and Amazon in September 2009:

How much does this book contain about social structure versus social change? Well, there is one chapter on social change, but 17 chapters on other things. There are some changes noted in some of the other chapters, such as individual change in Chapter 4 (the Life Cycle) and organizational change in Chapter 10 (The Rise of...). The authors undoubtedly touch on change in some of the other chapters, but is it "more or less" evenly distributed, as Comte suggested? Hardly.

Giddens's book is not unique. In a review, in September 2009, of the tables of contents of the top ten Introduction to Sociology textbooks, only seven even had a chapter on social change. And it was always the last chapter of the book, just like Giddens's. (How much time and attention do teachers and students spend on the last chapter as they are preparing to wind up the semester?) In total, those ten books devoted only 3% of the total pages to the chapters on social change.

There are lots of reasons for this emphasis on social structure rather than social change, most of which are based on the need for graduate students and assistant professors to publish as much as they can and as fast they can – publish or perish! It's easier and quicker to study a static structure than a changing one. They would have to wait, sometimes for a long time, for organizations and societies to change.

But the oddest part of this emphasis on social structure is that it takes place in a society that is enamored with and perhaps even addicted to change. People are treated to dozens if not hundreds of news sources – literally what is *new*. Improvement and innovation are key to success in every institution, particularly business and technology. Whole libraries are full of books on leading change. But has anyone described how social change actually occurs? Not many.

So this chapter fills that gap, as do a few excellent books on social change. (Thankfully, some sociologists do study social change!) The future is about change. Plausible differences between the present and the future are the most interesting and, to some extent, the most important things to know. The purpose of this chapter, then, is to understand how those differences come about. How do we explain the changes that occur? And what are the implications of those changes for the future?

GENERALIZATION

Explaining social change

The good news for explaining change is that some sociologists and many other thinkers have been writing about social change for a long time. The bad news is that they have not come up with any single theory of social change that everyone agrees with.

Unified, consensus theories of change are common in many scientific disciplines, particularly in the physical sciences. So in physics there are theories of gravity and the ideal gas law; in chemistry, the theories of chemical bonding and heat transfer; in biology, evolution and protein synthesis. While there remains much not understood about these theories, every member of those disciplines subscribes to the basics.

The same cannot be said of the social sciences. While social scientists approach their study with the same philosophy – objectivity, conclusions based on evidence, critical thinking – and use many of the same methods and tools – experiments, statistics – they still lack a fundamental unifying theory of their discipline. So economists have classical theory, rational expectations, and behavioral economics amidst a host of others. In anthropology, there are structuralists and cultural anthropologists. In political science, there are realists and idealists. And the list goes on and on.

So how does one explain social change when there is no theory for doing so? The answer is that there are many theories for doing so. Granted that it would be easier with one theory, as is the case in physics, but that's not the situation. Perhaps there will be one theory someday, but today there are many theories. So to explain social change in the present, it has to be explained in light of that fact. While most social scientists are arguing about which theory is the *right* theory, futurists need to explain change today rather than wait for the right theory to emerge.

Fortunately, there is an analogue in the physical sciences that will help justify the use of multiple theories. In the early part of the 20th Century, physicists were puzzled about the behavior of photons and electrons. In some experiments, they behaved like particles, such as pebbles or bullets. In others, they behaved like waves. The details are not important here. The point is that they had one thing (a photon, for instance) that looked like a particle in some circumstances and like a wave in other circumstances.

Could it be both? Well waves and particles are quite different things. It is hard, and maybe even impossible, to think of one thing being both. And that was the key. It is not what they are intrinsically, which will probably never be known, but how they are understood by using the conceptual tools available. Neils Bohr explained this duality in his theory of complementarity.[1]

Bohr's "solution" was that fundamental matter was something that people would never fully comprehend. The best one could do was to

---

[1] See http://www.upscale.utoronto.ca/GeneralInterest/Harrison/Complementarity/CompCopen.html.

use the complementary concepts of wave and particle simultaneously. The image is that quantum phenomena and other inconceivable parts of reality, like social change, are locked in a container with many windows. People see different mechanisms for change depending on which window they look through. They believe that change is a unitary phenomenon within the container, but it can only be explained using the apparently incompatible, yet complementary theories available.

Social change occurs in the macro world, not in the world of quantum physics, and our ancestors were aware of change – the seasons and the cycle of life and death, for instance. But what makes social science, and social change in particular, so difficult is that it involves human consciousness. The nature of consciousness is still not understood, and the earliest ancestors probably did not even know that it existed. So any phenomenon that involves humans as conscious, active entities is currently beyond our conceptual apparatus to understand in any unitary fashion. Someday consciousness might be understood, but social change needs to be explained today rather than waiting for a unified theory to emerge.

In that case, the multiple theories of social change are not a problem; they are a blessing. Bohr's complementarity principle can be used to study social change through the lenses of the different theories.

Just because there are many theories of social change in the literature does not mean that people don't already *believe* they can explain social change. They do it every day. People often say, "This is *really* what is happening, what is *really* going on." That's an explanation of some observable change using unobservable causes and mechanisms – an explanation of change. "It's all about money, or power, or technology," or whatever. Different people use different theories, and hence they get into disputes about what *really* is going on.

When using the principle of complementarity to explain social change, however, the claim to know what is *really* going on is forfeit. What is *really* going on is beyond people's ability to comprehend. Rather different, sometimes multiple and indeed sometimes incompatible theories to explain change are used, depending on the situation. That is still an explanation, though albeit not as satisfying as one theory that works all the time.

But getting to the point of explaining social change using multiple theories is not as easy as it sounds. The first step is realizing that people each have one or two favorite theories that they tend to use most of the time. They are not wrong, but if they only use one or two, then they are probably using them too much and ignoring the other theories that could be used instead. The second step then is to place those theories alongside a host of others that can be used at the appropriate times. This course leads one through both of these steps by considering the validity of ten or so different theories of social change – some of which are already used, most of which are not. Which of those does one use? What might one consider using instead?

Critical assumptions

But what makes different theories different? Why do people choose to use one theory over another? Explanatory theories are basically chosen, not revealed in nature. Social change does not come with a label or an instruction manual that says "This happened because of power" or "This change is driven by money." The change is observable, but the explanation is not. People construct an argument to support their explanation using that theory.

Arguments consist of two types of statements: evidence and assumptions. There is lots of evidence for the theories reviewed here, evidence that has been accumulating for centuries. Each of the theories, however, also rests on a set of assumptions about human nature, the nature of society, and the world. People accept and use these assumptions implicitly, usually without thinking about them. For instance, many people believe that people are naturally good, and they are taught to be bad. Or the opposite. Society needs strong leaders or else it will fall apart. Or the opposite of that.

There is no way to *prove* which of these assumptions is true. There is plenty of evidence for each one *and* for its opposite as well! Therefore, one has to *choose* which assumptions to use. And since one tends to use the same assumptions in almost all cases, one also tends to explain change using the same theories in those cases as well.

Part of the course on social change, then, is recognizing the assumptions people use that lead to the theories they adopt, and considering perhaps using alternative assumptions and theories in some cases. There is no way to tell that one is using the *right* assumptions and theories. That is unknowable. But one can make a reasonable *argument* to support one's choice, an argument that reasonable people will at least consider, if not accept. So the test of whether one is *right* or not is whether other people accept the argument, or at least consider it a reasonable one to make. Again, not as satisfying as being *right* in any absolute sense, but that is unknowable as well.

There are a certain class of assumptions, called critical assumptions, which distinguish between one theory and another. If one accepts a certain assumption, one gets a certain theory; if one accepts its opposite, one gets another. The term is borrowed from science which uses critical experiments. A critical experiment is one that has two outcomes. If one outcome occurs, then a theory is accepted; if it does not, then the theory is rejected.

One of the most famous critical experiments was used to disprove the theory of phlogiston. In 1667, in the early days of chemical science, Johann Becher proposed a theory that flammable substances contained a substance called phlogiston which burned off when the material burned. He pointed to the fact that a block of wood is heavier than the ashes left after it has burned so something must have been consumed in the fire. Pretty obvious, right?

But Mikhail Lomonosov in 1753 and then the famous chemist Antoine-Laurent Lavoisier in the 1780s burned substances in closed vessels that did not allow any of the gases of combustion to escape. Had the weight of the vessel changed, then something was obviously being consumed; if it stayed the same, then nothing was being consumed. The weight of the vessels did stay the same, and the phlogiston theory was dead – the result of a critical experiment.

Of course, critical experiments cannot be performed in social change because there is not the same level of control of societies that chemists have over substances. Sociology is largely an observational science, like astronomy. It deals with what can be observed; the conditions of a critical experiment cannot be constructed.

But the analogy holds: Choosing one assumption gets one theory; choosing its opposite gets another. It's like a plant that grows underground but which shoots sprouts above ground. A stand of bamboo, for instance, is actually one plant connected by an underground system, called rhizomes, which are actually stems that grow underground. In the same way, different theories may share a common set of assumptions. One path to the surface leads to one theory; another path leads to another one. So throughout this chapter, be on the lookout for the critical assumptions that distinguish one theory from another.

One last point before getting into the actual theories. This book is about teaching the future. Different theories of social change and their embedded assumptions are a critical element to the three functions of foresight – understanding, mapping, and influencing the future. Theories not only explain how a change came about (from the past); they also support how that change will continue (or not) and influence the future.

Different theories result in different images of the future and alternative scenarios, the core of foresight. Different theories also recommend different strategies for intervening in the system to influence it toward a more preferable future. Alternative theories of social change lie at the root of many alternative scenarios and strategies. The ability to conceive of as many alternative scenarios and strategies as possible is directly related to the ability to apply different theories to the same social change. Not all of the explanations will be plausible, and some might even be downright ridiculous. Of course, one can deal with multiple explanations in forecasting by simply identifying alternative scenarios. One must be more careful, however, in picking strategies based on multiple theories because the right strategy for one theory might be horribly wrong for another. So in the end, one might have to choose, but at least one realizes one is making a choice rather than picking the strategy blindly. Or one might even be able to craft a strategy that will be pretty good if either one or another theory is correct.

So while one often cannot decide for sure what is *really* going on, knowing something is better than knowing nothing. And more importantly, knowing what the choices are is better than blindly and implicitly believing that only one explanation is always true.

APPROACH

The course currently teaches ten theories of social change. This number has grown slightly over the years; the initial version of the course had eight.

The ten theories are:

1. **Progress Theory**: general improvement over long periods of time
2. **Development Theory**: consistent direction on key characteristics
3. **Technology Theory**: materialism and the means to manipulate it
4. **Culture Theory**: ideas, goals, intentions
5. **Cycle Theory**: recurrence of macro states
6. **Conflict Theory**: struggle among interest groups
7. **Market Theory**: competition among producers and consumers
8. **Power Theory**: inordinately influence a specific group
9. **Evolution Theory**: variation, selection and replication
10. **Emergence Theory**: interaction of independent agents

Progress Theory

The course begins with Progress Theory because it is the dominant explanation of social change in Western culture. Robert Nisbet (1979) catalogues how the theory of Progress appeared in ancient and medieval writings, but it was not until the Enlightenment that the theory gained the pre-eminence that it has today.

From the earliest schooling, children are taught that biological species and human societies have traced a path of

> **Progress Theory assumptions**
>
> 1. Today's society is better than the societies of the past.
> 2. Future societies will be better than the present.

increasing capability and sophistication, not to mention comfort, convenience and standard of living. Progress Theory proselytizes that while most Westerners respect other societies and their cultures, they believe that modern Western society is the pinnacle of human development and that indeed it is likely to get even better in the decades and centuries to come. Westerners are, just like everyone else, concerned with the challenges of the day, whether it is poverty, disease, terrorism, or global warming, to name just a few, but, the theory states, they also believe that human ingenuity and persistence will conquer those problems the way it has conquered so many in the past.

The theory sounds hopelessly optimistic and perhaps even a bit naïve to the casual observer. But proponents of Progress Theory can point to

Progress theorists argue that, as proof of people's satisfaction with the progress of the present, when asked, few would want to trade places with any person of equal standing in any previous historical period; *et sequitur*, if they thought that any other period was better, wouldn't they want to live then instead?

Two pieces of evidence undermine this: (1) some people, usually older people, would happily go back and live in "The Good Old Days" of their youth. (2) Progress Theory would suggest that, because the future will be better than the present, people would want to trade places with someone in the future; however, few want to live in the future either. Two explanations for this come to mind: (1) the risk of landing in a time that might not be so good – a war, famine, or some other cataclysm. After all, Progress says that society is better *overall* and *in the long run* and there will be some difficult periods along the way. (2) A more persuasive explanation might be that people are more comfortable in their own time than in any other. They have been socialized in this time; they know how it works and would prefer to remain here and not take the risk that they wouldn't like the future or would not fit in or be successful there.

increases in many indicators of long-term improvements in the human condition: life expectancy, literacy, and wealth, to name just a few. Opponents point out that this is an average and for many people – perhaps most – things have not necessarily improved.

Critical assumption. So what do Progress theorists assume that no other theory does? What does one have to assume to use progress as the primary theory of social change? The answer is simply that some universal standard of value can be used as the criterion for judging which changes are progressive and which are not. Some common values across many societies might act as a universal standard – security, liberty, justice, sufficient water, food, or even material comfort. Some would argue with these; but even if we accept them, not every person or society has experienced change in that direction. These are the values of Western society today, and many others aspire to them, but many peoples have also suffered at the hands of Western societies.

What is more, many people today see the West not as a progressive state, but as a decadent one – a decline from a better, simpler, holier and more moral time. One may not agree, but one must admit that proponents of this view have a point. Modern society is no picnic, what with poverty, crime, drugs, unemployment, pollution, and the rest of the litany of ills one could suffer today. So whether a universal standard exists is an assumption. It is neither right nor wrong. But one must make that assumption in order to be a Progressive theorist.

Development Theory

But there is another theory that rescues some aspect of Progress Theory because it does not incur the overhead of assuming the same values for everyone, like individual freedom or material comfort. That theory is the Development Theory of social change, the second stop in the journey through the explanations of social change.

The concept of Development is related to another set of familiar changes – the cycle of life from birth, through growth and maturity and eventually to the decline that every organism goes through. The newborns of all species *develop* into adults using generally the same process as all other members of the species. Thus the adults of the species are larger than infants and

> **Development Theory assumptions**
>
> 1. Society grows increasingly complex over time.
> 2. Societies are moving in a consistent direction over time not necessarily better or worse

are significantly more capable of doing whatever that species does – running, climbing, vocalizing, defending, and, of course, procreating.

Herbert Spencer used the analogy that a society, including human civilization itself, is like an organism that develops these new capabilities over time. One does not necessarily say that the adults of the species are *better* than the infants of the species, even though they possess capabilities that the infants do not. They are just at a different point in the developmental cycle. The essential point is that societies become more complex over time. They have more parts and more relationships among the parts than earlier societies do. For example, one indicator of complexity is the increasing division of labor and specialization in the workforce.

People know from their own experience that they do less for themselves today than their ancestors did. Farmers of previous times not only grew their own food, but they also made their own houses, clothes, and whatever furniture they had. They educated their own children, took care of each other when they were sick or old, and provided whatever entertainment or recreation they had. Today there are countless organizations and occupations to do those things, of course for a price – food producers and grocery stores, manufacturers of all types, teachers, doctors, home repairmen. Most people in modern society work at a specific, narrowly defined job to make the money to be able to purchase the goods and services from others who are also working in specific jobs. In the process, the number of organizations and occupations that provide those goods and services grows, leading to an even greater division of labor.

So Development is like Progress in that it asserts a direction to change in human societies over time. It is unlike Progress, however, in that it makes no judgment on whether or not that change is better or worse. Development is agnostic about the value of the change overall, simply stating that there is a consistent direction to that change.

Or it is supposed to be. Development Theory is the core of the belief that some societies are more "advanced" than others. Herbert Spencer famously used the theory to argue that all societies would eventually "develop" a standard of living comparable to the British of his day. He and others saw a train of development leading down from the most advanced societies to the lowliest tribe. The theory was even used by racists and eugenicists to argue that there are superior and inferior races.

So according to Development, societies develop like organisms in some ways, but not in others. One important difference is that organisms develop according to a genetic code which acts a blueprint for the production of its proteins, cells, and organs. There is no such clear internal mechanism for society as a whole. Aside from the tendency in a capitalist society to produce ever more goods and services as efficiently as possible, there does not seem to be any code that directs society to develop in a particular way. So Development simply points to the growth of overall complexity of modern society, even though it does not seem to have a specific mechanism for directing that growth.

Critical assumption. What do Developmental theorists assume that no other theory does? What does one have to assume to use Development as the primary theory of social change? Of course, one must assume that the apparent direction that has been going on for a long time will continue indefinitely for all future time. That the complexity of society will increase even further for a while is a pretty good assumption.

But what about after that? Smil (2006) points out that increasing social complexity has been accompanied by increasing energy use per capita. It takes a lot of energy to maintain all this complexity. Should the energy per capita go down, will complexity follow? Could the world return to a simpler way once the energy-rich fossil fuels are depleted? And if so, would Developmental Theory hold? The long-term direction suggested by Development could actually be "temporary," or at least come to an end at some point. The assumption of indefinite Development is not right or wrong, but Developmental theorists must assume it in order to use that theory as the primary theory of social change.

Technology Theory

Progress and Development are Shape theories of social change. They do not include the drivers or mechanisms that produce the shape of change; just that their shape or direction is somehow built in to the nature of society over time. Another category of theories is Driver theories. These are the engines of change. Technology is often considered as a driver of Progress and Development.

Technology Theory assumptions
1. There is a primary driver in the first place. (Progress and Development did not point to a specific driver.)
2. Technological development proceeds mostly on its own – the march of technology overall is inexorable.
3. Technology is indefinitely capable – that it will be able to support perhaps ten billion people at a high standard of living.

As with Progress, Technology is a common explanation of change in Western countries because they have been so transformed by technological developments that people can hardly see any other explanation for change.

Two major schemes of technological development describe the broad outlines of how technology has changed societies over time. Karl Marx first described three types of societies based on three types of social arrangements, each one based on who controlled the technology of its day – the Master–Slave society (the ancient empires), the Noble–Serf society (the feudal societies), and the Bourgeoisie–Worker society (the industrial society). In each case, the ruling class controlled the technology of production, and thereby the means by which that society supported itself and provided for its needs. Of course, Marx also predicted that communist society – with no class structure at all – would follow industrial society after the proletarian revolution, but that did not happen. The point is that he used technology as the primary driver of social change through history.

Alvin Toffler popularized his own arrangement of societies based on technology with his books *Future Shock* (1970) and *The Third Wave* (1980). He, too, describes three types of historical societies based on three types of subsistence technologies, each one separated by a radical wave of change. The first societies were tribal that provided for themselves by hunting, gathering and perhaps small horticultural plots. The first big wave to transform that society was the introduction of agriculture using domesticated plants and animals about 10,000 years ago. Agriculture changed food production and just about everything else, such as the creation of permanent settlements, class structure, organized militaries, supernatural religions, writing, transportation – to name just a few!

The second wave was the development of industry based on machines powered by fossil fuels. Again, a lot changed in the process – large cities, the nuclear family, wage labor, individualism, science, engineering, religious and political freedom, long-distance transportation, and communication. Much like Marx, Toffler predicted a third wave society based on information and communication technologies and that this society would be as different from the industrial society as the industrial was from the agricultural or the tribal.

A variation of Technology Theory called Materialism takes a more fundamental position, emphasizing not so much the manipulation of the material, but people's relation to the material world itself. Humans throughout history have, by necessity, had to make do with the resources that the material world provided them. So marine societies are close to the sea where marine life is plentiful, nomadic societies inhabit the desert where travel is relatively easy, hunting societies locate where big game is available, and so on.

A noted historian and anthropologist, Jared Diamond (1999), hypothesized that the major waves of technological development, like agriculture and industry, actually occurred in places that were conducive to their development in the first place. So large-scale agriculture was first practiced in the Eastern Mediterranean, in what was called the Fertile Crescent, because of the variety of plants and animals available to be domesticated in that region.

The materialist logic can be applied to the beginning of industrial society itself. While many factors presumably affected where industrial society first developed, the scarcity of wood and the abundance of coal in places like Britain and Northern Europe set the conditions for the first large-scale application of fossil fuels. Human ingenuity clearly played a large role in that development, but even humans cannot create something from nothing. Nature provides some raw material in the first place. Even more fundamentally, science and technology use the properties of the material world, like gravity, friction, electricity, combustion, to do work that in turn produces what people need.

The materialist variety of Technology Theory is gaining more support these days as the human population grows in size and affluence, putting pressure on that same nature that provided the means to grow in the first place. Modern society has clearly transcended the geographic limitations of early societies. Humans can now live anywhere on the globe, including small colonies in the coldest, most desolate places and even in outer space.

But is technology infinitely productive? Can there be as many people as possible living at the highest standards of living without affecting society's ability to maintain itself in the future? That, of course, is the current debate about resource scarcity, global warming and the sustainability of human civilization itself. The Technologists assume that human ingenuity will find a way to support people even under increasingly challenging conditions. If they are wrong, however, then human society is in for the kind of massive changes witnessed only in the agricultural and industrial waves of the past. In any case, technology (or the lack of it) will be the major force for social change.

Critical assumption. What do Technology theorists assume that no other theory does? What does one have to assume to use Technology as the primary theory of social change? Their assumption is that humans are fundamentally material beings. Marx believed that people's role in society was largely a function of the work they did. "We are what we do" is a common belief in modern society. Another assumption is that the technology we use in that work has a life of its own, that it is not caused by anything else. It does seem that the march of technology is inexorable.

But where does all this technology come from? Does it spring direct from the ground or the air? Of course not. Technology is created and developed by people. So technology might not be the prime mover that Technological theorists think it is. But they must assume that Technology has a life of its own, is *sui generis* as the philosophers say, in order to make it the default theory of social change.

Culture

As opposed to Technology Theory, Culture Theory assumes a society is based on its culture more than on its material environment or the technologies that manipulate it. It argues that technology is part of culture and that different cultures have different attitudes towards technology. Those attitudes can allow technology to be the main driver of change, as it has been in Europe, or only a sideline activity, as it was in China until recently. Sounds pretty persuasive! The Technologists counter, however, that a clear pattern of differences emerges among societies with different subsistence technologies irrespective of culture. Modern societies are larger, more complex, and more productive than tribal or agricultural societies were regardless of differences in culture. Even cultural differences seem to flow from the technology.

> **Culture Theory assumptions**
>
> 1. Society is based on its culture more than on its material environment or its technologies – the theory argues that technology is part of culture.
> 2. Ideas are the key components that give culture its ability to drive change.

Technology theorists hold that the material world and what people do with it is the primary driver of social change. Culture theorists agree that technology is an important driver of social change, but they hold that technology is actually part of the larger system of human culture.

Culture is a shadowy concept in Western thought. The West is ultimately materialistic – what Westerners see or what they can understand mathematically is what is. Abstract concepts like personality, values, relationships, and ultimately culture are there, but they are not accorded the status that physical things are – people, machines, and goods. So the Culture Theory of change is not as substantial as Technology Theory in Western circles, but it has some powerful advocates and evidence nevertheless.

First of all then, what is culture? Merriam-Webster provides an extensive definition:

- the integrated pattern of human knowledge, belief, and behavior that depends upon the capacity for learning and transmitting knowledge to succeeding generations
- the customary beliefs, social forms, and material traits of a racial, religious, or social group; a way of life
- the set of shared attitudes, values, goals, and practices that characterizes an institution or organization.

In general, then, culture is the sum total of knowledge, beliefs, values, attitudes, norms and conventions shared by a certain group of people at a particular place and time – a pretty big concept, to be sure! But can it create social change?

Well, the first point is clearly that technology is a part of a society's culture. What society knows how to do is part of its overall knowledge, and knowledge is part of culture.

Secondly, the value and the role that technology plays in a society is also part of its culture. The West celebrates technology as the source of change and innovation. Some societies, in fact most societies throughout history, did not value change and innovation as much, if at all. Rather they valued stability. They wanted to keep things exactly as they were.

The most extreme example of a stability oriented society was ancient China. The Chinese actually invented the compass, gunpowder, papermaking, and printing and a host of other inventions long before the Europeans did. Then why were the Chinese not the first to create a modern, industrial society? Explanations vary. The political explanation is that the ruling dynasties did not want to upset their power in running the country. The philosophical explanation is that Taoist philosophers did not believe that the universe was subject to universal causal principles or at least ones that humans could understand.

So the European culture valued change and innovation, at least since the Renaissance, while most other cultures in history did not. But does culture itself change? And do cultural changes create other social changes? Most certainly, but very slowly.

Cultures are conservative and traditional by nature. A people's culture is the sum total of their historical experience passed on to the next generation in the process of socialization. Socialization makes people social. It allows them to live and do well in a particular society. So they acquire language and, through language and imitation, they learn how "to be" in that society – what is important and how to be accepted and successful there.

Socialization is a powerful process because most of it occurs before people are even aware that it is taking place. Culture is acquired first from parents and siblings, and then from teachers and peers, and finally from religious, political and economic leaders, from celebrities, and from the media in general. But sooner or later most people are exposed to another culture which on first meeting may seem unusual, strange or even wrong. "How can people think or behave like that?" Exposure to other cultures often challenges people's assumptions. What was obviously true and good and accepted without question becomes suddenly relative, even arbitrary. The first reaction, of course, is to reject the other culture. "They are simply wrong." The second reaction is to reject any form of culture whatsoever, the so-called sophomore attitude – the wise fool – completely rejecting any truth or standard. And finally, most come to accept both their own culture and other cultures as good, just different. No culture is perfect, and others have aspects that might even be better than one's own. So it ends up not completely relative and arbitrary, but not universal and absolute either.

So that describes the typical cultural journey of most Westerners who come to accept living in a pluralistic society, a society with different beliefs and values, most of which have some validity. But not everyone is a Westerner and not all Westerners accept the plurality of cultures. Even in the most pluralistic society, such as the United States, some cling to their cultures to the point of rejecting all others. And some parts of whole cultures, such as ideological Islam or Communism, consider themselves and their way of life correct, and they have no intention of accepting or living in a pluralistic manner. The conflicts in Afghanistan and Iraq in the first part of the 21st Century are based, to some extent, on those cultural differences. So again, culture does make a difference in creating social change.

But do cultures themselves ever change? Of course they do. The cultures in today's world are different from all previous cultures in important ways. People today need to be socialized into a different world than our ancestors were – different technologies, laws, family relations, lifestyles, and so on. Culture changes when those items change, but ever so slowly. Culture preserves and passes on the knowledge, skills and wisdom of the past. It is deliberate if not skeptical about new developments, and wants to be sure they are important and long-lived enough to be worthy of attention. So it is no hurry to change lest something of value be lost.

But change it must, eventually, and sometimes in startling and even violent ways. The drivers of cultural change are called anomalies – pieces of the puzzle of how the world works that do not seem to fit. Merriam-Webster again on *anomaly*: "something different, abnormal, peculiar, or not easily classified." The world is full of anomalies, most of which one simply puts up with. "All men are created equal," except for those who are slaves. Women usually make less money than men for the same work. Rich and powerful people get to speak to the public through the media, a platform denied to most poor people. And so on.

One anomaly does not change a culture. Even a number of anomalies do not until they mount up and eventually the damn breaks. Even then, however, an alternative paradigm needs to be available that explains the same things that the original paradigm did. Religious conversion or rejection is just such a change. It can be troubling or upsetting, but most people look back on such ideational changes as the most important events in their lives.

And whole societies can go through a similar process of culture change, even though it might take a little longer than it does for individuals. Political revolutions are good examples of sudden cultural change. In these cases, there is no time for deliberation. The problems with the old regime mount up. The vanguard of the new regime point them out as they offer a better alternative. Finally, the weight of anomalies becomes so great that the old system collapses beneath them.

Critical assumptions. What do Culture theorists assume that no other theory does? What does one have to assume to use Culture as the primary theory of social change? The assumption is that society is essentially a collection of beliefs, attitudes, values, and norms that defines the world for its members and prescribes what they should do in that world. Advocates assume that people are cultural beings more than material ones. People clearly need the material world to survive, but that world is mediated through culture. So culture is primary.

But is culture as independent as its proponents assume? The Technologists have already pointed out how different subsistence technologies give rise to different cultures. Compare the culture of modern society with that of medieval Europe. Almost everything is different – work, family, learning, religion, money, war, political power. In fact, it is hard to find things that are the same between these two cultures. So did one culture just decide to change itself? And how would it do that if each generation is socialized into the culture of the previous generation? Even if socialization is not perfect, could it account for that much change? "Of course not," say the Technologists. It was the external force of technology that pushed people out of one culture into another. The printing press undermined the power of the Catholic Church. Science undermined religion. The factory created wage labor. The railroad pushed different cultures together. And on and on. A Cultural theorist has to assume that culture is generally impervious to these external influences if it is to be the primary theory of social change.

Cycle Theory

Another critical assumption of the first four theories of the journey is that change occurs in a specific direction. Whether or not the direction is progress or whether the change is driven by technology or culture, those four theories assume an accumulation of technologies and ideas over time. They are heading somewhere. The next theory disputes that assumption.

"What goes up must come down." "Nothing goes on forever." "In the long run, we are all dead" (Keynes, 1923). These well-worn phrases capture the essence of the Cycle Theory of social change. Everything moves in cycles. Any indication that change moves in any specific direction is a short-term illusion. In the end, every change, indeed every entity, ultimately ages, and dies.

> ### Cycle Theory assumptions
>
> 1. No directional change is uniform in any one direction – long-term directional change contains short-term peaks and troughs.
> 2. Directional change eventually reverses itself over sufficiently long timeframes – nothing goes on forever, even the universe itself.
> 3. Selecting the timeframe is crucial when explaining whether change is largely directional or cyclic – it can appear as either at different timeframes.

Cycle Theory is clearly true in the longest of timeframes. Astronomers note that the sun will expand beyond the Earth's orbit in a billion or so years, burning our little planet to a crisp. They are still debating the ultimate fate of the universe, whether it will continue to expand into a lifeless uniformity or collapse into another Big Bang. In either case, however, the universe as known today will eventually be no more. Everything ultimately dies.

It appears that cycles dominate in shorter timeframes as well. The planet has cycled through periods of heat and cold throughout its history. Life itself has blossomed in one form or another only to be snuffed out and transformed in one of the planet's great extinctions. Human societies come and go – tribal societies as well as the empires of China, India, Egypt, Persia, and ultimately Rome. All living organisms progress through a life cycle of birth, growth, maturation, and death. The seasons of the year, the tides, the daily cycle of light and dark – the world is full of cycles.

On the social level, fads come and go; new technologies mature; hot products and trends cool off; celebrities age and fade away. Is there no direction to any of this or is Elbert Hubbard right: "Life is just one damn thing after another"?

In the longest timeframe, probably it is, but is there a way to rescue any part of the previous directional theories? Yes, one way is to shorten the timeframe to reasonable limits. Who cares about the ultimate fate of the earth or the universe or even a society hundreds of years in the future? People care about the future for the rest of their lives, the lives of their children and grandchildren, and maybe more. And there is a general feeling for generations farther into the future, but people expect so much change before then that their feeling for future genera-tions is necessarily quite abstract.

Another way of rescuing the directional theories is to combine them with the Cycle Theory, assuming that directional and cyclic forces operate at the same time. There seems to be strong evidence that societies do develop over time. There is no doubt that they have become larger, even spanning the whole planet, and more complex over time. Even though they will not survive the explosion of the sun a billion years from now, they seem to be doing pretty well in the meantime and over some fairly long timeframes – tens of thousands of years, at least. At the same time, one cannot dispute the existence of peaks and troughs of human civilization throughout that period which provides support for Cycle Theory as well.

The technological eras described in a previous section are an excellent example of long-term development that also contains cyclic change. Each era in modern history is led by a technology whose productive capacity drives the engine of economic growth and increasing standards of living. Just like the runners of a relay race, that technology even-tually hands the baton to the next technology whose job it is to add even more capability and productivity to society. Overall, growth and development (direction) proceed nevertheless, but in a cyclic fashion.

The most important question for the future then is how long a directional change will continue before the cyclic nature of change takes over. In other words, when will it come to an end? Surely it will, eventually? Traders ask that question when riding a trend of increasing prices. Should they continue to buy or is the end in sight? Product managers and government analysts ask the same question – how long will the product or the policy continue to be effective?

The biggest question of all, however, is how long the overall technological, economic, and social development that societies have experienced since the beginning of the modern era at least, if not from the beginning of agricultural society, continues. Will it go on indefinitely or will it come to an end in our lifetimes? The optimistic Technologists assume that such growth is inherent in human society and that it will continue indefinitely. Cyclic theorists assume the opposite – that nothing goes on forever and, more specifically, that modern society requires the unsustainable exploitation of finite resources and emission of planet-changing waste products, all of which will conspire to reverse the trend, probably in this century. The changes experienced in this century will go a long way to deciding whose set of assumptions is more nearly correct.

Critical assumptions. What do Cycle theorists assume that no other theory does? What does one have to assume to use Cycle as the primary theory of social change? The answer is obvious: Nothing goes on forever. Sooner or later every directional change, be it progress or not, comes to an end. The directional change may last a long time, for generations or even centuries perhaps, but it will end someday.

Yet Technologists disagree. While they do not dispute the eventual death of the Sun or even the Universe, they see an upwardly trending ability of humankind to improve the human condition indefinitely, at least until then. It used to be coal and steam that supported such optimism. Today it is digital technology. No matter the source, they believe strongly that technology will continue to advance for as long as the Earth exists; that change will take place in a consistent direction over time. Those who believe otherwise are Cyclic theorists.

Conflict Theory

Even though the Directional and Cyclic theories disagree on the nature of change, they do share a common assumption – namely that society (or an organization) is one unified thing that changes as a unit. But what if the unity of societies and organizations is an illusion? What if

Conflict Theory assumptions

1. Society is not a unitary entity, but a collection of different groups in conflict with each other, working to achieve their own goal and implement their own agenda.
2. Social change affects different people and groups in different ways and at different times.
3. Being in conflict binds people more closely together, as long as radical conflict does not threaten the very existence of the society.
4. Conflict among groups motivates people to work harder for their goals and increases the amount and the rate of social change.

societies and organizations are not things, but rather consist of groups and individuals, each with its own life, goals, agenda, and resources. There are obviously attributes of groups and individuals that are common in a society or an organization. Most speak the same language, vote in the same elections, or purchase goods from the same companies. Which is it then: a unified thing or a collection of things?

The answer probably varies depending on which society or organization one is talking about or when in the history of that entity one focuses on. One could hardly describe as an entity a society during a civil war or a marriage during a divorce. But some societies and organizations are quite homogeneous, with strong cultures that exhibit more commonality than difference.

Conflict Theory says that change occurs as a result of the conflict among different groups and individuals in a society or organization. There is no doubt that conflict exists in all societies and organizations no matter how homogeneous they are. Different people with different goals and agendas are continually jostling, cajoling, or coercing others in order to get what they want. And that might describe the reality of society and organization better than the unitary descriptions do, even in societies that are apparently unified. The apparent unity might be an illusion or a temporary condition to be broken once the next source of conflict appears. And if diversity does describe the reality better, then Conflict Theory is a better explanation of social change than the other theories because they all rest on a false premise.

Their false premise is that society moves through time as one entity; that the whole society experiences progress and development in the same way and at the same time, that everyone in society is affected by changes in technology and culture in the same way and to the same extent. When stated like that, the premise is clearly false. Some groups experience the benefits of progress and development more than others do, or at least sooner. In many cases, in fact, they make progress because other groups do not. Progress for some groups is based on decline for others. And the same is true of technology and culture. Some groups have and are affected by technology and culture more than other groups are.

Karl Marx was quite critical that society gave more wealth, status, and power to those he called the ruling class. In fact, he opens the first chapter of *The Communist Manifesto* with these words: "The history of all hitherto existing society is the history of class struggles." For Marx, everything in society, including social change, was the result of the struggle between the classes. Marx is the prototypical Conflict theorist.

Marx's criticism was muted by 20th Century Conflict theorists for a number of reasons, the most important being that his prediction about the future of class struggle was wildly incorrect, and the Communist societies that tried to follow his prescription of a classless society failed. But his observation that some groups have more influence over the changes in society, and often for their own benefit, still stands as a major tenet of Conflict Theory.

Another Conflict theorist, Lewis Coser, actually saw some benefit to the conflicts in society. Conflict (or competition, another word for the same concept) motivates people to get things done. It also binds those in the same camp more closely. Political and military leaders have used that process by pointing to real or exaggerated threats from outside the group to scare people into supporting them. "Us against them" is a powerful motivator.

Coser described two states of conflict in a society in order to distinguish the beneficial conflict from the dysfunctional conflict. He used the term "cross-cutting" conflicts to describe the beneficial type and "radical" conflicts to describe the dysfunctional type. The difference is that radical conflict divides most everyone in the society along one particular line of conflict, like a civil war. More commonly, cross-cutting conflicts are the many intersecting lines of conflict that exist in most societies, such as conflicts over wealth and money, over political offices, over cultural norms and values, over resources, and so on. People often participate in many cross-cutting conflicts simultaneously, and they are allies with some people in some conflicts and adversaries with those same people in other conflicts. So a husband and wife might vote the same in an election, but disagree over women's rights in the workplace. By the same token, some poor people have very traditional values so they ally with the rich over preserving the status quo even as they struggle to make ends meet at home. Ultimately, cross-cutting conflicts can lead to more social unity rather than less, as long as none of those conflicts gets out of hand and splits the society in two.

Critical Assumptions: What do Conflict theorists assume that no other theory does? What does one have to assume to use Conflict as the primary theory of social change? The assumption is that the unity of society or even groups in society is a façade. "We are in this together," is a common phrase, but Conflict theorists don't buy it. They agree more with the early political philosopher Thomas Hobbes, who describes society as "the war of all against all." Conflict theorists see society as an Us versus a Them. There may be many Us's and many Them's, but the story is the same. People are in constant conflict with those who oppose them – management and labor, owners and managers, producers and consumers, government and business, one party and another. The list goes on and on.

But Cultural theorists respond this time with the concept of a "we." The We's are clearly part of different groups – age, gender, ethnicity, or social class. But they are also part of the same culture, to some extent at least. And even many of the groups themselves promote a "we" that may be more cooperative than collaborative. Successful organizations or teams, for a time at least, use a high degree of collaboration as a way to succeed. So if one believes that the divisions within society dominate, then he or she is a Conflict theorist. If one believes the similar and cooperative elements are more important, then not.

Market Theory

Conflict Theory is a third type of theory called a Mechanism theory. It is not a Shape theory because the direction that conflict takes, whether directional or cyclic, is unclear. It is not a driver because it is not a specific thing. Rather it is a state of being

Market Theory assumptions

1. There is no limit to what humans want.
2. Conflict and competition are the overriding motivations for human action.
3. The production of goods and services is the most important mission of society and its economy.
4. Capital investment is the best mechanism for continued progress in the future.

(in conflict) that produces behaviors that create social change. But there are specific drivers of this mechanism just as there are specific drivers of Progress and Development.

Cycle Theory challenged the assumption that progress and development can go on forever and Conflict Theory challenged the assumption that society itself is a unitary entity. One form of conflict is even celebrated as the engine of progress over the last few centuries – economic competition in free markets, better known as capitalism. Trading has been found in almost all societies, going back to the beginning of tool making. But only in the last few hundred years has economic competition (or conflict in the marketplace) become so important in creating social change.

The economies of the past were tribal in which most goods were obtained and shared in common. The appearance of agriculture allowed societies to grow well beyond tribal limits, thereby introducing new forms of competition. Competition in those days, however, was rarely economic. Goods and services flowed up and down the social hierarchy rather than horizontally from producers to consumers. Slaves and peasants worked for their masters and lords and received some modicum of support and protection in return. No money changed hands. The occasional fair or bazaar allowed traders to exchange goods and sometimes money, but few people participated in them.

Industrial capitalism transformed the peasant into a wage earner who purchased the means of his subsistence in the marketplace, using the wages he received in exchange for his labor. The market then set up the conditions for all types of competitions to emerge – among workers for the better paying jobs and among the firms for the most qualified workers. Firms also competed among themselves in the marketplace to get the most money from the workers in their role as consumers. Workers were in conflict with managers over wages and working conditions. Even consumers were in conflict with firms for the most product or service for the least money. And finally, both firms and consumers were in conflict with government who would tax the wages and profits and regulate their behavior. Seen in this light, conflict is an endemic, if not the essential trait of modern society – each group fighting to increase its returns on the effort they expend.

The result of this conflict has been an incredible, almost unbelievable increase in the standard of living for hundreds of millions of people over a relatively short time. Look at the social changes of the 20th Century alone – living in electrified, air-conditioned homes with indoor plumbing, moving around at speeds of 70 mph/112 kph on the ground and 500 mph/805 kph in the air, sending and receiving messages by voice and data instantaneously from around the world, curing and managing dozens of diseases over an increasing life expectancy. Few can doubt the progress made over that time period, almost all of which was due to the ingenuity and commitment of people competing with each other in the marketplace.

But the marketplace also set up the conditions for radical conflicts – conflicts that divided people along one particular fault line. The most obvious one, already revealed by Karl Marx, was the difference between capital and labor. The other major one is that capitalism has set up an even more insidious conflict, one that cannot be resolved by increasing wages – the conflict between human civilization and nature itself.

Part, if not all, of the essential genius of industrial capitalism is the ability to turn natural resources (resources from nature) into economic goods and services using innovative technologies. Human society has always depended on nature to meet its fundamental need for air, water, food and material goods. But no society, until now, has been so clever and so aggressive in appropriating resources from nature for the purpose of winning the competition of the marketplace, turning raw land into food, converting ancient fossils into fuel, and extracting all manner of minerals from the earth. The growth of the human population from less than two billion in 1900 to over seven billion today and the exponential growth of the human economy are based on the exponential extraction of resources from nature driven by the demands of the marketplace.

Can such exponential growth continue? Yes, but it is not assured. For it to continue, one has to assume that human ingenuity will create the technologies to extract even more benefit from a declining supply of natural resources. The easy stuff is gone. But a lot remains. Can what remains be used to achieve a sustainable, middle-class lifestyle for most of the nine billion people who will be alive by the middle of this century? Or is that goal simply unattainable, no matter how much firms and individuals want to win the competition in the marketplace? And if so, what is the alternative? A return to a lower, yet still decent standard of living – one that is more modest and less materialistic? Or worse, to a lifestyle that is quite primitive by modern standards?

People have bent nature to their will for so long and so aggressively that it might actually break. And frankly nature doesn't care. Though it is a protagonist in that conflict, it will outlast human civilization by a long shot. Life's extraordinary power of adaptation and rebirth will win out, not to return to the way it was before, but to a new and perhaps even more vibrant form. She's been here before – times where more than half of all species went extinct in a relatively short time. Each time nature returned with even more glorious species. It is people who should be concerned. The marketplace giveth, and the marketplace may therefore taketh away.

Critical assumptions. What do Market theorists assume that no other theory does? What does one have to assume to use Markets as the primary theory of social change? The assumption is that money is the primary driver of modern society. Everyone needs money to survive, thus the Golden Rule: those with the gold make the rules. Gone are the days of subsistence agriculture and barter. And those with more money have more power to create social change, for themselves, to be sure, but also for their employees, customers and often for society as a whole. In this theory, it is the ingenuity of capitalist competition that has created more social change than all the other theories combined.

But back again to the critics. Are people merely slaves of the capitalist machine? Is life merely the pursuit of wealth? Are businesses the most powerful force for change on the planet? Those who believe it are Market theorists.

Power Theory

Many of those who come to explain social change initially place great faith in human agency, in the ability of humans to influence the future. Western society in general and Americans in particular believe that people are fundamentally responsible for their future. One's future is the direct result of one's decisions and actions

> **Power Theory assumptions**
>
> 1. People are free to influence the future as they wish, to a large extent at least.
> 2. People make conscious choices to influence the future so that they can achieve certain goals for themselves and for (or despite) others.
> 3. The best explanation of the past (history) is the story of individuals acting to create change.
> 4. Some people are more able to get what they want than others are.

in the present. The past is taught as the story of remarkable individuals who "changed the course of history." Among the social sciences, psychology is more popular than sociology or anthropology. Psychology studies the individual person, a nice recognizable entity. Sociology and anthropology, on the other hand, study the relationships among people. Relationships are not as visible as people are so they seem not quite real to most Westerners. It is no wonder then that many Westerners believe that individuals are the single most important explanation of social change.

Most people realize, of course, that they have little influence over the course of history. One may have great influence over their individual future, but they have little influence on the future of the larger entities in the world – organizations, communities, and nations. But people extrapolate from their belief in the power of human agency to those larger entities and assume that someone, somewhere is powerful enough to influence the course of history – that some individuals have their hands on the controls, that someone is steering the ship, and that someone is calling the shots to create social change at the macro level.

Power is the ability of individuals to achieve what they want. In physics, power is the use of stored energy to create change – to build, move, heat, light or destroy objects. By the same token, social power is the ability to create social change – to move groups and institutions to achieve certain goals. So in this theory, it is people themselves who create change, not the impersonal forces of technology, culture or even the marketplace. Influential people have enough power to create change in the world that the rest must deal with.

That people have different amounts of power and influence in the world is beyond doubt. Weber (1958) identified power as one of three layers (strata) in society. Presidents, ministers, CEOs, chairmen, generals, and bishops clearly have more power to achieve what they want than others do. The question is how powerful are they compared to the other forces of change?

It is easy to see how Power Theory quickly devolves into conspiracy theory. The difference between the two rests on the size and coherence of the powerful people in society. A conspiracy is a relatively small group that shares common goals and works together in secret to achieve them. A football team is a small group that works together to achieve common goals, but they are not a conspiracy because their goals and actions are quite public. But what of the executives in a company or the ministers in a government? Are executives always working for the good of the company or might they have other goals? They clearly do have other goals, such as their own enrichment, in addition to their working for the company. One may believe that Warren Buffett and Bill Gates became rich by working for the good of their customers and their shareholders in addition to themselves. But what about Bernie Madoff?

Shy of an actual conspiracy, Karl Marx believed that the ruling class was such a coherent group working for itself. They pursued common goals and, based on their economic power, affected everything that went on in society – technology, ideas, government and, of course, people's chances to get ahead. C. Wight Mills (1957) focused on what he called "the power elite [that] today involves the often uneasy coincidence of economic, military, and political power." He preferred that term to Marx's ruling class because he saw less unity and coherence among the powerful than Marx did. "...this instituted elite is frequently in some tension: it comes together only on certain coinciding points and only on certain occasions of 'crisis.'" President Eisenhower, a man with deep experience in both the military and in government, called it the military–industrial complex.

At any rate, Power Theory does not require an outright conspiracy to explain social change. It only must assume that the most powerful people in society or even in the world at large are a relatively small group compared to the number of people they affect. It also assumes that the members of this group share some attributes, such as coming from the same families, going to the same schools, or joining the same organizations. It does not have to assume that the group is completely closed nor that the group always agrees on common actions. Nor does one have to assume that any one family, group or even institution dominates the group, only that individuals can move freely among institutions. So, in the US, the political families of the 20th Century (Roosevelt, Kennedys, Bush) had roots in business. Others moved freely among the major institutions in society – Cheney and Rumsfeld from government to business and back again, Rubin and Paulson from Wall Street to government. In the UK, out of information gathered from 616 MPs (from a total of 650), 20 went to Eton and a quarter to Oxbridge (Smith Institute, n.d.).

And one does not have to assume that the power elite only work for themselves. All the members are quite wealthy, to be sure, but many earned their wealth as a result of service to their businesses or their country. So the degree to which the power elite is closed, unified and selfish is an empirical question that varies depending on the organization or community under study. The group may be open to new members through mechanisms of social mobility; the members may be in conflict with one another over some policies, and they may be motivated by corporate or societal goals as much or even more than their own personal advancement. Power Theory asserts only that a relatively small group with similar attributes and interests influences social change more than the macro forces considered so far; that human agency is the dominant source of social change, and that even macro history is the result of individual actions and decisions more than the macro forces of technology or culture.

Critical assumptions. What do Power theorists assume that no other theory does? What does one have to assume to use Power as the primary theory of social change? The assumption is that a relatively small group of people create an inordinate amount of social change based on their positions and the influence they have. Power is the one theory that places human agency, the power of individuals, above impersonal macro forces as driving change in the world. Power is a conflict theory because not only might these powerful people be working more for themselves than for the good of society and thus be in conflict with many ordinary people, but they are also in conflict among themselves in business, government or civil society.

No doubt some people have more power than most, but is it enough to drive social change more than the other enormously powerful theories? The President of the United States is arguably the most powerful single person in the world – the head of the richest country with overwhelming military might and strong diplomatic influence. Yet ex-presidents often remark that they never realized how constrained they were by the forces around them. Even presidents have to deal with technology, with culture, with businesses and with the many conflicting groups, each contending for their own agenda. So a power elite? If so, then the Power Theory may be the primary driver of social change. If not? Read on.

Evolution Theory

Many of the explanations of social change covered so far have been around a long time. People knew that ideas, cycles, and powerful people changed the world, even though they may have been only dimly aware of the direct causal links that we know today. Other theories are more recent. There were optimists in the ancient

---

Evolution Theory assumptions

Three elements are required for evolution to work:

1. differences among the individuals in the evolving entity (variation)

2. A higher probability that some of the individuals will produce offspring based on their fitness in the environment (selection).

3. The ability to pass traits from one generation to the next (replication).

world who believed in a theory of progress, but progress was only acclaimed as the universal direction of social change at the beginning of industrial society. The marketplace likewise emerged as a powerful force of social change only in the last few hundred years. And the next theory, Evolution, is even more recent than that.

The early scientists of the industrial age, going back to Galileo in the Renaissance, lived in a world with powerful beliefs that they had to challenge in order to come to know the world as it is known today. Copernicus challenged the belief (actually supported by everyday observation!) that everything in the universe revolved around the Earth. And he turned out to be right once Galileo saw the moons of Jupiter and the phases of Venus. That finding was the first of many blows to the human ego as the center of the universe.

Jean-Baptiste Lamarck, Alfred Wallace, and most famously Charles Darwin held that species had changed over time as well. These men were asserting the Development Theory considered above. Today it is hard to imagine understanding the world in any other way, but the static nature of the forms was as much a part of their world as the geocentric theory of the universe was to the Renaissance.

Development is one thing; evolution is another, although the two are commonly used interchangeably. The distinction is that development follows a fixed path, largely determined by the developing entity itself. So stars develop through a fixed sequence, called the Main Sequence, over time. Living organisms develop over time, from birth through maturity to death, directed by their genetic structure. People develop psychologically and socially over time, from childhood through adolescence to adulthood and beyond. Even technologies develop over time, from innovation to mature commercial products. The development can be changed or stopped altogether by death or some other external shock, but most entities of a same type pass through the same stages of development.

Evolution does not follow a fixed line of development because its changes are not directed by the entity itself. The environment plays a much larger role in evolution than it does in development. In evolution, the environment is an essential part of the mechanism of change. What is more, different types of entities, from stars to organisms, develop in their own way and according to their own principles. Evolution, as we will see, is a mechanism of change across many different phenomena, from change in biological species to social phenomena.

Evolutionary Theory is actually quite simple so it is curious that it took so long for people to recognize it. It consists of three steps:

- *Variation*: the individuals within an entity to be changed, such as a species, must first be different from each other. Variation is achieved in various ways depending on the phenomena being considered. In biological evolution, variations are created by genetic mutation and by sexual recombination.
- *Selection*: some individuals within the entity are fitter for the environment in which they find themselves than others. The more fit individuals have a greater chance of going onto the third step and producing offspring.[2]
- *Replication*: individuals, particularly those who are more fit, are able to pass their attributes along to the next generation. So, assuming that the environment does not change, the next generation is more fit on average than the previous generation was since the more fit individuals had more offspring than the less fit did.

Evolution even underlies many of the other theories of social change. With Technology, for example, inventors propose new technologies to society (variation). Those that are found to be useful (they increase productivity) at a reasonable cost are adopted (selection), and they are then disseminated throughout the rest of society (replication).

Evolution would seem to explain Progress, too; but there are two important assumptions that must be true for the evolutionary mechanism to deliver progress. The first assumption is that fitness in the short term is the same as fitness in the long term. Evolution operates from one generation to the next. It is blind to any effects after that. So an invasive species can populate a new ecosystem and grow exponentially for a while; but eventually it might change the ecosystem so much that it cannot survive, and it becomes extinct. Systems analysts call that behavior "overshoot and collapse." Financial analysts call it a "bubble." A species or a process grows so rapidly that it destroys the infrastructure it depends on and collapses as a result. Short-term fitness may not be

---

[2] It is popularly thought that the environment selects the more fit individuals for reproduction, but in *natural* selection the environment is actually passive. Individuals are fit (they possess fitness) in that environment so they have a greater chance of reproducing. Actual selection does take place, however, in *artificial* selection, such as breeding animals, where the breeder does actively select the individuals for reproduction.

the same as long-term fitness, particularly when changes are rapid and exponential.

The second assumption required to see evolution as the mechanism of progress is that the environment must remain stable. In a stable environment, successive generations will gradually become more fit until they reach maximum fitness for that environment. In order to become maximally fit, however, the variation within the evolving entity (species or society) must decrease as the less fit individuals are gradually weeded out. In early agriculture, for example, farmers used many thousands of varieties of grains that were grown throughout the world. Today there are relatively few. The grains with the highest yields have been replicated, and those with lesser yields have been abandoned.

When the environment changes, the evolving entity must adapt or go out of existence. In natural selection, the only way that a species can adapt to a new environment is to already include individuals who are fit for and who can succeed in that new environment. Those individuals, however, tend to be less fit for the old environment so they will tend to be weeded out over time. If the environment changes enough, the species might not have any individuals fit for the new environment, in which case it goes extinct. So emphasizing fitness over variety is a risky strategy. It's a good strategy if the environment stays the same, but it runs the risk of losing it all if the environment changes.

So the Evolutionary Theory of variation, selection, and replication is a powerful theory that seems to subsume all the others. It explains Progress and Development when the environment is stable, and Cycle Theory when it is oscillating. It explains how technology and culture are adopted and disseminated throughout society. It explains how conflicts appear, and who prevails in the markets and in the halls of power. Can Evolutionary Theory really be that good? Is this the one theory that explains it all, despite our assumption that no one theory can explain all of social change?

Well, it depends. Evolutionary Theory challenges the assumption that social change is caused by a thing, such as technology, ideas (culture), or power. It introduces the central role of the environment for the first time. Changing entities are not changing on their own. They do so only in interaction with their environment; and how successful they are depends, to a large extent, on the environment. Fitness is not an absolute quantity; it does not reside within the individual; rather it depends on the environment in which the individual lives. So variation, selection and replication may explain change, but one has to know the environment and what is fit in that environment to understand what direction change may take. One can explain successful technologies, ideas, products and powerful groups and how they came to be. But the only way to explain such change is to accept that all change is the result of a successful fit between a varying entity and a selecting environment. Does that really get us anywhere?

A number of thinkers have stumbled over the problem of telling just how fit individuals are. One mistake was to see every attribute of a successful species or society as perfectly fit for that environment. The fallacy is to equate what has evolved to what is universally right and good – to confuse *is* with *ought*. One example is the evolution of the upright posture for humans. Walking upright frees the hands for hunting and tool making, a trait that made early humans more fit in their environment. But the human spine is not the optimal design on which to hang the human frame, as many generations of people who suffer from chronic back pain will attest. But the spine evolved from the vertebrae of other primates that used their hands when walking and, before that, from four-legged mammals. Evolution could not create an upright structure from scratch. It had to work with what it had and vary from that. So while upright posture is more fit, the human back is not.

A mistake of using Evolutionary Theory was to assume that there was some absolute level of fitness that successful individuals and groups had that others lacked. That misinterpretation led to the eugenics movement of the early 20th Century and perhaps even to the racism of Nazi Germany.

So the generality of Evolutionary Theory might be its weakness as well. It subsumes all the others, but in doing so, it might have lost any utility, particularly for forecasting changes in the future. One can say that all fit variations will be selected and replicated, but what variations will be proposed in the future? And how does one estimate their fitness before the environment has done its selecting? So a general theory? Yes. But a useful one? Not so sure.

Critical assumptions. What do Evolutionary theorists assume that no other theory does? What does one have to assume to use Evolution as the primary theory of social change? Compared to all the others theories so far, evolution identifies the central role of the environment. The environment cannot create or force change by itself. Rather it relies on an evolving entity (from an individual to a species as a whole) to present some type of variation before it can "select" that variation as more fit and thereby allow it to replicate and multiply. In biology, replication is standard procreation. In technology, it is the dissemination of the fit products using that technology. In culture, it is the transmission of more fit ideas (memes) from one person to another.

But is the environment all that important? Some technologies are adopted that are clearly not the most fit for the environment. The most common example is the QWERTY keyboard that was developed to *slow* down typists of manual typewriters so the next key would not run into the last key. QWERTY is not ideal by any means, but it's still here. In other contexts, powerful individuals have had their way and produced change that was not only unfit, but even disastrous for many. Look to the many wars that were undertaken with little or no consideration to their utility for the future. And so on. Does the environment select the social changes that will go forward? Those accepting that assumption are Evolutionary theorists. But those who believe that people or technology or ideas can produce change despite the environment are not.

Emergence Theory

Evolutionary Theory was developed in the 19th Century. The next theory was developed in the 20th, and mostly in the later part of that century.

The story begins with the origins of and subsequent practical application of systems theory, as discussed in Chapter 2. General systems theory was first developed in the 1930s, notably by Ludwig von Bertalanffy and others. The first real application of systems emerged during World War II when Norbert Weiner developed cybernetics, the mathematics

> **Emergence Theory assumptions**
>
> 1. Social change "bubbles up" from the bottom rather than "top-down."
> 2. Systems consist of a multiplicity of agents, each operating to achieve goals in an environment of other agents.

of control, for which he received the Nobel Prize. Control theory led to systems engineering, a discipline that formed the basis of most of the complex machines developed in the second half of the century.

As mentioned in Chapter 2, mathematician/scientist John von Neumann was developing another approach to systems thinking at the same time. He called this branch cellular automata, independent agents that acted to achieve goals in an environment that included resources and other agents. He laid the groundwork for the field, but it did not take off because no equations described the behavior of these systems the way differential calculus described control theory (cybernetics). These systems had to be simulated to see what they would do. So the field had to wait for powerful computers to be invented, which they were in the 1980s, before the field could develop. The field is now called complexity science and it is forming the basis of everything from the understanding of networks to prediction markets.

The agents in a complex adaptive system produce macro behavior in systems in a process called emergence. Emergence is the appearance of a macro pattern based on the actions of independent agents. Living organisms, for instance, can be considered emergent phenomena consisting of billions of independent agents (cells) operating only on information contained in their local environment. Digestion, for example, is carried on by thousands of bacteria in the guts of animals. No central processor tells them what to do. They just do what they do when presented with the right conditions. The amazing result is food broken down into its nutritious elements and distributed throughout the body. Neurons are also agents that produce movement in animals and consciousness in humans. The market price for oil is an emergent phenomenon as is the public perception of public policies or politicians. Getting right down to it, most systems, particularly social systems, are much better described by the actions of the millions or billions of agents than by the macro variables of economists or social scientists.

Emergence can be used to explain social change, such as the collapse of the banking system in 2008 or the revolutions in the Middle East in 2011, because those systems displayed large-scale patterns based on the actions of individuals. Emergence is the bottom-up process of social change compared to the top down process of all the other theories considered so far. Emergence operates at the individual (agent) level. The others operate at the societal level. As with the other assumptions, neither is right nor wrong. Pick your assumption, however, and you get an entirely different theory of social change.

Critical assumptions. What do Emergence theorists assume that no other theory does? What does one have to assume to use Emergence as the primary theory of social change? An Emergence theorist has to assume that systems consist of a multiplicity of agents, each operating to achieve goals in an environment of other agents. In that sense, Emergence Theory is like Conflict Theory, but at a much more elementary level. Conflict exists largely between groups, which themselves consist of agents, rather than the agents themselves. But most social phenomena can be seen as the emergent patterns of agents – in the economy, in governance, in culture.

The problem with that assumption as an explanation of social change, however, is that no one knows how emergent patterns arise. There is no science of emergence that can tell which conditions will produce which patterns. In that sense, the theory can say that the change is the result of the action of millions of agents operating in the system, but it cannot tell exactly how those agents came to be so organized. Emergence might even be a universal theory of social change, since all social patterns are based on the actions of individuals, but it is not very satisfying or even explanatory because we cannot tell how those patterns arose.

CONCLUSION

Social change is a curiously neglected topic among sociologists. Since the future lacks facts and direct empirical data, it is less comfortable to work in than the present. The fit with foresight, however, is quite snug, given its emphasis on the study of change.

This course studies ten different explanations for large-scale social change. No single explanation is offered as the correct one. Most students enter the course with a preferred theory, often implicit. By the end, most report that they believe that some if not all the theories account for part of the explanation. While they may still see one or two as more influential than others, they see the influence of each as important to consider.

Another important outcome of this course is the learning around the role of assumptions and the future. Each theory hangs on a few critical assumptions – if one changes the assumptions, one changes the theory. It also reveals how a particular theory or theories that one holds influences their point of view about the future. If one is a believer in technology as the key driver of social change, for instance, they will tend to see the future through technology-colored glasses.

Table 4.1 lists the essential critical assumptions of each of the ten theories covered here. They are illustrated in Figure 4.1. The assumptions are the scaffolding that supports the theories or, as described above, the common root structure that lies beneath stands of bamboo or aspen.

Table 4.1 Critical assumptions supporting theories of social change

Theory	Critical assumption
1. Progress	Universal standard of value and worth
2. Development	Consistent direction
3. Technology	Materialism and the means to manipulate it
4. Culture	Power of ideas
5. Cycle	Recurrence of macro states
6. Conflict	Struggle among interest groups
7. Market	Competition among producers and consumers
8. Power	Direction by a specific group
9. Evolution	Successive interactions with the environment
10. Emergence	Bottom-up independent agents

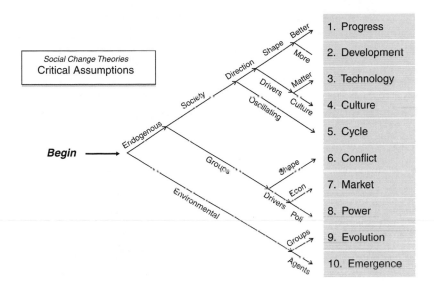

Figure 4.1 Critical assumptions
Source: Bishop (2009).

Understanding that structure is the key to understanding the theories as a network of assumptions rather than as a simple list. One can begin with Figure 4.1 at the left and traverse the paths from the most general assumptions to the most specific or one can begin at the top in the same order that the theories were presented above. Taking the latter path, the first two theories are Progress and Development, two of the most common theories in modern Western thought. They are both Shape theories; they describe what the change looks like, but they do not explain why the change looks that way. And they are different on one crucial assumption. Progress theorists believe that the world gets better over time; Development theorists that change moves in a particular direction, such as more complexity, but they do not believe that that direction is necessarily better over time.

The next two theories are Driver theories, explaining the movements of Progress and Development. They differ in the priority they place on the material versus the cultural aspects of society. Technologists see society as essentially a continual quest to provide the basics of life: water, food, shelter, security or even information, communication, and entertainment. Culture theorists recognize the value of technology, but they see technology as part of culture and its ideas, not outside it. Ideas drive social change, some of which are technological.

All four theories share a common assumption, however, that change is directional, that society is moving somewhere. Advocates of Cycle Theory, also a Shape theory, disagree. In their view, everything exhibits a life cycle of birth, maturity and death so that nothing goes on forever. Change may look directional for a time, even for a long time, but it will always come to an end.

All five of these theories also share another assumption, that society is a thing that can progress, develop or cycle as one thing. Conflict theorists disagree. They assume that the apparent unity of society is an illusion. Behind that illusion is the reality of perpetual conflict of individuals and groups each pursuing their own goals and interests.

Conflict is a Mechanism theory, a description of how change occurs, rather than why it occurs the way it does. But conflict can be driven by two primary drivers, just as with Progress and Development – the market and the political arena. In the first instance, Market Theory, conflict (competition) within the economy drives change – among companies in the same market, between labor and management, between consumers and producers, between lenders and borrowers, between companies and government. Conflict in the economy drives innovation, a necessary ingredient to long-term success in a competitive environment.

The other arena, Power Theory, is political – not just government, but any individual or group that uses their power to influence change substantially more than most people can. The powerful group drives change, sometimes for the good of society, as in the aristocratic view of a republic, or for themselves, as in the Marx's view of the ruling class. With whatever outcome, political theorists see a relatively small group of individuals as the primary drivers of change.

All eight theories, so far, share a common assumption, namely that change is endogenous, that it arises from the society itself. Evolutionary theorists disagree. They claim that society does have a role in change, but so does the environment. Individuals, groups or the society as a whole propose changes to their respective environments, but it is the environment that determines which changes survive and thrive and which come to an untimely end.

And finally, the last theory, Emergence, disagrees with all of the previous theories in assuming that everything arises from the interaction of agents pursuing their individual goals in a system of other agents. Emergent theorists assume that even conflicting groups are a figment of the theorist's imagination. The true reality is small-scale, low-level, local interactions, which create larger patterns and changes, to be sure, but they are all based on those local interactions.

Stands of bamboo and aspen share common root systems. So do the various theories of social change.

RESOURCES

Lauer, R. (1977) *Perspectives on Social Change* (Boston: Allyn and Bacon).

- Laments that sociology has not paid more attention to the study of change and attempts to fill the gap. Excellent overview that aligns fairly well with the curriculum, but is now out of print (though available online).

Noble, T. (2000) *Social Theory and Social Change* (London, UK: Palgrave).

- The text used for the Social Change course.

Progress

Bury, J.B. (1932) *The Idea of Progress* (NY: Macmillan).

- Classic on the origins and evolution of the idea of progress.

Coates, J. F. (1990) "There Is Much to Celebrate," *Technological Forecasting & Social Change*, 38, 307–11.

- Coates has taken up a very positive message about the future first promulgated by Herman Kahn, who wrote *The Next 200 Years* largely in response to the pessimistic forecasts of the *Limits to Growth* in the early 1970s. Other articles by Coates may be found at: http://joseph coates.com/articles.html.

Durant, W. & Durant A. (1968) "Is Progress Real?" in *The Lessons of History* (NY: MJF), 95–102.

- After reviewing the most important changes in the major institutions in society, the Durants ask the question, "Is progress real?" See what they say.

Kahn, H. & Simon, J. (1984) "Introduction" in Simon & Kahn (eds) *The Resourceful Earth: A Response to Global 2000* (London, UK: Blackwell).

- Kahn and Simon are unabashed Progressive theorists, taking direct aim at the many "gloom and doom" books that came out of the 1970s.

Nisbet, R. (1979) "The Idea of Progress," *Literature of Liberty: A Review of Contemporary Liberal Thought*, 2 (1).

- An extensive essay on the history of the idea of progress throughout Western thought.

Simon, J. (2008) *The State of Humanity* (West Sussex, UK: Wiley-Blackwell).

- Along with Herman Kahn, Simon was one of the most vocal critics of the *Limits to Growth* and other negative extrapolists in the 1970s, asserting progress was endemic to human society.

Spencer, H. (1857, April) "Progress: Its Law and Causes," *The Westminster Review*, 67, 445–65.

- Spencer is the best known of the early Progressive theorists, basing his theory of progress on the newly formed Darwinian theory of evolution. In fact, Spencer, not Darwin, coined the phrase "survival of the fittest," saddling Evolutionary Theory with its most popular sound-bite and image in the popular mind.

Development

Bunting, M. (2001) "The End is Nigh," *Guardian of London*, August.

- A review of all the reasons that theories of decline are so appealing.

Rosenberg, M. (2008) *Rosenberg New Countries of the World: The 33 New Countries Created Since 1990*, 18 February.

- Characterizes the 33 new countries created in the world since 1990.

Zakaria, F. (1997) "An Optimist's Lament," *New York Times Review of Books*, 30 March.

- Not all developmental change is positive. Zakaria's essay reviews a book that documents the deep strain of pessimism in Western culture. In this rendering, the world started out not in the primitive slime, but rather in the Golden Age; and it has been all downhill from there!

Technology

Diamond, J. (1999) *Guns, Germs and Steel: The Fates of Human Societies* (NY: Norton).

- A classic work that explores why white Eurasians prevailed over other cultures by means of superior guns, population-destroying germs, and steel. His thesis is that it owed chiefly to advantageous geography and environment difference that enabled the spread of ideas and technology. He provides a compelling case to support this view.

Kurzweil, R. (2005) *The Singularity Is Near: When Humans Transcend Biology* (NY: Viking).

- How exponential growth in information technology is leading toward machine intelligence surpassing human intelligence, called the "singularity," in which life as it is known is unrecognizable on the other side.

Meyer, C. & Davis, S. (2003) *It's Alive: The Coming Convergence of Information, Biology, and Business* (NY: Crown Business).

- Forecasts the arrival of the "molecular economy" – biotechnology, nanotechnology and materials science-based on biological processes or things that mimic them. Suggests that these technologies will force business and society to adapt to them and describes how that can be done.

Toffler, A. (1970) *Future Shock* (NY: Random House).

- This best-seller helped put foresight on the map with Toffler's controversial thesis that the pace of change was proceeding so rapidly that it was creating a condition known as future shock, in which people would be incapable of keeping up with change – essentially highly stressed and disoriented by the change.

Toffler, A. (1980) *The Third Wave* (NY: William Morrow).

- Human history can be divided into three patterns or waves. The transition of hunter–gatherer societies into agriculture societies about 10,000 years ago characterized the first wave. The second wave was the Industrial Revolution in which energy powered machines to replace human labor. The third wave, in place today, is characterized by information or knowledge becoming the central engine of economic productivity.

Culture

Fairbanks, J. K. & Goldman, M. (1992) *China: A New History* (Cambridge, MA: Belknap Press).

- This comprehensive history of China demonstrates the influence of culture on a society; by one of the great experts on Chinese culture.

Inglehart, R. (1997) *Modernization and Postmodernization: Cultural, Economic, and Political Change in 43 Societies* (Princeton, NJ: Princeton U Press).

- Describes the role of values and cultural change in moving societies from a traditional to modern and postmodern orientation.

Polak, F. (1973) *The Image of the Future* (Amsterdam, Netherlands: Elsevier).

- Seminal work on the influence of ideas, in the form of images of the future, in shaping the development of cultures.

Cycles

Keynes, J. M. (1936) *The General Theory of Employment Interest and Money* (Cambridge, UK: Macmillan Cambridge University Press).

- Challenges conventional thinking on business cycles; for instance, arguing that the way to end depressions is not to cut expenses, but to stimulate spending.

Schumpeter, J. A. (1934) *Theory of Economic Development* (Cambridge, UK: Cambridge University Press).

- Describes his cyclical view of economics in which long periods of equilibrium are disrupted by a creative destruction of the old order instigated by an entrepreneurial wave of innovation.

Conflict

Coser, L. (1957) "Social Conflict and the Theory of Social Change," *The British Journal of Sociology*, 8 (3), 197–207.

- Puts forth the idea that social conflict can actually unify and reinvigorate loosely structured groups.

Marx, K. & Engels, F. (1998, 1st published 1848) *The Communist Manifesto* (NY: Signet Classics).

- Lays out the argument for how class conflict between the bourgeoisie and the proletariat would bring down capitalism.

Markets

Friedman, T. (2005) *The World Is Flat: A Brief History of the Twenty-First Century* (NY: Farrar, Straus and Giroux).

- Asserts that technological innovation and the near universal adoption of free market economics have levelled the global playing field for developing countries vis-a-vis the developed ones.

"Homo Economicus?" (2005) *The Economist*, 7 April.

- Presents the argument of Jason Shogren of the University of Wyoming and his colleagues that trade and specialization are the reasons *Homo sapiens* displaced previous members of the genus, such as *Homo Neanderthalensis* (Neanderthal man), and emerged triumphant as the only species of humanity.

Rostow, W.W. (1990) *The Stages of Economic Growth: A Non-Communist Manifesto* (Cambridge, UK: Cambridge University Press), 1–16.

- Suggests that there are five stages of economic development that societies can progress through: the traditional society, the preconditions for take-off, the take-off, the drive to maturity, and the age of high mass-consumption.

Power

Kleiner, A. (2003) *Who Really Matters: The Core Group Theory of Power, Privilege, and Success* (NY: Currency/Doubleday).

- Asserts that many organizations have been co-opted by elites, whose purpose is to serve their own, and their children's, needs.

Mills, C. W. (1957) *The Power Elite* (Oxford, UK: Oxford University Press), 269–97.

- Describes how the American power elite have managed to stay in power through four eras and into a fifth.

Evolution

Darwin, C. (1859) *On the Origin of Species by Means of Natural Selection, or the Preservation of Favoured Races in the Struggle for Life*, 1st edn (London, UK: John Murray).

- Classic work outlining his ideas on evolutionary biology.

Dawkins, R. (1989) *The Selfish Gene* (Oxford, UK: Oxford University Press).

• Introduced the idea of memetics, in which Evolutionary Theory is adapted to explain the success of prominent ideas.

Hofstadter, R. (1955) *Social Darwinism in American Thought* (Boston: Beacon Press).

• Used the work of Herbert Spencer to describe society as a living organism, to which the theory of natural selection could be applied. Spencer did coin the phrase "survival of the fittest" after reading Darwin, but did not describe himself as a "Social Darwinist"—this came primarily from Hofstadter's interpretation of his work.

Emergence

Gleick, J. (1988) *Chaos: Making a New Science* (NY: Penguin).

• A layman's guide that was instrumental in helping to popularize chaos theory with the general public.

Laplace, P. (2007, 1st published 1818) *A Philosophical Essay on Probabilities* (NY: Cosimo Classics).

• Classic work on probability that lays out his system for reasoning based on probability.

Wolfram, S. (2002) *A New Kind of Science* (Champaign, IL: Wolfram Media).

• Included in this intellectual tour de force is his idea of intrinsic randomness generation – that natural systems can generate their own randomness.

Part II
Mapping

Inbound change is the change that happens to people. It comes at people from the "outside" world. Forecasting is used to map out the anticipated shape of that change. By mapping out the future landscape, one has a starting point from which to begin planning and working towards one's preferred future.

Research and scanning support the creation of forecasts. Research provides the basis for understanding the history and context of the topic being forecast. Scanning explores for the signs of change within the topic. Together they create the raw material from which the forecasts can be constructed. The curriculum recommends the creation of a baseline forecast, aka the most likely future, and plausible alternative future forecasts.

- Chapter 5, Research: covers the basics of solid primary and secondary research techniques as tailored to studying the future. Futurists tend to spend more time on secondary research, since there is no actual first-hand information about the future, with primary research being complementary and most often involving the gathering of expert judgment. The aim of research is to teach students a process for quickly learning the basics about a domain or topic they are studying.
- Chapter 6, Scanning: covers how to explore for the signs of change in a domain – or for change in general. The scanner is a lookout for change, searching for signs that change is coming. The signs are weak at this point, and the art of scanning is about developing the ability to recognize and evaluate them.
- Chapter 7, Forecasting: covers the creation of forecasts to describe the anticipated shape of change. Forecasting results in a baseline forecast, which is the extrapolation of present conditions and trends into the future. Knowing where one is most likely headed provides a departure point to talk about the alternative forecasts. The alternatives describe what might happen if the baseline does not.

5
Research

INTRODUCTION

Futurists are not exempt from research. There may be a perception in some circles that it's all about intuition, deep discussions, and sophisticated computer techniques. After all, how can there be data about the future? Futurists do indeed make use of data.

Three uses stand out:

- Data from the past and present helps to set the context for the future
- Data about a domain (topic being forecast) directs scanning, that is, points to where to look for the signals of change
- Data in the form of signals of change can then be extrapolated from, analyzed, and plugged into methodologies as ingredients for forecasting

The two primary types of research are primary and secondary. Primary research is about gathering first-hand information – usually interviews or questionnaires are used for gathering individual expectations, expertise, and preferences. That said, some futurists emphasize primary research, such as Hallal's Techcast[1] and the Millennium Project's use of Real-time Delphi.[2]

Secondary research involves gathering second-hand information that has already been published, such as articles, websites and data sets. It involves the basics of how to find and evaluate existing information relating to the future.

---

[1] See http://www.techcast.org.
[2] See http://www.realtimedelphi.org/.

Futurists tend to spend more time on secondary research, since there is no actual first-hand information about the future. Primary research in futures largely involves gathering expert and other judgments about the future. It almost always complements secondary research.

The emphasis on research is to support the preparation of a forecast – the creation of the baseline and alternative futures. The aim is to teach students a process for quickly learning the basics about a domain or topic they are studying. While some futurists make a career by specializing in one domain and become expert in it, most cover a wide range of topics, and thus need a process for quickly and effectively getting up to speed on a new domain. This background information is vital context for making informed forecasts. It also supports the development of trends and drivers that provide the key components of a forecast.

HISTORY

The nature of futures research has evolved along with its theory and methods. The early days of foresight relied heavily on expert judgment. Herman Kahn, for instance, one of the early US-based futurists, relied heavily on his own judgment to create his scenarios and forecasts, a technique popularly known as genius forecasting. Kahn was clearly a genius, as other futurists have been, but it is hardly a technique to support a whole discipline. Expert opinion was an essential input into the forecasts of this era.

The need to harness expert opinion more effectively led to the development of the Delphi technique. Analysts at the RAND Corporation, after Kahn, sought a means to tap expert opinion from a wide variety of perspectives without one perspective dominating the outcome as so often happens in face-to-face meetings. The method therefore relied on a multi-round anonymous survey of expert members to express their expectations for the future and then see what their fellow experts thought. Discussion followed in which members described their reasoning, particularly for different expectations. Members then responded to the survey again, presumably making adjustments to their initial forecasts in the second round. In particular, it was valuable for the experts to see the outlying estimates, hear the reasoning for those estimates, and then decide whether to adjust their own thinking (Gordon, 2003).

The next phase of foresight introduced quantitative forecasting techniques, so research focused on gathering quantitative data. Demographic projections were an area where solid quantitative information was available and could be plugged into forecasting models. The use of computer models for forecasting broke into the field with the publication of the *Limits to Growth* (1972), which used systems dynamics models to forecast the possible demise of society as a result of growing faster than the ecosystem could handle. At the same time, much of the quantitative approach still relied on expert judgment, with a set of tools developed for quantifying that judgment.

Quantitative forecasting eventually fell out of mainstream favor, though it remains alive and well in some circles, such as economic and technological forecasting. Newer methods emerged that relied more on qualitative inputs. Scenarios for forecasting and planning became the emblematic method of this phase, and continue to be the most popular tool in foresight today. Scenarios incorporated quantitative data where possible, but relied much more heavily on the qualitative. Research focused on gathering supporting data that would be analyzed and interpreted for input into qualitative forecasts. Qualitative approaches still required underlying evidence to be credible. This shift from quantitative to qualitative also enabled a greater range of factors to be considered, as limits around the availability of quantitative data became less of an issue. This shift in turn expanded the scope of research. A key skill for futurists entailed finding, interpreting, and evaluating this information.

GENERALIZATION

Research is taught primarily as an input to forecasting. There are three principal considerations in carrying out this type of research.

- *Choosing a domain*: while the client often defines this, in many cases the futurist has latitude in framing the research, sometimes changing the topic boundaries as the research leads to greater understanding and then refinement
- *Primary research*: information from first-hand sources
- *Secondary research*: information from second-hand sources.

Choosing a domain

Futures research involves assembling all the information necessary to make a valid and useful forecast about the future of a domain. A domain is any topic that can be forecast; and since everything has a future, a domain is just about any topic whatsoever. A domain might be a geographic region, from a neighborhood to the world as a whole, such as all the countries and their sub-regions. It might be an organization, from the local church to the United Nations, including businesses, government agencies, and non-profit organizations. It could be an issue like AIDS or greenhouse gases. It could be an industry like chemicals or automobiles. It could be an institution like education or transportation. In other words, a domain could be just about anything that has a future. A domain could even be an individual person, such as with "personal futures" (Wheelright, 2010).

Futurists choose a domain and then set about the research. The domain is typically their client's industry or a topic they want to write or speak about. So Alvin Toffler's domain is information technology and all its implications. For Donella Meadows, it was the interaction of population, technology, resources and the environment for the world as a whole – one of the largest domains. As noted, many futurists stick with a domain they find interesting or valuable because it takes some time to get to know a domain and become an expert in it. Having made that investment, one doesn't want to leave it and immediately move on to something else. Other futurists cover a wide range of domains as they work for clients in different areas.

Choosing one or more domains, then, is one of the strategic decisions that a futurist makes, or is made for them by clients. The chosen domain, all other things being equal, should be:

1. *Interesting*, because one will stay with it for some time
2. *Changing*, because that is the value that futurists bring to their work
3. *Important*, because it has significant consequences for people and for society as a whole.

Once the domain is chosen, the research begins.

Primary research

Primary research involves gathering first-hand information directly from a source. There are many different types of primary research: interviews, questionnaires, focus groups, and observational (ethnography) are probably the most common.

The curriculum emphasizes interviews and questionnaires, which gather judgmental data – what is in people's heads rather than what is published or what is observed. There are two fundamental ways in which gathering judgmental data differs – the degree of structure and the manner of administration. The structure varies from unstructured or open-ended to highly structured or closed-ended. The administration varies from interviewer-administered (synchronous, same time) to

Table 5.1 Taxonomy of judgmental data-gathering techniques

		Open, unstructured	Closed, structured
Administration	Interviewer	Face-to-face interview	Market research
		Focus group interview	Political polling
		Telephone interview	US Census
		Electronic interview	
	Respondent	Write-in questionnaire	Mailed questionnaire
		Email questionnaire	Internet questionnaire

respondent-administered (asynchronous, different time). Putting those two dimensions together creates the following four-fold taxonomy of judgmental data-gathering techniques.

So interviews are forms of data collection in which an interviewer and a respondent are both engaged at the same time (synchronous), such as in a face-to-face meeting or over the telephone. A questionnaire, conversely, is a form of data collection in which the respondent responds to an instrument by themselves (asynchronous), such as by written questions over Email or an online survey tool.

Interviews can be structured or unstructured (or in between). They are used in a new area of research in which one is looking for new ideas and perspectives. Information about the future actually begins in people's heads before it appears on the Internet. In other words, the newest, freshest, most timely information emerges before an item appears in public – what knowledgeable people know about what is happening or what is about to happen.

Open-ended interviews can be a good way to explore for the key issues influencing the future of a domain. Table 5.2 outlines the recommended preparation. Stakeholders or experts can often provide a shortcut to what really matters in a domain. Once the issues are better defined, a more structured approach such as the Delphi is useful, because it gathers data more efficiently from a larger number of people, albeit in a narrower and more structured way. A challenge with open-ended interviews is that their speculative nature is only as good as the respondent that provides it, so it is necessary to cross check that speculation with research.

At the opposite end of the spectrum is a highly structured questionnaire. Questionnaires are the correct tool when one wants precise information from a relatively large number of people. One must be generally familiar with the domain in order to construct a questionnaire because it must be completely self-administered. Therefore, wording of both the questions

Table 5.2 Sample interview plan

Module	Question
1. Objective	What do we want to learn from the interviews?
2. Content	What specific information do we need? Is there any information we'd like our interviewees to respond to?
3. Interviewees	Who has the information we need?
4. Interview guide	How will we conduct the interview?
5. Analysis	How will we analyze the interview data?

and the response categories must be clear and unambiguous. Designing questionnaires is an excellent skill to bring to the marketplace.

Traditional interviews and questionnaires have equal and opposite advantages, depending on the state of knowledge of the field and the objectives of the research. Interviews are flexible where the interviewer can pursue new lines of questioning or new ideas that come up in the interviews. They are easy to prepare for, but hard to analyze afterward. Questionnaires, on the other hand, are not flexible, but they provide a consistent set of data that is easier to analyze afterwards. New domains are usually best explored with flexible interviews and only later verified with structured questionnaires. Well-known domains can skip the interview phase altogether and go right to structured questionnaires.

Secondary research

Futurists tend to rely heavily on secondary research (aka "desk research"). It involves the summary, analysis, and synthesis of existing research done by others, since primary research about the future tends to be difficult and expensive.

Being able to do secondary research is thus an important capability of futurists. In the early days of the Futures program (pre-Internet), much time and effort was spent on how to find information. Most research was done in the library leafing through physical periodicals and books. The Internet, as everyone knows, changed all that! The challenge now is not finding information but rather not drowning in it. There is still a need to teach where to find information but the emphasis now is on quality rather than quantity of sources. Being able to evaluate the quality of research is an increasingly important skill.

The temptation for many is to rely solely on a Google search. Undoubtedly, Google and other search engines typically return a large quantity of information…and fast. But how much of that turns out to be useful? It turns out that there is a role for good old-fashioned library research. Electronic versions or collections in libraries have closed the gap with search engines. It takes some convincing of today's students, but the extra time invested in more traditional, library-based resources actually saves time over the long term. And most of those resources are increasingly electronic, although they do not appear in search engines. Thus, the techniques for good information searching, such as how to select sources and databases, identifying search terms, creating Boolean expressions, and so on, are still useful and taught. As suggested above, concepts and techniques for evaluating research have become increasingly important.

APPROACH

Research supports framework forecasting

Research along with Scanning (Chapter 6) are positioned in the curriculum to provide input to Forecasting (Chapter 7). Research and scanning are, of course, separate activities in their own right, but the primary function of both is to enable forecasting. The principal approach to forecasting taught in the curriculum is called Framework Forecasting. Domain selection, research, and scanning precede and inform the creation of the forecast in this approach.

While everything changes, things change at different rates. Futurists add most value when a domain is changing rapidly and/or in a turbulent manner, such as when the outcomes are uncertain. So research, in the narrow sense here, is gathering all necessary information to make a valid forecast in a specific domain. While that sounds simple, the question arises: What is "all necessary information"? Most people just start collecting and reading and thinking and stop when they have enough. One never stops when the information runs out because it never does. The universal experience of doing research in a new domain is how complicated it becomes. What looks simple and straightforward from the outside always contains a mass of conflicting stakeholders, trends and forces.

Rather than simply leap into the fray, however, the framework forecasting approach is used to guide the research. Framework forecasting uses categories of information that are useful in developing well-supported forecasts. Categories contain elements, the specific items within a category. So a specific text, statistic, or trend is an element of the framework. The categories also have relations with each other, forming a theory and a process of forecasting. The framework forecasting process will be explained fully in Chapter 7. Here, the categories relating to research will be described.

The framework categories act as containers to organize the outputs of the research of the process. They provide the appropriate "raw material" upon which forecasts will later be built. To help guide the research process itself, experienced researcher and program graduate Cody Clark typically lectures the Futures Research class each fall with his tips on how to carry out research. He organizes the searching of a domain into four categories (Clark, 2010):

Table 5.3 Clark's research strategy

Target	Where to look
1. Find the center of the domain	Terminology, experts, authoritative sources, history, standard measures, and current values
2. Find the edges of the domain	Research centers, discussions, blogs, "fringe" elements
3. Find the ecosystem (transactional environment) of the domain	Applications, markets, customers, suppliers, enabling technologies, competitors
4. Find the future of the domain	Assess the "velocity" of the domain Catch people talking about the future Discern trends from your own research

Table 5.4 shows the research categories from a framework forecast template (categories 1, 3, and 9).

1 Domain definition

Sometime a domain is clear from the start. A client asks for a particular study around a specific question or objective. Or the futurist has an intended audience in mind around a particular topic. In other cases, the domain is murkier. There may be a general sense of a need, challenge, or problem, but it is not specific. For instance, an organization might be interested in new business opportunities relating to water, but not sure about what aspect. The research might start with a broad view of water. It might reveal that desalination is a promising opportunity space. If the client agrees, then the domain could be narrowed to the future of desalination. The domain definition and research, as with the entire framework approach, is an iterative one.

Another method for defining the domain is called "What's In and What's Out." What parts of the domain are definitely going to be

Table 5.4   Research aspects of framework forecasting

1. Domain definition: A paragraph that defines the scope of the domain, including what is and what is not in the domain. A domain definition may include one or more of the following three levels:

The organization level	The internal environment of the region, organization, industry, or issue that is to be forecast
The immediate level	The external environment that directly affects the organization in the short or medium term. (The stakeholders within the organization are usually quite conscious of this level of the environment.)
The global level	The external environment that indirectly affects the organization in the long term (includes STEEP: social, technological, economic, environmental, and political trends)
Geography	The area of the forecast
Time horizon	The future date of the forecast

3. Current assessment: A review of the domain up to and including the present. Each of the following may be divided into any of the three levels (organization, immediate/transaction or global) and/or into the STEEP categories.

Current conditions	An overview of how the domain is structured and how it operates. Key quantities that characterize the domain
Stakeholders	The major actors in the domain (individuals and organizations) along with their values, political interests, and relationships with one another
Past events	Recent events within the domain that have created the current conditions and stakeholders, with particular attention to recent discontinuities that began and define the current era

9. Information: lists of relevant items in each of the following information categories

	Research	Scanning
Texts	Overview publications that describe the structure, statistics and/or future of the domain	N/A
Periodicals	Journals or magazines that carry overview or summary material about the domain	Journals or magazines that report on the latest developments in the domain
Organizations	Professional, trade or research organizations and institutes that publish relevant material on the field	
Experts	Knowledgeable people who are often consulted about the domain	
Websites	Sites that contain important information for understanding the future of the domain (portals and destinations)	Sites that carry the latest information about the domain

considered; what parts not. Gray areas can then be discussed and decisions made about the close calls.

The reason for spending time on getting the domain right is to avoid the explosion of the domain during the research. "Everything looks interesting; everything affects the future; of course, we need to consider that." "No, we decided upfront that we were not going to consider that." Of course, new components can be explicitly included as they come up.

It is also useful to set a geographic scope. Where is the forecast taking place?

A final element of the domain definition is the time horizon – how long into the future is the forecast for. Analogous to the spatial horizon, the time horizon is how far one is intending to look into the future. The time horizon is usually expressed as a year, and usually a round number like 2020 or 2025. The year is not used as a strict twelve-month period of time, however, such as forecasting for 2020 and not 2021. The year actually stands for how much change one is going to allow in the forecast. Transformational events can happen any day, but the probability of significant change increases as the time horizon gets longer. So a time horizon of 2050 will include a lot more change than will a time horizon of 2020.

A more technical reason for a specific time horizon is that the elements of the expected future, such as constants or trends, can be assumed to continue over medium times, such as ten years, where they are unlikely to continue over longer times, like thirty years. So the time horizon even influences what elements are included in the rest of the framework.

3 Current assessment[3]

The first detailed section is the current assessment, basically assembling the pieces and the recent history of the domain. It emerges directly from the research. This section provides a snapshot of the domain in the present. The subsequent components of the framework process will put that snapshot into motion and take it into the future. Even though it appears simple and straightforward, the current assessment is a difficult category to define. The current conditions contain all the structural elements that an individual would need to know in order to understand the domain. It is Cody Clark's ecosystem or transactional

---

[3] Note that 2. Summary and the rest of the non-research categories of the framework forecasting process will be covered in Chapter 7, Forecasting.

environment described above. It contains key variables, quantities, and structural arrangements. In the domain of petrochemicals, for instance, it might include the total annual sales, perhaps by major product category and by application area. It could also cover applicable standards or regulations that govern actions in the domain.

The current assessment also includes the stakeholders, the individuals and organizations that work in and could affect the future of the domain. In petrochemicals, for example, the stakeholders would be the primary producing companies, their suppliers and customers, service providers like transportation companies or equipment manufacturers, government regulators and not-for-profit groups like trade associations or environmental organizations. The stakeholders contain all the people involved in the domain just as the current conditions contain all the quantities and structural elements.

The framework also includes a little history, but just a little. Some would like to go back to the Roman aqueducts in describing the history of water. While immensely interesting, that era is long gone and has little practical value in understanding the present era or forecasting the next one. So history in the framework is confined to understanding the previous era, the one before the last major discontinuous event, and its influence on the current era. Past events are those significant events that signal a transition from one era to another. It may be a technology breakthrough, such as the iPod marking the beginning of a new era in digital music.

The purpose of the history section is to identify the previous and current eras of the domain. An era is a generally cohesive period of time that begins and ends with discontinuous events. So the Cold War was a previous era that began with the events of 1946–9, such as the Berlin Airlift and the Soviet acquisition of nuclear weapons, and ended with the events of 1989–91, such as the fall of the Berlin Wall and the Soviet Union itself.

The period within an era is called the equilibrium period, a quieter time when trends shape the future and incremental change dominates. The periods of discontinuity and equilibrium together form a model of change called punctuated equilibrium, a term borrowed from the study of biological evolution. Contrary to Darwin's idea that biological evolution proceeds smoothly, the fossil record shows that significant change in biological capability is infrequent yet rapid when it does occur. So the era of the dinosaur ended 65 million years ago in the fiery catastrophe of a meteor that hit the earth. With the dinosaurs out of the way, the mammals could exploit ecological niches previously closed to them, ushering in the current biological era. Paleontologists have actually recorded five such Great Extinctions in the history of the planet. The model applies equally well to economic, political, and even socio-cultural domains.

The two areas of concern in the framework are the previous and the current era. The current era is more difficult to define because it lacks historical perspective and because it is not known how it will end. Geopolitically, the current era might be the Age of Terror of the Conflict between Islam and the West, beginning with 9–11. Economically, it could be the Age of Globalization, beginning with the fall of the Soviet Union and the dominance of capitalism as the preferred economic system throughout the world.

Although difficult, it is nevertheless important to try to define the current era and how it began because the current era captures the "spirit of the times" and, most importantly from a forecasting perspective, it captures most of the major trends and issues that are shaping the future. When the era changes, however, those trends and issues go away or change significantly. So in the Cold War, the nuclear issue was how many nuclear missiles the US and the USSR had pointed at each other. In the current era, nuclear weapons are still an issue, but now the issue is nuclear proliferation.

Comparing the previous and current eras can also be highly illuminating. In fact, people and institutions are usually struggling with the trends and issues of the current era, but they are using the ideas and tools of the previous era. Making that comparison explicit reveals the novelty of the current era, and it allows one to jettison old ideas and habits more readily in order to confront the current era on its own terms.

A simple device for doing such a comparison is a small chart that requires people to identify the differences between the previous and the current eras. An example of a discontinuous event that started the current era in information technology might be the release of HTML and the creation of the World Wide Web (~1993-4). The comparison between the era before the World Wide Web and the era after it is illustrated in Table 5.5.

Those comparisons are commonplace today because the Internet era is more than ten years old, but more insight could be gained from domains that began more recently, like the Wireless Era, or the Genomic Era, or the Age of Terrorism. Those eras are not so mature that people are fully aware of their import or of the appropriate responses and strategies required to be successful.

In fact, some eras are so new that the domain may be in the midst of the short-term effects of its opening discontinuity when the framework

Table 5.5 PC era vs. Internet era

Discontinuity	Creation of the World Wide Web	
	Old Era: PC	*New Era: Internet*
Conditions, Arrangements	Print	Digital
Trends	More paper, mail	Less paper/mail as a percentage of information and communication
Issues, Conflicts, Controversies	Cost Distribution	Privacy IP Rights
Responses, Strategies, Plan	Push In house development	Pull Open source development

is constructed, but that is rare because eras are long compared to the turbulent times that get them started.

In many domains, it is possible to identify more than one discontinuity that began the current era. Multiple discontinuities indicate that the present is layered with a number of equilibrium periods. For instance, the current era of public education in the US might have begun with the publication of *A Nation at Risk* (1983), a US Department of Education study that described the deplorable state of public education throughout the country, or with the arrival of the Internet (~1994), a communication medium that could change the very delivery of education itself, or the passage of the No Child Left Behind Legislation (2002) that required standardized testing in all states. All three are significant events in the recent history of public education in the US, and together they define the trends and issues in the current era.

Though eras are thought of as exact periods of time demarcated by discontinuities, their effects linger well beyond their formal end. More specifically, the immediate past era is still quite influential in the current era, even though its influence may be waning. Understanding that tension between past and present, between the new and the old, between the receding and the emerging is extremely important to understand the present. Multiple eras in different domains are also emerging simultaneously. So in the first years of the 2010s, the breakthroughs in wireless technologies are opening a new era of communication, just like the attacks of 9/11 opened a new era of geopolitics, and the financial collapse of 2008 opened a new era of economics. So the framework calls for "the" previous era, but there could be more than one that is relevant to the domain.

The history category, however, is not a complete history of the domain. Such an exercise might be interesting, but it would not be especially relevant to the domain's forecast. Events and trends involved in eras before the previous one have usually faded from consciousness, and though their residue may continue to shape the present, their effect is not as strong as the events and trends in the current era. Thus a complete historical study of the domain is different from and generally unnecessary in constructing a forecast.

Finally, the current assessment also lists those quantities, structures, and stakeholders that are likely to continue unchanged throughout the forecast period. Constants provide a reminder that not everything changes before the arrival at the time horizon. Hence some of the elements of the baseline future will be the same as they are today. In fact, most things do not change, but identifying the most important constants is not trivial. In fact, directly after articulating some constants, others will think of ways in which they might change. So a discussion of constants is an excellent probe into the assumptions of the baseline forecast.

The current assessment is the snapshot of the domain as it exists today. The elements in the current assessment tend to be unremarkable. Nevertheless, it is good to articulate what they are so that any questions or issues concerning the domain can be raised and dealt with, particularly the assumptions about what is likely not to change in the forecast period. With the snapshot taken, the framework is set in motion with the consideration of the driving forces of change.

9 Information sources

This last section catalogues the most important information sources used in the framework to date (research) and the sources that will be most useful in the next phase (scanning). The framework is the sum total of what is most important to know about the future of the domain at the present time. Scanning is the on-going effort to keep up with new changes, ultimately to keep the framework current. So anything that might change the framework, even in the slightest detail, is a worthy scanning hit. Scanning in turn provides the material to adjust the framework to new changes that occur after it was originally created. The framework therefore is a living document, periodically reviewed and revised in light of recent change revealed by scanning.

The information section lists where information about the domain and, more importantly, change and the future of the domain are presented and discussed. Information about change exists in standard publications like texts and periodicals. It also resides in the human sources of information – individuals and organizations. Websites, the ubiquitous source of information these days, also contain a wealth of information. Important and useful websites come in two varieties: portals contain links to many other websites in the domain; destinations contain the best information themselves. Portals are characterized by many links going out of the website. They are often nothing more than a long list of links. Destinations are harder to determine since they are linked to by many other sites. One can tell a good destination site, however, by using the Google "link:" command. Entering "link:URL" into the Google search box lists all the sites that link to that URL. The more sites that link to that site, the better a destination site it is.

While the Internet is vast and growing rapidly, some of the best information is still obtained from other sources, notably experts. Experts know things about the domain that have not yet been published. True, in-depth forecasts will always require querying the experts for what they know.

CONCLUSION

Students are provided with a mix of concepts and tools for doing research in support of making forecasts. Secondary research generates ideas and evidence, with a key emphasis on the ability to analyze and interpret what is found. Primary research is also used, but to a lesser extent; interview and questionnaires are the principal tools used, mostly to gather expert judgment.

An important emphasis is on helping students do their research efficiently. It is easy to drown in information, so a process and template with the most futures-relevant categories for most quickly identifying and collecting the necessary information is provided.

RESOURCES

Glenn, J. & Gordon, T. (eds) (2009) *Futures Research Methodology, V2.0* (Washington, DC: AC/UNU Millennium Project) [CD-ROM].

- The best single compilation of futures research methods.

Gordon, T. J. & Helmer, O. (1964) *A Report on a Long-Range Forecasting Study* (Santa Monica, CA: RAND Corporation).

- Arguably the most famous Delphi study ever conducted.

Markley, O. W. & Wygant, A. C. (1988) *Information and the Future: A Handbook of Sources and Strategies* (Westport, CT: Greenwood Press).

- Covers both primary and secondary research approaches, specifically applied to finding information for futures research.

Primary research: Interviewing

Several links to overview pieces include:

- Doyle, J. (2006) "Introduction to Interviewing Techniques." Worcester Polytechnic Institute. Available at http://www.wpi.edu/Academics/ GPP/Students/ch11e.html#g.
- "Interviewing Techniques" (2003) *NY Times Learning Network*, http:// www.nytimes.com/learning/general/specials/weblines/461.html.

Primary research: Questionnaires

Several links to overview pieces include:

- Barnes, S. (2001) "Questionnaire Design and Construction. Institute for Learning & Research Technology," http://www.cros.ac.uk/ question_design.pdf.
- Borgatti, S. (1998) "Principles of Questionnaire Construction," http://www.analytictech.com/mb313/principl.htm.
- *Air University Sampling and Survey Handbook* (2002) *HQ AU/CFA*, http://www.au.af.mil/au/awc/awcgate/edref/smpl-srv.pdf.

Secondary research

Several links to doing secondary research include:

- "Boolean Searching" (n.d.). Surrey Institute of Art & Design on behalf of the ADAM Consortium. Art, Design, Architecture & Media Information Gateway (ADAM) Consortium, http://adam.ac.uk/info/ boolean.html.
- "Finding Information on the Internet: A Tutorial" (2009). UC Berkeley Library, http://www.lib.berkeley.edu/TeachingLib/Guides/ Internet/FindInfo.html.

- Google Web Search: Web Search Help (n.d.). Google, http://www.google.com/support/websearch/bin/answer.py?hl=en&answer=1368 61&rd=1.
- Harris, R. (2007) *Evaluating Internet Research Sources*. Virtual Salt, http://www.virtualsalt.com/evalu8it.htm.
- *University of Utah Research Guides* (n.d.). Willard Marriott Library at the University of Utah, http://campusguides.lib.utah.edu/browse.php?o=g&gid=30.

6
Scanning

INTRODUCTION

Surprise is an odd emotion. People like to be surprised – an unexpected visit from a friend, a gift from our spouse, a beautiful spring day. Sometimes people even pay to be surprised – at the fair or the cinema. But surprise is not a good thing at work. Being surprised means that either something that was expected to happen didn't or something that was not supposed to happen did. It's just not right even when the surprise is a good thing. At work, one is supposed to know what is going on and what is  about to happen all the time – to know and be prepared for everything that occurs. One is not supposed to be surprised at work.

Of course that is unreasonable. Everyone is surprised, even at work, even though they try not to show it when it happens. So people basically cover up – "never let them see you be surprised, even when you are." But rather than just wait, steps can be taken to reduce surprise – even if it cannot be eliminated altogether. Horizon or environmental scanning warns about change coming in the future. The term evokes images of lookouts on old ships or modern-day radars scanning the horizon. Lookouts and radars report sightings or signals from objects that are far off before they have the chance to harm a vessel, a plane, or a fortified encampment. It takes time for the objects to get to the lookout or the radar's location, time that people can use to prepare. The farther away the object is, the longer it takes for the object to arrive and the more time there is to prepare.

At the same time, most potentially threatening objects at sea or in the air pass off to one side or the other without interacting with the ship or plane. But woe to the lookout who does not report the object anyway. He would not be doing his job if he only reported objects that were about to hit the ship. He is allowed a lot of "misses," objects that have no consequence in the end, but not even one "hit."

The scanner is to the future what the lookout is to the sea. Most change does not occur suddenly, out of the blue, even if it appears that way at first. When looking back, one usually finds precursors, signs that the change was coming. Of course those signs are not as clear as the outline of a ship or the blip on a radar screen. In fact, the signs are often so weak that they are ignored completely, until it is too late. And most signs do not amount to anything anyway, so it is usually safe to ignore them. As a result, people develop the bad habit of ignoring all signs of change. "Oh, that's nothing. That will never come to anything." And being right almost all the time reinforces the habit. The signs do not come to anything, usually – until they do!

Environmental or horizon scanning ... or just scanning?

Environmental scanning was the first term used to describe the process of scanning an organization's external environment for signals of change. In recent years, horizon scanning has emerged as a synonymous term. The folklore is that it emerged from the UK government as a way to avoid the potential confusion of "environmental" with the physical environment, thus the substitution of horizon for environmental. In practice, the term environmental scanning is predominant in North America, while the use of horizon scanning is more prominent in Europe. Both terms are used pretty much interchangeably in Australia/New Zealand. Some innovators have even begun making a distinction between the two terms, with the scope of environmental scanning being closer to the organization's operating context and horizon scanning further away – well beyond the operating context. For this work, the simple term "Scanning" will be used. *Source: APF Listserv Discussion, August 2010; thanks to Sara Robinson, Andrew Curry, Kate Delaney, James Gillespie, Seongwon Park, Marcus Barber.*

Scanning attempts to break the habit of ignoring the early signs of change. It forces people to look at the novelty happening around them and report those signs that *could* have a significant impact on the organization, not just those that are sure to have an impact. Scanning is part of strategic foresight because it recognizes the inherent uncertainties in preparing for the future and allows people to report plausible outcomes rather than just lock-solid certainties.

Despite its obvious utility, scanning is many times more difficult than being the lookout on the ship, thus it is a core piece of the curriculum.

HISTORY

Aguilar opened the literature on environmental scanning in 1967 with his book *Scanning the Business Environment*. He identified four modes for collection (Morrison, 1995):

- *Undirected viewing* consists of reading a variety of publications for no specific purpose other than to be informed
- *Conditioned viewing* consists of responding to this information in terms of assessing its relevance to the organization
- *Informal searching* consists of actively seeking specific information but in a relatively unstructured way
- *Formal searching* is a more actively organized attempt to devise methodologies for obtaining information for specific purposes.

This was foundational work that many others built upon. For instance, Choo based his work on Daft & Weick (1984) who in turn built on Aguilar's work. Choo (2001) developed a model for scanning that was essentially a contingency framework that specified two conditions influencing organizational scanning: environmental analyzability and organizational intrusiveness. In the 1970s, Arnold Brown set up a well-regarded formal scanning process for the Institute of Life Insurance that scanned for trends outside of the insurance industry that might impact it in the future (Cornish, 2004, 81). STEEP (social, technological, economic, environmental and political) – and variations of it, such as ESPT (Aguilar's initial framework), PEST (E stands for economic in both acronyms) and PESTLE (where L stands for legal) – became popular in the 1980s. It provided an easy-to-recall popular shorthand for key categories in which to scan for developments.

Michael Porter's (1988) five forces model (see Figure 6.3, 185) helped to further popularize the concept of scanning the external environment for change. Another addition was issues management. United Way of America, the fifth largest charity in the US, put out an influential scanning report in 1980 that was often used as a model by other organizations. A more specialized form of environmental scanning emerged in the 1980s; known as Issues Management, it focused on controversial issues that might arise and harm the organization.

In the last decade, the new approach known as Integral Futures (see Chapter 3) has been applied as a means to expand the breadth and depth of environmental scanning. Australian Futurist Richard Slaughter introduced the idea and his students and others have been exploring various approaches to applying it to scanning. A key insight from this work is that scanning cannot be separated from the worldview and state-of-mind of the practitioner, that is, what the individual scanner believes has an important influence on what they decide to report on as a scan hit.

Another thread of work in scanning comes in the search for wildcards, low-probability, high-impact events that have significant consequences. A primary contributor to the understanding of wildcards is John Peterson who has been hunting wildcards for decades. His 1997 book *Out of the Blue* contains an extensive taxonomy and system for  evaluating the importance of different wildcards. Wildcards were also the subject of Nassim Nicholas Taleb's 2007 bestseller *The Black Swan*. The title of the book refers to the widely held medieval assumption that "All swans are white." That was true in Europe because all the swans in Europe were white, but *Cygnus atratus*, a species of black swans, was discovered in Australia in 1697. Taleb argues that Europeans had no way of knowing that their "fact" was wrong. In an extension of this principle, he argues that wildcards are essentially unknowable before they occur. They are random events that no amount of forecasting can prepare for. But if one understands genetics and mutations, is the possibility of Black Swan unknowable – perhaps not! He defines Black Swans as lying "outside the realm of regular expectations," but this is exactly what scanning is doing in searching for the weak signals of change.

A more recent treatment (Markley, 2010) further expands the scope and thinking around the wildcard concept by adding the element of credibility to the dimensions of probability and impact to the evaluation of wildcards. He asserts that some future possibilities actually have a reasonably high probability of occurring, as judged by experts, but are discounted because important non-expert stakeholders don't believe the projections.

GENERALIZATION

Day & Shoemaker (2006) offer a diagnostic test on whether an organization needs to do scanning and a common-sense seven-step process from identifying the right scanning sources to acting on the results, complete with many business examples that illustrate how scanning works (or doesn't, as the case may be).

One would think that, having been developed for so long and with so much written about it, the practice of scanning would be more advanced, but there are three key reasons why scanning is difficult.

Why scanning is difficult

Scanning is inherently subjective

A weak or early signal of change is called a scanning hit – an event or a new piece of information that signals that change is coming. The hit itself is something new or different, something out of the ordinary, a discrepancy in the pattern. It is not itself a significant change, but it could someday develop into a major change with important consequences for a domain or an organization. But what is new, extraordinary or discrepant to one person is not to another. Therefore, what counts as a scanning hit depends on what that person already knows and expects to happen. Discrepancies are only discrepant compared to some background pattern. Scanners therefore are sensors comparing new items on the horizon with their knowledge and experience of what is usually there.[1] Thus scanning is inherently subjective, making it very hard to teach or practice with any degree of repeatability. It is also difficult to achieve credibility as an objective function since a significant event to one person may not be significant to another.

Weak signals are, well, weak

The signal to noise ratio is very low. Strong signals are widely reported in the media. While a scanner might draw novel implications from a widely reported news story, the event or information itself is not special or unusual since everyone knows it already. The best hits are those that are not widely reported. The problem is that they appear in an ocean of information of no consequences whatsoever.

---

[1] A growing emphasis on the mindset/worldview of the scanner has been a key point of the Integral Futures perspective, highlighted in Chapter 3.

The signals are there, but they are surrounded by noise. Finding the signal amidst the noise is the difficulty.

Early signals are also early

Signals take a long time to develop into full-blown change. While early is good because it gives time to prepare, early also allows time for a lot of other things (or in fact no things) to happen. So the signals are not that reliable; they may not result in any change at all. And the earlier they are, the more likely they are to produce no change at all.

So, on balance, scanning involves one or more individuals picking up weak and early signs of change, and making subjective judgments based on their knowledge and experience by selecting what they believe are real signs of change in a sea of noise, most of which will probably not amount to anything anyway. Thus, the monumental task for scanners!

In fact, the task is so difficult that most people just ignore almost all signs of change. They simply don't have time to comb through the ocean of new information looking for real signals. When they do find what they think is a real signal, they wait to see what effect it has, which is usually nothing. So scanning takes a lot of time that usually does not result in real change anyway. Not only is scanning difficult, therefore, it probably does not get the attention or respect it deserves because the number of hits that result in real change is quite small. The lookout on the ship reports every object that comes over the horizon whether or not it is on a collision course with it. The scanner is held to a different standard, an impossibly high one, in fact, namely "only report the signs of change that will have real consequences for the organization. Don't bother us with the rest." Since the standard is impossible to meet, very few people do it. As a result, the organization is essentially blind to the real signs of change out there and surprised when that change suddenly comes upon them.

APPROACH

So is it worth doing? Put another way, should one be on the lookout for wild animals in a dense forest? The answer, of course, is that people should, and that they should be extra careful the denser and things get. There is a point of diminishing returns, of course, where the added benefit does not outweigh the added cost, but the benefit–cost ratio is almost certainly positive in a modest effort to scan the future horizon. Simply closing one's eyes to the signs of change would not be prudent in turbulent times like the present.

So, as hard as it is, scanning must be done anyway and others need to be taught to do it as well. Here are some of the techniques for scanning that the curriculum teaches.

- Identify scanning hits
- Scan a wide range of sources
- Operate at different levels of the domain
- Keep an eye on wildcards
- Keep track of your hits
- Distinguish types of scanning hits
- Establish criteria for evaluating scanning hits.

Identify scanning hits

Scanning items come in the form of hits. The best scanning hits are events or solid pieces of information that indicate a plausible change in the future. Items of opinion or speculation may be included, but with care. People are speculating about the future all the time, few with any solid rationale for the speculation. Sometimes those speculations are truly valuable. New

Title		Author	
Brief source		Date	
STEEP Category/ies		Keywords	
URL			
Type (*bold one*)	Actual event New trend New cycle New plan Potential event New information New issue		
Brief description of the item			
How could the future be different as a result?			
What are the potential Implications for...?	...Stakeholder name:		
Overall effect (*bold one*)	Confirming (baseline scenario) Creating (a new scenario) Resolving (between two scenarios)	Impact (0–5)	Plausibility (0–5)
Baseline, new or resolved scenario(s)		Novelty (0–5)	Timeliness (0–5)
Scanner		Date Submitted	

Figure 6.1   Scanning hit form

ideas and perspectives have to start somewhere. Usually, however, they add little to our image of the future. The best hits are attached to a solid news hook that can actually change the future. They are changes, really new things in the world, which can cause additional change down the line.

Table 6.1 Diffusion of ideas

State of idea	Source (where it appears)
Visionary uninhibited	Aesthetic, poetic works Science fiction Fringe media, underground press, Usenet
Rendering idea to specifics	Unpublished notes and speeches Monographs, treatises, individuals' web pages
Corroboration of details	Scientific, technical, professional journals Highly specialized, narrow viewpoint publications Statistical documents, social indicators, statistical services Abstracting journals, services
Diffusion of an idea among opinion leaders	Data search services, scouts Egghead journals (*Science, New Scientist*) "Dopesheets," product safety letters
Institutional response	Popular intellectual magazines (*Harper's, Spectator, New Statesman*) Network communications, small-time newsletters, pamphlets
Mass media	Journals for the cause (*Consumer Reports, Which?*) General interest publications (*Time, Newsweek*) Compilations of general literature (*Reader's Digest*)
Politicizing the issue	Poll data, public opinion, behavioral and voter attitudes Legislative, governmental services, reports
Instantaneous coverage for mass consumption	Books – fiction, novels, social analyses of the times Books – nonfiction, pull together discordant themes in poorly understood areas Newspapers (*New York Times, Washington Post, The Times*, early Southern rural papers) Radio-TV networks
Educating people to the norm	Education journals
Historical analysis	Historical analysis Doctoral dissertations

Timeliness is one of the important criteria for a good scanning hit. Finding something out a few hours before it runs on CNN is not particularly useful. At the same time, the lead time might be so long that it is irrelevant for any meaningful future today.

Graham Molitor (1986), one of the most experienced scanners in the field of foresight, has developed a more detailed taxonomy of sources that ranks them on how much lead time they offer (see Table 6.1).

The sources are ranked from the most novel to the most significant. Each level selects certain things to report from the previous level and filters out the rest. So new items appear at the top of the list and filter their way down the list until they become major issues reported in the mainstream media. Identifying items early at the top of the list increases the lead time. Unfortunately, keeping up with the vast selection of sources at the top of the list is particularly difficult. And now the Internet, with all its new web pages, listservs and newsgroups, adds another layer of complexity to the whole mess. The "right" items are out there – finding, identifying, selecting, and reporting them is the trick.

The list also displays the gamut of what one might call risk. Risk is the probability that a scanning hit will *not* change the future. The further up the list one scans, the longer the lead time and the higher the risk that the item will "pass off the side" without ever changing the future. One must assess one's own or one's client's "risk tolerance" – that is, how "far out" the scanning hits should be on likelihood or impact. Different situations call for different levels of risk tolerance.

Operate at different levels of the domain

Scanning involves three levels of the domain and typically somewhere from five to eight distinct sectors. The levels, introduced in Chapter 1, related to change (see Figure 1.2, Levels of Change).

The three levels are defined as follows:

Table 6.2   Three levels of scanning

Level	Definition	Examples for a University
Organization	The individual, family, group, organization or community that the scanning is for	Faculty, administration, facilities, equipment, policies, procedures
Immediate environment	Factors that affect the future of the organization directly in the short term	Students, employers, academic disciplines, other universities, State and Federal/local government
Global environment	Factors that affect the future of the industry indirectly in the long term	Population, technologies, the general economic and political climate, public opinion

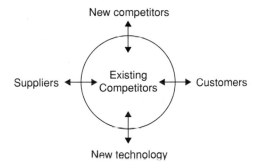

Figure 6.2 Porter's five forces

The organization is the center of Figure 1.2, surrounded by the immediate environment. The immediate environment affects the organization directly; and for that reason, most organizations know their immediate environments better than any general futurist would. Porter's (1988) five forces are probably the most common set of categories for the immediate environment, in this case of a business organization: existing competitors, new competitors, customers, suppliers, and new technology.

Just as the organization knows its immediate environment better than anyone, so the futurist knows the global environment – the collection of forces of change that affect the organization only indirectly and over the long term through changes in the immediate environment. The most common list of sectors for the global environment comes from STEEP.

It is important to recognize the interconnected nature of the various elements of the future. The diagram in Figure 6.3 begins at the bottom with *Social*, or people in a natural habitat, or *Environment*. Humans are species like every other living thing, and they ultimately depend on the physical world to supply their needs. Humans are special, however, because they can use *Technology* to manipulate that habitat to get resources from the world and put them to more productive use. The technologies that get developed and the products and services that they produce are determined the *Economy*. The economy itself operates within the larger frame of *Politics* or government, the mechanism that society uses to make collective decisions. Government, in turn, operates in the largest frame of all, culture, depicted in the figure as the language, beliefs, values and norms that are prevalent in a society at any one time.

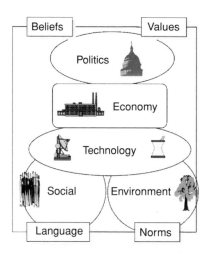

Figure 6.3   STEEP

All of these sectors are changing, and changes in one affect all the others over time. So technology affects population (the contraceptive pill) which affects the economy (more women and older workers in the workforce) which affects government (laws on sexual harassment and the provision of Social Security) and on and on. It is impossible to catalogue all of these interactions, but recognizing that change comes in all of these sectors in a good beginning. Most people use the STEEP categories more as a checklist, in order to prevent neglecting or discounting change from any sector, than as a comprehensive causal diagram.

Those indirect effects take time to affect the organization so they are some way off into the future. As a result, most people discount those effects, believing that they do not have time to deal with them now. But the effect of preparing for them can be quite important.

Keep an eye on wildcards

Figure 6.4 shows the emerging issues life cycle curve originally proposed by Graham Molitor, which identified the typical trajectory that an emerging issue followed. *Wildcards* are those very low-probability but high-impact events that could have enormous consequences for the organization. Even more important are *Emerging Issues*, just below the surface of general public awareness. The emerging issues are known, but they do not get much attention because they have not popped above the surface yet. They do so when an event occurs that puts the issue

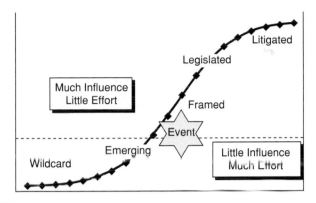

Figure 6.4 Molitor's emerging issue curve

on the public agenda, a process called *framing*. Once an issue is framed, watch out. It becomes a focus of intensive media attention; political leaders sensing danger or advantage begin to be involved, and finally lawyers take over to settle the score. The point is that no organization wants to be caught on the wrong side of a framed issue.

Scanning is the obvious solution to becoming aware and acting before an issue explodes. The problem is that there are an uncountable number of possible wildcards and a very large number of emerging issues, all of which cannot be monitored at once. Good scanning nevertheless involves being generally aware of many emerging issues and being sensitive to changes in the issues that could lead to framing. As described before, most emerging issues do not get framed, and they recede from view. But those that do can have significant consequences so getting even a few right puts an organization in a better position than just letting the issues be framed without any preparation.

The levels themselves are not mutually exclusive, nor is it necessary to be sure to get the "right" scanning item at the "right" level. The purpose of identifying the levels is to be sure to cover them all in some fashion – that is, not concentrating so narrowly on the industry itself that one misses items of change in the larger, global environment.

Keep track of your hits

There are many approaches for capturing, storing and reporting scanning hits. The most widespread public service for doing so is *Shaping*

Table 6.3   Types of scanning hits

Type	Definition	Examples for a "Parenting" Domain
Confirming	A change that indicates that the baseline forecast is more likely	A report that shows an increase in mothers going to work
Creating	A change that indicates that a new alternative future is more plausible	A lawsuit by non-parents in the work place contesting the family benefits offered to parents
Disconfirming	A change that makes an alternative future less plausible	Newly elected government vows to cut spending on any new initiatives

Tomorrow.[2] It has a large database of up-to-date scanning hits with lots of features for reporting and analysis.

Another tool for scanning is the form used for capturing and reporting hits at the University of Houston (see Appendix 3). The form contains a comprehensive list of the characteristics of a good scanning hit. However, in actual use it may not be necessary to collect all this information. The form is used for education and training to encourage students to think of all aspects of the scanning hit; organizations that collect scanning hits on a systematic basis would probably use a subset of these attributes.

The single biggest problem to organization-level scanning is to encourage members of the organization to contribute to the database. While a rich source of scanning hits benefits the whole organization, it is hard for individuals to justify spending much time making contributions in the face of the many other pressing demands on their time. While the mechanisms of open source and crowd sourcing have produced volumes of information on the Internet, in the form of computer programs, blogs, Facebook pages, and the like, the routine collection of scanning hits or other pieces of intelligence at the organization level is a still a goal to be achieved.

Distinguish types of scanning hits

Scanning hits come in three types, with each type having a different effect on the framework.

---

[2] See http://www.shapingtomorrow.com/.

Unfortunately, almost all scanning hits are confirming hits that support the baseline. While it is good to know that the baseline is still the expected future, it does not take many of these hits to confirm that. Confirming hits should therefore be reported sparingly.

The real value lies in the creating and disconfirming hits – those that modify the plausible alternatives. Even more important are those hits that elevate one of the alternatives to the baseline itself, but these are extremely rare. The fall of the Soviet Union was a discontinuous event that changed the baseline for all sorts of domains. Advanced warning of such discontinuities has been some of the most important information to come from the scanning function since it can have a profound impact on the forecasting framework.

Establish criteria for evaluating scanning hits

At a more detailed level, good scanning items range from best to worst according to a set of criteria. Those criteria are described in Table 6.4.

Using these criteria, then, the best scanning hit is:

- an event or a new piece of information
- from a credible source

Table 6.4 Criteria for evaluating scanning hits

Criteria	Description
Credibility	Is the source reputable? Has the source reported good hits before?
Novelty	Is the hit new? Or has it been widely reported? Is it new to the client/audience?
Likelihood	Will the hit amount to something over time? Could it change the future?
Impact	If it does, how big a change will that be? Will it change the framework document, our current image of the future?
Relevance	How important is that change to the client or the domain? Is the change direct or indirect?
Timeliness 1 (time to awareness)	How long before this information is widely known? When will it appear in a mainstream newspaper or magazine?
Timeliness 2 (time to prepare)	How long before this hit begins to change the future? Is it too late to do anything about it? Or is it so far off that action now would be premature?

- that is unknown to the client or audience
- that has a high likelihood of changing the future
- in a relevant way
- and for which there is some time before it is generally known and some time left to do something about it.

These criteria apply to scanning in a particular domain for a particular client or audience. A second and shorter set of criteria is more appropriate for general scanning hits – events or information that could change the future in a general way. In that case, a good scanning hit needs to be *novel* (it is generally unknown or unexpected) and *important* (it could have a measurable impact on the future).

CONCLUSION

So scanning is hard, but also necessary. It is hard because finding the truly novel requires knowledge of experience in the domain, but the most experienced people are often the most locked in to the current mindset which filters out anything new. Scanning is also hard because the signals are weak – looking for a needle in a haystack. Finally, they are early – even most good hits do not amount to much in the long run. Asking experienced people to look for novelty in a sea of noise, most of which will not change the future anyway – no wonder the future tends to get ignored!

But scanning is also necessary in order to be prepared for change, particularly for sudden and surprising change. The saving grace for scanning is that one does not have to get the future "right" for scanning to be useful. The obvious benefit of scanning is to pick up an early signal of change, evaluate its implications and prepare contingency plans in case it does occur. But even scanning hits that do not occur are valuable because they sensitize the organization to the fact that some change is guaranteed to happen. The current era will not go on forever because nothing goes on forever. So those who look for signs of change have already implicitly bought into the concept that the organization needs to be ready for change no matter where it comes from. As a result, even if the organization is surprised, it is more ready to deal with the implications of change than if it first has to realize that the past is over.

As a result, scanning for change should be part of every organization's portfolio of strategic activities.

RESOURCES

Aguilar, F. (1967) *Scanning the Business Environment* (NY: Macmillan).

- Often cited as the work that kicked off formal environmental scanning inside organizations. He came up with a four-dimension scanning framework, based on interviews with 137 managers from 41 companies, which subsequent researchers were able to build upon.

Choo, C. W. (2001) *Information Management for the Intelligent Organization: The Art of Scanning the Environment* (Medford, NJ: Information Today).

- Solid overview of environmental scanning.

Coates, J. F. (1996) *Issues Management: How You Can Plan, Organize and Manage for the Future* (Mt. Airy, MD: Lomond).

- A how-to book on scanning for emerging issues.

Day, P. & Shoemaker, G. (2006) *Peripheral Vision: Detecting the Weak Signals that Make or Break your Company* (Cambridge MA: Harvard Press).

- One of the best current treatments of how to do environmental scanning. Estimates that less than 20% of firms are doing it. They provide a systematic approach for organizations wishing to do so.

Hines, A. (2003) "Applying Integral Futures to Environmental Scanning," *Futures Research Quarterly*, Winter.

- Makes the case for how Integral Futures can revitalize environmental scanning by providing an example from his organizational experience.

Klein, C. (1999) "Overcoming Net Disease: The Risks in Depending Solely on the Internet for CI Research," *FID Review*, 1 (4/5), 27–30.

- Provides a needed caution about relying too much on the Internet for research sources.

Markley, O. (2011) "A New Intelligence Methodology for Anticipating Disruptive Surprises," *Technological Forecasting & Social Change*, 78, 1079–97.

- Important addition to the literature on wildcards that introduces a new typology with added dimensions for assessing wildcards. A significant advance in the thinking around this topic.

Molitor, G. (2003) *The Power to Change the World: The Art of Forecasting* (Potomac, MD: Public Policy Forecasting).

- Contains a definitive guide to scanning sources and a model for how different types of sources tend to reveal different types of scanning hits in a fairly predictable fashion. Based on his years of experience in forecasting the emergence of public policy issues.

Morrison, J. L., Renfro, W. L. & Boucher, W. I. (1984) *Futures Research and the Strategic Planning Process: Implications for Higher Education*, ASHE-ERIC Higher Education Research Report No. 9 (Washington, DC: Association for the Study of Higher Education).

- Places environmental scanning in the context of doing strategic planning.

Morrison, J. L. (1995) "Environmental Scanning," in G. Kurian & G. Molitor (eds) *Encyclopedia of the Future* (NY: Simon & Schuster).

- Concisely and capably summarizes the mainstream literature on environment scanning, and reviews different types of scanning and provides tips on how to do scanning well.

Petersen, J. L. (1997) *Out of the Blue: Wild cards and other Big Future Surprises: How to Anticipate and Respond to Profound Change* (Toronto, Canada: Madison Books).

- Contains an extensive taxonomy and system for evaluating the importance of different wildcards.

Slaughter, R. (1999) "A New Framework for Environmental Scanning," *Foresight*, 1 (5), 441–51.

- Advocates the application of Ken Wilber's Integral Theory as a means to reinvigorate environmental scanning, in particular redressing what Slaughter sees as an over-reliance on empirical sources at the expense of the interpretive.

Taleb, N. N. (2007) *The Black Swan: The Impact of the Highly Improbable* (NY: Random House).

- Identifies and discusses "Black Swans," random events that no amount of forecasting can prepare for.

7
Forecasting

INTRODUCTION

The methods of foresight deal with change in all its variety for two purposes: (1) to map change and (2) to influence it. Mapping change means describing expected and other plausible future states for which one needs to prepare. Influencing change means to bring about the best possible future given the time and resources available. People who understand the dynamics of change and the changes that are going on around them are not often surprised. People who then influence those dynamics toward their vision of a better future will have a greater chance of getting that better future.

The two big divisions of foresight, therefore, are mapping and influencing. The "products" of mapping are forecasts of the baseline and alternative futures. It requires an understanding of which futures are plausible; planning is the action side of foresight. The "products" are visions, plans, and ultimately, actions. The goal is working to bring about a better or preferable future, covered in Part III.

Forecasting results in two types of forecasts: baseline and alternative. A baseline forecast is the extrapolation of present conditions and trends into the future. It is also called the expected or surprise-free forecast. It would be the future that would occur if nothing really surprising or interesting occurred, if present trends continued uninterrupted. No one really expects the baseline forecast to occur, at least futurists don't. But it is a useful place to begin the forecast. Knowing where one is headed provides a point of departure to discuss the other and more interesting forecasts, the alternatives.

Two basic approaches to generating alternative futures are critical and creative thinking. A brief module on each outlines how the curriculum draws upon these approaches to help generate alternative futures.

Alternative futures happen when the baseline does not. As a group they are more probable than the baseline even though each of them individually is less probable than the baseline. The total of all futures, baseline and alternatives, is represented as an expanding cone (see Figure 1.13). The longer the time that elapses, the less probable the baseline becomes and the more probable something else will occur. In the far reaches of the cone, enough time passes to allow unexpected events or issues to turn the trajectory of the future one way or the other.

HISTORY

The desire to know the future is as ancient as humans themselves. It is the unique ability to conceive of states that are not present at the moment that got people thinking about the future (and about the past). And just as history was based on myth and legend before the first historians (Herodotus and Thucydides) decided to write down exactly what happened, so trying to know the future (forecasting) was based on a set of beliefs and superstitions that were of little use, except perhaps to make people feel better. Some wonder whether forecasting is much better today even with fast computers and Internet resources! At any rate, while knowing exactly what will happen in the future is impossible, foresight is nevertheless taking its place alongside other disciplines, such as management, marketing, and policy making. These are not done perfectly either, but they are better than they used to be. By the same token, foresight will never reach the accuracy of prediction that the physical sciences have. Nevertheless, some knowledge of the future, imperfect though it may be, is better than no knowledge at all.

But is being aware of what will happen in the future the only benefit of foresight? If one cannot know the future exactly, is it worth looking at all? Yes, there are other benefits of looking into the future even if it cannot be predicted accurately. One of the other benefits is to appreciate the dynamics of change – how the future is unfolding. Even though predictions are inaccurate, one can still get a sense of how things change.

In fact, that was the rationale for the very first scenario work done in the Pentagon and at the RAND Corporation in the 1950s. Military planners were faced with a new type of warfare with the appearance of intercontinental ballistic missiles tipped with nuclear warheads. Conventional wars take a while to get going. Moving men and material into position takes time, and that time is used to plan the campaign. Not so with nuclear weapons. A nuclear war could be over in hours rather than months or years; planning time was over once the missiles appeared on the radar screen. But strategists did not just wait for that to happen. They conducted war games with one side playing the US and the other side the Soviet Union. The record of those simulations is probably still classified, but one can imagine that a lot of it was, "We will do this, and then they will do that, and then we will do the other thing," and so on. Each of these simulations was a mini-scenario about how a nuclear war might progress. In the end, the teams were exploring the space of possible moves, and counter-moves, and counter-counter-moves. In essence, they were getting a feel for how things might happen even though they could not tell which scenario was going to occur.

And simulating the future is not confined to the military. Shuttle astronauts and emergency preparedness agencies run through dozens of risk scenarios in order to be prepared for the one that does occur. Sports teams will have their reserve team run the opponent's plays just to get a feel of the game. And even if none of the scenarios actually occurs as simulated, at least those in charge have a better idea of how the things work and the tools they have to influence the outcome. In the same way, scenario forecasts are simulations of what might happen – not to predict what will happen or even to hedge our bets by making multiple predictions, but rather simply to understand the dynamics of change.

Looking into the future can help people to know themselves better as well. Forecasts, like all inferences, are based on two types of knowledge: evidence (data) and assumptions (beliefs). Data is used in constructing forecasts, but the assumptions are more important and more suspect than the data. How do things work? What leads to what? What's possible or impossible? No one knows the answers to those questions, particularly in human systems, so one makes assumptions. Ironically, even though assumptions are the key to making good forecasts, people are often not aware of the assumptions they are using. For good forecasting, discovering and challenging assumptions is essential. Rather than simply waiting to see if the forecast comes true or not, which is what many people do, futurists imagine how it might turn out differently. Each of the possible scenarios rests on the same data but uses different assumptions. Thus one can proceed with a little more assurance of not being blindsided by an assumption that they did not even know they had.

GENERALIZATION

Regrettably forecasting is not taught in school despite the fact that people think about the future all the time and a lot is riding on how well it pans out. Will the light change before I get there? What's for dinner? How long before it rains again? And over longer timeframes: When's the best time to buy a car? What should I major in? Where should I put my savings? So it's unfortunate that forecasting is not taught because it's a skill people could use in life!

Nevertheless, people do get ideas about the future in school even though it is not regularly taught. In science class, for instance, one learns how to predict natural phenomena, like the period of a pendulum, the force of a lever, the time it takes an ice cube to melt. Scientists are making predictions all the time – the phases of the Moon, the weather for the coming week, the heat of a reaction in a chemical plant, the warming of the planet. And most of those are quite accurate and useful for managing our world. So people learn from science that forecasting is prediction.

Where science covers the world of things, history covers the world of people. History is taught as a series of events – wars, elections, revolutions, or natural disasters. Each of those events did happen, but they did not *have to* happen. They were not determined by known laws the way the phases of the Moon are. They are contingent; they depend on the circumstances and the context.

Psychology, sociology, anthropology and political science take a different look at the social world, a presumably more scientific one. Can one make predictions in society the way they are made in the physics lab? Unfortunately not. Economists are pretty good at telling people what the economic growth will be over the next year – that is, of course, until they are not. For instance, few predicted the housing collapse and the banking crisis of 2008. That type of massive error rarely occurs in physical science, but it happens in social science all the time. In fact, social scientists often do not make just one prediction; they make multiple predictions based on different theories. There are patterns in human behavior that are known, but predicting human behavior accurately is not one of them.

It is confusing. Is the future predictable or not? And the answer is – sometimes it is, sometimes not, but one can't tell when it is and when it is not until it occurs, which of course is too late to do anything about it! And just to make matters worse, there is a third set of people telling us how to predict the future. Alan Kay famously said, "The best way to predict the future is to invent it." A nice catchy phrase, if it were only true. But parents, teachers, ministers, and every motivational speaker on the planet say that humanity's future is up to individuals. "You can be anything you want to be; you can reach any goal you choose." Well, that is not entirely true, but it does raise the question about how much influence individuals do have over the future. I can have any flavor of ice cream I want, but can I have any career? Probably not.

At this point there are three ways of handling the future. Each comes from reputable sources, but they appear to contradict each other:

- Science says that the future can be predicted
- Historians and social scientists say no, the future is contingent
- Alan Kay and many others say the future can be created, but that doesn't always seem to work.

So which is it: the predictable future, the contingent future, or the chosen future? In the end, it is all wrapped into a model of change. The future is predictable to some extent because the expected, surprise-free future is more likely than any other single future. But the expected future will probably not happen exactly as expected; something else is bound to happen instead (alternative futures). And the future can be influenced to some extent (outbound change), but the world will influence the future as well (inbound change).

So forecasting is the process of discovering and describing plausible futures – those that are more likely than any other (the baseline future) and some of the others that might happen instead (the alternative futures). Planning is taking that information and combining it with our values, aspirations, preferences, needs and desires to design a way to influence the future toward our vision and goals, literally to bend the trajectory of the future to a more preferable future and away from a less preferable one.

Forecasting theory

An entire volume could be written on the topic. For present purposes, three principal ideas behind the theory are briefly introduced.

1. Forecasts are inferences

Forecasts are statements about the future. The future cannot be observed directly so any statement made about the future is an inference. People make inferences all the time in science, in history, and in everyday life. No one has directly measured the distance from the Earth to the Sun, but people know that it is 93 million miles because it is inferred from other information. No one alive today was in the American Revolution, but people know (infer) that Washington crossed the Delaware and surprised the Hessians at Trenton in 1776. One knows (infers) that the train will leave the station at 11:00 am although they are not there yet. Each of these cases involves knowing something that cannot be directly observed. They are all inferences.

2. Any forecast can be wrong

Forecasts are inferences, too, just like the knowledge people have about the world that they cannot directly observe. Any inference can be wrong. (Direct observations can be wrong, too, but much less often.) So people say they *know* things that they cannot directly observe, but that knowledge is always uncertain. Rene Descartes touched off a philosophical and scientific revolution when he realized that he could doubt everything except his own existence, that everything he *knew* about the world was uncertain to some degree. So forecasts could be wrong just like any other inferences.

3. Forecasts are supported using evidence and assumptions

An inference cannot be proven the way that mathematical theorems are. Rather they are supported using two types of knowledge: evidence (data) and assumptions (beliefs). Evidence consists of facts accepted as true. They can be wrong, too, but only rarely so. The evidence used to support inferences is usually pretty solid.

Comparing futures forecasting and traditional forecasting

Forecasters of human systems cannot simply borrow techniques from the physical sciences. Human systems are a different class of phenomena that requires a different approach to forecasting.

The most comprehensive review of forecasting techniques is *The Principles of Forecasting* (Armstrong, 2001). It is immediately evident that futurists tend to use qualitative techniques rather than quantitative because of the breadth and time horizon of their forecasts. Quantitative techniques are suitable for relatively short time-horizons and relatively narrow domains. But the synthetic power of human judgment and expertise is more appropriate when forecasting over longer time-horizons and broader domains. Quantitative data does exist for many variables, but extrapolating that data over 10–20 years is quite risky. Futurists also tend to focus on potential future discontinuities and transformations for which quantitative analysis is not appropriate at all.

No, the weak links in supporting inferences are the assumptions required to use the evidence to support the inference. A scientist's assumption could be that an anomalous reading from a measuring instrument is due to the instrument not working properly. When an airline pilot receives a warning signal, the assumption always occurs, is it a real warning or a faulty sensor? That assumption actually played a role in the discovery of the destruction of the ozone layer in 1989. It turned out that instruments aboard satellites were already measuring less ozone for most of the 1980s. Scientists assumed, however, that the instruments on the satellite were decaying and sending back erroneous readings. After all, nothing could destroy the ozone! It was not until they received corroboration that they had to revise their assumption, make a different inference and begin to address the problem.

Historians and paleontologists make assumptions as well. The process of dating fossils assumes that Carbon-14 decays at a set rate. The use of photographs assumes that the photograph has not been altered. Referencing eye witness accounts of historical events assumes that the observer was there and able to see the event as it happened. It also assumes that the account was not unduly biased by the observer's values or prejudices. All of these assumptions are pretty strong and so are the inferences they support.

Forecasters use evidence and make assumptions just like scientists and historians do. The evidence includes quantitative trends over time (trend extrapolation), goals and plans of individuals and organizations (stakeholder analysis), past situations that are similar to the present one (historical analogy). The evidence is solid – those trends have been going on, individuals and organizations did announce those plans, and the present is like an historical situation to some extent. But the assumptions that forecasters make are considerably different from those that scientists make. The speed of light and the decay of Carbon-14 are well-established rates, but will a trend continue? Will that individual or organization be able to execute the plan and achieve the goal? They probably will, but there are many ways in which they could fail. Everyone makes inferences, and all inferences use assumptions. Therefore all inferences are uncertain to some extent. The degree of uncertainty, however, varies among disciplines. Assumptions in the physical sciences are usually very good, but in the social sciences, such as forecasting, the assumptions are weaker. As a result, the inferences are more uncertain. Forecasting is a useful, even necessary activity, but one must deal with the inherent uncertainties involved.

APPROACH: FRAMEWORK FORECASTING

Framework forecasting (introduced in Chapter 5) is a process for categorizing information and placing the categories in relation to each other to generate the expected (baseline) forecast and a set of alternative forecasts (scenarios). The process begins with a characterization of the present era – when did it start? What are its conditions and trends? It then explores the forces of change, beginning with trends that, after a while, generate the expected future. Discontinuities are then introduced in the form of plausible events, emerging issues (issues that have not yet made the news) and new ideas. The discontinuities are collected into dimensions of uncertainty, each of which has the potential to kick-off a new era. The result is a baseline forecast and scenarios of alternative forecasts whose implications can be explored for opportunities and threats to the organization or client in question.

The outcome is called a framework because it is a rough outline of the future of a domain. It is not filled in and "fully furnished," so to speak, with lots of detail or with values, preferences, visions, or strategies. A framework is to the complete mission of a futurist what the foundation and the 2×4 studs are to a fully livable house. It indicates the general outline of the future. Everything else hangs on it or is contained within it, but it is by no means the complete job.

While the framework is a process that has a logical order, the information does not arrive in that order. Rather, information comes in as it will. One does not look for one category and then another. Think of the categories as a set of bins into which information is stored as it comes in, such as information sources, historical discontinuities, or current conditions. Only when the bins are relatively full and the ratio of new information to old starts to decline does one think of relating those categories to each other in a chronological order. Before that, it's toss it in the bins and sort it out later.

The other crucial aspect of the process is to recognize that it is a framework, not the fully furnished house. It has all the necessary information to make a forecast, but not all the information. In doing secondary research, one can drown in too much information just as easily as one can starve on too little (to mix the metaphor!). Therefore, the framework is inherently selective. It is the best information in each category. The framework document suggests about ten items as the target for each category, but that is completely arbitrary. It might be more or less, depending on the quality of the items and the purpose of the forecast. It is never all the information in a domain or even in a category, which is impossible. One selects the best from all the information collected to focus attention on those most important items and not let them get lost in too much detail. The human mind can only handle a limited number of items at once. The ultimate purpose of the framework is to break the problem of forecasting down so that one can literally see all the pieces of the forecast at once. That comprehensive picture is lost if the categories contain too much detail.

At the same time, one runs the risk of leaving out something important in making the selection. True, but that risk is counterbalanced by the risk of leaving too much in each category and overwhelming the truly important stuff. What to leave in and what to take out is a matter of professional judgment that can only be learned through experience.

The framework consists of nine sections describing the domain, as listed in Appendix 1:

1. Domain definition (covered in Chapter 5, Research)
2. Summary
3. Current assessment (covered in Chapter 5, Research)
4. Era analysis
5. Baseline forecast
6. Baseline analysis
7. Alternative futures
8. Scenario kernels
9. Information (covered in Chapter 5, Research)

Figure 7.1 synthesizes the key components of the whole framework process in one chart.

2. Summary

The most important item in the whole framework process is the summary. Although the summary appears early in the document, it should be completed at the end, once all the other sections are complete. The summary is the opportunity to look over all the material about this domain and select those items that are most important for understanding its future. It is easy to get lost in the details because the framework process is so information intensive. The summary prevents the product from being just a mass of facts.

Good candidates for the summary are surprising bits of information, important implications from the baseline, interesting scenarios developed, and significant information sources. The summary contains the highlights of the best material in the framework.

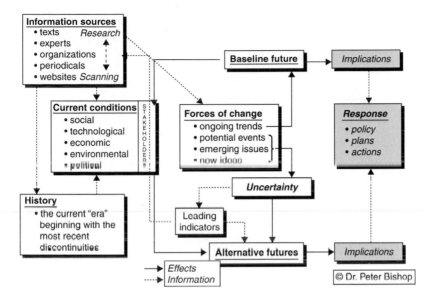

Figure 7.1 Framework forecasting

4. Era analysis

As noted in Chapter 1 (where eras are described in detail), eras are periods of relative stability and coherence that have a distinct identity. They begin and end with a discontinuity, such as Mao's Communist revolution in China after World War II and Deng's opening up of the economy beginning in 1978. When doing a framework, one "locates" the current era. Is the domain in a period of equilibrium, or is it on the cusp of a discontinuity? Either way, this is noted in the document to help set the context of the forecast.

5. Baseline forecasting

The research phase of the framework described in Chapter 5 sets the stage for the forecasting process. It defines the domain, describes its key elements (conditions and stakeholders). The current conditions of the domain are like a snapshot, a magic camera taking one picture of the domain. Forecasting is then putting that picture in motion to describe the domain in the future.

Putting the snapshot in motion requires a consideration of the drivers of change. The three basic drivers of change in this theory are trends, events, and issues. Trends and other relatively predictable drivers of change lead to one type of future, the expected or baseline future, and the other drivers lead to other futures, the plausible alternative futures. Together they describe the major regions at the end of the cone of plausibility, an ever-expanding region of alternative futures as time goes on. The big difference between trends and the other drivers is the degree of uncertainty. Trends do reverse themselves, but rarely. Hence they are fairly predictable. Potential new events, emerging issues and new ideas, however, are quite unpredictable. Trends, therefore, lead to the expected future, the baseline, at the center of the cone, and intervening events, issues and ideas can twist and turn the trajectory to some other region in the cone. Hence there are two types of futures – the expected and the alternative futures.

The expected future is called the baseline because it is the fundamental future with no surprises. It is *more likely* to occur than any of the other single futures, but it is not *likely* in itself because of all that could intervene in the meantime. As Herman Kahn is reported to have said, "The most likely future isn't [most likely]." It is called the baseline because it is a good place to start, as the surprise-free default future against which more interesting alternative futures are developed.

Listing trends that drive the expected future is usually not too difficult. In fact, selecting the most important ones from the vast number proposed is usually more challenging. One must guard against two dangers, however, in proposing trends. The first danger is to select almost all negative trends that lead to unpleasant futures. Is this a human trait to imagine negative futures first? Perhaps so, but for whatever reason, it occurs all the time. It is doubly strange that people think of negative trends much more readily than positive ones given the overall progressive view of change in Western culture.

It is perhaps this primeval view of change, that any change would be negative, that sees catastrophes more often than opportunities even in today's world. In selecting trends, therefore, it is important to balance the bad with the good. Although people may rarely feel it, good things do happen. Positive and negative trends do not have to be exactly equal, but the positive should be strongly represented nevertheless.

A second tendency is to draw trends from certain sectors of society, especially the technological. The American or Western view of change sees technology as the big driver, particularly during these heady days of the electronic revolution. But technology is only one of five sectors if one uses the typical STEEP approach. Trends should be distributed across all categories. Again they do not have to be equal, but there should be representatives in most categories.

In addition to trends, four other factors contribute to the development of the baseline future: constants, plans, cycles, and projections.

- *Constants* are those quantities, structures, and stakeholders that are likely to continue unchanged throughout the forecast period. Not everything changes. Constants are those things that are changing so slowly, or not at all, such that they can be considered static for the purpose of the forecast. That is not to say that constants cannot possibly change in some plausible set of events, but the probability is that they will remain the same, at least until the time horizon. Those assumptions can and should be challenged, however, when considering the alternative futures because presumed constants that start to change are excellent sources of alternative futures. The constants are also called the boundary conditions for the baseline future because they are unlikely to change during the period under study.
- *Trends* are quantities or changes that move incrementally in a specific direction over a long period of time; the value of the quantity and its rate of change (if known). One always says "more" or "less," or "increasing" or "decreasing" when describing a trend. Similar trends can be clustered into macro themes.
- *Plans* are intentions to act. They are announced by individuals, organizations, or governments. People who announce plans do not always carry them out, but they are usually sincere in their intention to do so. Hence they represent a driver of the future. A government's plan to reduce taxes or to start a new program is not guaranteed to occur, but it is more likely having been announced than if it were just a possibility.
- *Cycles* are predictable oscillations of some variable. So the seasonal cycle of sales, the boom and bust of different commodities, or even the swing from one political extreme to another can be part of the baseline. It might be impossible to predict where in the cycle one is at the time horizon, but at least the repetition of cyclic variables is not confused with the secular increase or decrease of trends
- *Projections* are forecasts of the baseline future made by others. Again these are not guaranteed to be accurate, but most forecasters are technically qualified and generally good at describing the baseline. Projections also increase their own likelihood by the process of self-fulfilling prophecy, that is, what people believe is going to happen is more likely to occur than if they do not believe it will happen. Self-fulfilling prophecy may be stronger or weaker in different domains, but the projections themselves and their effect on the future is important for understanding the baseline.

The baseline then is the result of constants, trends, plans, cycles, and projections that create differences in the future. The top five to ten of each type should be included in this section. The baseline future is the result of these driving forces and their consequences for the domain being forecast.

It is sometimes hard to distinguish a trend or a plan from the baseline future. Trends and plans, however, exist in the present. They are changes or intentions going on today. It is a subtle difference, but an important one. Describing the baseline requires extrapolating these trends and plans and projecting them into the future. What will the future be like at that point? What are the big differences between the present and the baseline future? And what difference will these differences make? The most important realization is not just that trends will continue, but that the future will be quantitatively and qualitatively different as a result. Highlighting the most important differences is the beginning of understanding the future.

The baseline future is the expected future, and expectations about the future are already fairly well known. As a result, one might expect the baseline future to have no interesting or surprising elements, but that is a misconception. While the basic elements of the baseline future might be expected, the implications of those elements can still contain surprises. A pair of trends, for instance, might set up a conflict, even in the baseline future. What if a government agency's mission is expected to increase over the next ten years, but its budget is expected to shrink. Could both of those trends be strong and almost irrefutable? Sure, it's happened before. But that convergence of contradictory trends sets up interesting differences between the present and the future.

A tool that futurists often use to investigate the implications of the baseline is a futures wheel. A futures wheel is essentially a mind map centered on a significant change in the future. What are the implications of that change? What will change as a result of the central change? Those changes go in a set of circles: the first-order changes connected to the central circle containing the focal change. Second-order changes result from the first order ones, and so on. One can conclude with implications for the enterprise.

The futures wheel is a brainstorming technique; it is not analytical truth. As with other brainstorming techniques, most of the material is well known or questionable. But a few nuggets emerge, elements of the baseline future that were not immediately evident on first impression, particularly if all the aspects of the global (STEEP) environment are

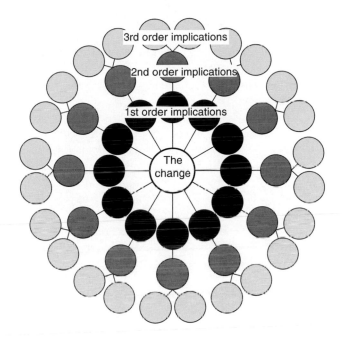

Figure 7.2 Futures wheel

represented. In that case, the baseline can be just as interesting and even as surprising as some of the alternative scenarios.

Critical thinking

Critical thinking is introduced here because it is a skill that is central to the process of generating alternative futures. The baseline forecasts or suggests what will happen if present trends continue and nothing changes (which rarely happens). Critical thinking provides a basic approach to challenging assumptions. The baseline rests on current assumptions continuing – alternatives, therefore, can be generated by challenging these basic assumptions.

Critical thinking is a process of discovering and testing the support for conclusions. Critical thinking skills are perhaps one of the most cherished goals of higher education. If one asks any member of a college or university faculty, from the president to the lowliest instructor, what are the goals of their institution for their students, the responses will suggest that one of the top three is to teach students to be critical thinkers. It is an anomaly, therefore, that nowhere in most college curriculums is critical thinking ever explicitly taught. It is true, nevertheless, that most graduates leave college better critical thinkers than when they entered. Their professors, by and large, are good critical thinkers themselves so students must pick it up by osmosis.

However, this curriculum is about to challenge established curriculums. It has developed a process that one can follow to become a better critical thinker. There are good parts to most treatments of critical thinking. Some of those good things are to consider the source, check for biases, be sure there is data to support the conclusions, and such. Good advice all. But they are not satisfactory in terms of a definitive process. The problem is that even sources that are questionable (bloggers, for instance), that are biased (propaganda, for instance), and that don't have data to support their positions (op-ed pieces, for instance) are still right some of the time!

A related – and one might argue even more important – contribution of the course is providing an understanding of the role of inferences and the evidence and assumptions that underlie them. Since one cannot directly observe the future, one must, as noted, rely on inferences about it. Ideally, these inferences are supported by some evidence, and they always rely on assumptions to a great degree.

There are two ways of rationally knowing something: by direct observation and by inference. Knowledge acquired by direct observation is immediate and irrefutable. Whether or not that car is blue, I saw blue; and you can't tell me that I didn't. ("You shouldn't feel cold." "But I do!") However, one acquires little of what one knows and less of what it is important to know through direct observation. Seeing a Space Shuttle lift off is a marvelous site, but the laws of physics, chemistry, biology, astronomy, and the other sciences that make space flight possible are not directly observable. They are based on inferences, the ability to know things that cannot be directly observed. The future is "known" through inference. Whether one predicts a single future or describes alternative ones, one obviously cannot observe the future directly.

Inferences are never completely true or false because one cannot prove or disprove them irrefutably or without some doubt or uncertainty. Rather they are distinguished by their degree of support. Thus, one must rely on an inference's degree of support to distinguish between inferences to accept and those to reject. Well-supported inferences may still be false, and poorly supported inferences may well be true, but the degree of support is all there is to go on.

The support for inferences requires two elements:

- *Evidence*: knowledge that is accepted as true with a high degree of certainty

- *Assumptions*: knowledge that is believed to be true in the face of uncertainty.

One gathers evidence, but one chooses their assumptions. Evidence is occasionally found to be wrong; assumptions, on the other hand, are frequently wrong. Incorrect forecasts are rarely the result of bad evidence and almost always the result of incorrect assumptions. Even evidence that includes numbers (numerical quantities) requires assumptions to support inferences, and those assumptions can be just as wrong as the assumptions required by qualitative evidence. As a result, two primary outcomes from the critical thinking module are:

- to recognize the evidence and assumptions that support inferences about the future
- to make well-supported inferences based on appropriate evidence and reasonable assumptions.

The assumptions required to make inferences from quantitative data are related to the methods used to collect and analyze the data. Therefore, the course is about those methods – recognizing the ones that others use and using them appropriately ourselves. However, learning to use the methods is not an end in itself or the primary purpose of the course. Making inferences based on those methods is.

One of the authors (Bishop) set himself the task of developing a process of critical thinking that relied solely on the text, leaving aside external cues on whether a source is credible or not. The process examines the support for inferences to tell how good that support is. It renders a judgment, not whether the claim is correct or not (a clear binary choice to be sure), but rather a qualitative assessment of how good the support is for a particular claim. That assessment can range from none to weak for some to strong to excellent and all the stages in-between for others. The process for evaluating the support for an inference is briefly summarized below:

1. Identify an important conclusion of the piece
2. Identify the evidence in the piece that supports the conclusion
3. Identify the assumptions required to use each piece of evidence
4. Reverse each assumption to create alternatives
5. Consider reasons that each alternative might be true
6. If there are such reasons, identify the modifications to the original conclusion or an entirely new conclusion that result if the alternative assumption is true

7. Make a judgment concerning the original conclusion and any other plausible conclusions that result
8. Synthesize them into one overall conclusion if possible.

The importance of critical thinking for futurists is indisputable. Not only do futurists use claims about the future made by others, usually forecasts, but the core of this approach identifies and evaluates the quality of the assumptions required to support such claims. Assumptions, not coincidentally, are also the basis for alternative forecasts, the primary product of professional futurists. If one chooses different assumptions, one automatically gets different futures! So critical thinking can be the beginning of developing interesting and important plausible futures.

6. Baseline analysis

Critical thinking in framework forecasting establishes the bridge between the baseline and the alternative futures, between traditional forecasting and framework forecasting. Traditional forecasting uses the baseline as its end product; it stops there. Framework forecasting begins there by evaluating the evidence that supports the baseline, identifying and challenging the assumptions required to use that evidence, and using the plausible challenges as the basis for alternative futures. If any one of the assumptions that support the baseline can be challenged (that is, an alternative assumption could plausibly be true instead of the original), then by definition an alternative future results. Baseline analysis is not the only way to arrive at alternative futures, as the next section will show, but it is the more rigorous since it rests on evidence and plausible reasons that the alternative might come true instead of the baseline.

So baseline analysis simply applies the process of critical thinking to the support for the baseline future. The process is quite simple, though it may not be easy at first:

1. Conduct research
2. Forecast the baseline (expected) future
3. State the evidence for the baseline future, such as constants, trends, plans
4. Challenge the evidence:
    I. Is it true? In this case, the operational definition of true evidence is that no one has a plausible reason to object to its truth. It is a social criterion, leaving absolute or metaphysical truth to the philosophers
    II. Is it relevant? Does it, in fact, support the inference? Many true facts have nothing to do with the baseline future

III. Is it sufficient? Strong claims require strong evidence. Is the evidence strong enough to support the strength of the claim?
5. Identify the assumptions that one must accept to use each piece of evidence that passes these tests
6. Challenge each assumption by stating its opposite. Stating the opposite brings to mind reasons the assumption might be true
7. Identify the alternative assumptions that are plausible, those with foundation, support, evidence, or reasons that they might be true
8. Extend plausible alternative assumptions into plausible alternative futures
9. The reasons for the alternative assumptions then become the reasons and foundation for the alternative futures (scenarios).

The key here is to distinguish between merely possible futures and truly plausible ones. A possible future is one that could happen, for which the probability is simply greater than zero, one that does not break any known laws of the universe. Plausible futures have higher probabilities than that. There are reasons, based on empirical evidence, that that future could indeed come about. That evidence does not "predict" that the alternative will come true. It is not another baseline. But the evidence does give some indication that the alternative future could occur. The distinction is subjective, to be sure, but important nevertheless. Selecting futures that have plausible foundations is the best way of developing scenarios based on some empirical evidence.

Creativity

Baseline analysis reveals plausible alternative assumptions about the future which in turn produce alternative futures. But the human mind is capable of imagining even more futures than that, and the process would be remiss if we did not harness that ability. Creativity is the companion to critical thinking in the process of developing alternative futures. Critical thinking requires the careful analysis of evidence. Creativity is open to possibilities. It breaks boundaries and reframes problems. It is a different, yet just as useful way of developing alternative futures.

This module provides a brief overview of creativity, which could be a course in its own right. As with most of the skills covered in the curriculum, creativity is a life-long pursuit. So the intention here is not to "teach" students to be creative, but rather to alert them to some important ideas and resources that they can use in their coursework and carry with them into their professional careers.

The terms creativity and innovation are often used interchangeably, thus they are distinguished upfront:

- *Creativity*: the process of coming up with new ideas
- *Innovation*: the process of implementing creative ideas into useful solutions.

There are hundreds, perhaps thousands, of different approaches, methods, and tools for enhancing creativity. One of the authors (Hines) surveyed the world of creativity and identified the best and most useful practices. His experience in evaluating the different approaches was that they shared a common framework, but that they differed in what they emphasized and how they carried out the basic steps of the framework. The framework taught in the curriculum is based on and adapted from the work of Gerald "Solutionman" Haman of the creativity firm Solutionpeople[1]. It uses the IDEA acronym to aid retention (see Table 7.1).

This framework provides the basic set of steps to aid any creative problem-solving. There are a wide range of methods and tools that can be used to carry out each of the steps. Many creativity firms offer their particular version of how to carry out these steps, or one can simply mix and match the best parts from the many different offerings.

Another insight from this survey was the close relationship between the creative and futures thinking. In fact, many of the tools of the fields are practically identical, except in terms of their intended application. For instance, mind mapping, a staple tool for creativity, is much the same as the futures wheel. One could say that the futures wheel is mind mapping adapted for futures purposes. There are many similar instances of overlap.

The course spends time on the psychology of ideating. Many people will tend to downplay their own creativity; "I'm not the creative type," as if creativity were an inheritance. They may have been using this assumption to avoid anything to do with creativity. The view here, however, is that creative thinking is a skill that can be learned and improved with practice. In fact, Robert Weisberg's (1993) study of some of history's great creative thinkers found that what appear to be sudden bursts in creative genius were in fact the product of years of hard work and study. Their great insights did not simply come out of nowhere, as the folklore implies. This point is captured best by Edison's quip that genius is 1% inspiration and 99% perspiration.

---

[1]See www.solutionpeople.com.

Table 7.1 IDEA framework for creative problem-solving

Step	What it covers
Investigate needs	What is the problem/challenge?
Develop ideas	What are the ideas for solving it?
Evaluate solutions	Which are the best ones?
Activate plan	How can the best ideas be implemented?

The point is that people can improve their ability to be creative and innovative. That said, there does appear to be some innate talent involved – some are more creative than others. However, all can improve with the proper training and practice. But since most people believe creativity is a gift, they fail to practice. But, even here, practice makes perfect (well, improves at least).

A common misconception regarding creativity among organizations is the perception that it is simply a matter of finding the "best" tools. Using the right method or tool or hiring the right creativity consultant is relied upon as the answer. The view here is that certain tools are more appropriate to particular challenges. Thus, if a creative problem-solving activity fails, the tool is often blamed. To put this in proper perspective, three "laws of tools" are suggested as relevant to creativity:

- Practicing with your tennis racket will improve your tennis game (practice is important to improving creativity)
- Tennis rackets don't work well for baseball (the tool needs to match the situation)
- A good tennis racket will help you play better tennis, but it won't necessarily make you play like a Grand Slam champion (a tool is only as good as those using it).

Another key, and often overlooked, facet of creativity is having a clear focus. Again, the myth is that creative insights just come out of thin air, but brain research suggests that the brain needs to have some direction. Simply having a focus will alert the brain to look for possible connections. Thus the advice to "sleep on it" has some basis in research in the sense that the brain will process and look for connection when it is properly focused and stimulated. Mihail Czikzentmihaly (1991) developed the idea of "Flow" to describe a state in which the mind is so perfectly focused and challenged that one loses all sense of time and is completely immersed and engaged in the task at hand.

Finally, Micheal Ray's (1988) concept of the Voice of Judgment introduces the tendency for people to downplay their creative abilities. He suggests that many have "voices" in their head, often authority figures from childhood, that tell them they are not creative. Consciously or unconsciously these authorities at some point suggested to the child that either they were not creative or they needed to get serious and grow up. This message gets internalized, and when confronted with creative challenges as adults, the message replays and the adult is often paralyzed by it. Ray developed a series of techniques at Stanford Business School to address the voice and thus re-open one's creative potential.

Creativity in framework forecasting identifies elements (below) that could lead to alternative futures. Some of them may have already been uncovered in baseline analysis. Others will be new. Even the new products of creativity require a foundation, a reason to believe the alternative future could come about. Simple creativity can produce possible futures, but creativity linked with a reasonable foundation produces a plausible alternative future.

7.   Alternative futures forecasting

A funny thing happened on the way to the baseline future – something else! That is the essential problem of forecasting. People can tell very well where they are headed, but no one really expects to get there. Something will happen between now and then to upset the most elaborate and well-supported baseline forecasts.

Can we tell what that will be? No, but it's guaranteed that something will. What is one to do then? Give up forecasting entirely? Hardly. Rather, futurists explore the range of variation in plausible futures by focusing on the uncertainties in the baseline forecast.

Bishop, Hines and Collins (2007) surveyed the techniques used in developing scenarios. They classified the twenty-three techniques found into eight major categories (refer to Table 7.2).

The study was intended to focus on techniques that futurists use to construct alternative scenarios. The authors realized early on, however, that any forecasting technique could be used to construct an alternative scenario, even the most quantitative technique, because all forecasts rest on assumptions and varying the assumptions automatically creates alternative scenarios. By the same token, any technique that futurists use to create alternative scenarios can also be used to forecast the expected future by selecting the most plausible assumptions. So there really is no difference between the techniques used in baseline versus alternative futures forecasting since all rest on assumptions. The more

Table 7.2 Scenario (alternative futures) techniques

Technique	Process
1. *Judgment*	
Genius	Thinking, imagining.
Visualization	Relaxation, stimulation of imagination.
Role Playing	Act out one or more pre-arranged conditions.
Coates & Jarratt	Define domain and time horizon, identify conditions or variables of interest, develop scenario themes, estimate values of conditions and variables under each scenario theme, write the scenarios.

2. *Baseline* (quantitative techniques involving one variable, including trend extrapolation and time series decomposition)

Manoa[2]	Implications, cross-impacts, elaboration.

3. *Elaboration of fixed scenarios*

Incasting	Elaboration on specific domains.
SRI	Specific domains in rows.

4. *Event sequences*

Probability trees	Sequence, assign probabilities.
Sociovision	Cluster similar alternatives into macro themes.
Divergence mapping	Place on one of four time horizons, link events in sequence.
Future Mapping	Sequence events to create end-state.

5. *Backcasting*

Backcasting, Horizon Mission Methodology	Steps that could lead to that end-state
Impact of Future Technologies	Highly capable scenarios, signposts leading to scenario, cost/benefit.

6. *Dimensions of uncertainty*

Morphological analysis, Field anomaly relaxation	Multiple alternatives for each dimension, link one alternative from each dimension.
GBN (Global Business Network)	Select two most important and most uncertain, create 2×2 matrix, title and elaborate.
Option development & evaluation	Multiple alternatives for each dimension, rate consistency of every alternative against every other alternative, perform nearest neighbor calculation.

(continued)

---

[2] University of Hawaii-Manoa Futures program approach.

Table 7.2   Continued

Technique	Process
MORPHOL	Multiple alternatives for each dimension, link one alternative from each dimension, excluding impossible combinations and rating more likely combinations more highly; can calculate probability of combination of probabilities.
7. Cross-impact analysis	
Cross-impact analysis	Initial probability of each, contingent probabilities of each given the occurrence of each other, Monte Carlo simulation.
IFS	High, medium, low values of the variables, initial probability of each range, cross-impact of ranges from different variables on each other, Monte Carlo simulation.
SMIC PROB-EXPERT	Initial probability of each, contingent probabilities of each given the occurrence of each other, correction of contingent probabilities for consistency, Monte Carlo simulation.
8. Modeling	
Trend impact analysis	Estimate impact of event on trend – time of initial impact, max impact, time of max impact, time of final impact.
Sensitivity analysis	Enter multiple plausible values for each uncertain boundary condition, possibly Monte Carlo simulation.
Dynamic scenarios	Build system model for each dimension, combine into one overall model.

plausible ones lead to the baseline scenario while the others lead to the alternative scenarios. All forecasting uses the same techniques whether the result is the baseline future or some of its alternatives.

The elements that lead to the alternative futures are the result of baseline analysis and creative imagination, all with some type of foundation for believing that the element is plausible. All the elements are uncertain to be sure, else it would not be alternative futures forecasting, but they are not just possible. Revealing and managing uncertainties in this manner is the heart of alternative futures forecasting. Where traditional forecasters may state their assumptions (though many do not), they rarely challenge them because they do not know what to do with those that are successfully challenged. Professional futurists use such uncertainties as the basis of their alternative futures.

The beauty of alternative futures forecasting is that one doesn't even have to get all these uncertainties right, though the better they are the more interesting and useful they will be. But even if one doesn't get the "right" alternatives, they are at least considering some of them. The effect is to remove the illusion of certainty or determinism, that feeling that what is going on is known and where it will end up is known as well. Plausible alternatives show that one can't be positive that the baseline will occur – hence the need for flexibility, contingencies, creativity. That attitude, more than the right alternatives, will prepare organizations for the unknown and the uncertain.

Uncertainties arise from the results of baseline analysis, largely trend reversals and unfulfilled plans, and from the other drivers of change: potential future events, emerging issues, and new ideas.

Trend reversals

Trend reversals occur when an assumed trend that supports the baseline could plausibly change its rate by slowing down, stopping altogether or even reversing. Most trends set up countertrends. Pushing society in one direction often creates a force that is pushing back. Countertrends sometimes overwhelm the original trend, as in a revolution, for instance, but at the least they alter the trajectory of the trend. Trends are uncertain; and if they change, they can lead to alternative futures.

Unfulfilled plans

Unfulfilled plans occur when influential stakeholders are not able to achieve their intended goals. No goal is guaranteed, and no plan is foolproof. Things happen, often unexpected and unintended things. The future could be quite different from the baseline if a major plan is thwarted. It's uncertain, but that is what alternative futures are for.

Potential events

Potential events could clearly change the future. Eras begin and end with events as described above. If they happen, the result is one future; if they don't, the result is another one. Will there be a major economic recession? Will the atmosphere suddenly shift into another warmer or colder mode due to greenhouse gases? Will AIDS mutate into another more communicable form? Will scientists develop the means to retard aging? Any of these events could shape the future dramatically. The events specific to the focal domain have the same power and the same degree of unpredictability.

Emerging issues

Issues also have the power to shape the future. Resolving current issues one way or the other could make the future different. Issues on the US agenda today include US involvement in the rest of the world, free trade or protectionism, assistance for or competition with the world's developing countries, universal healthcare, or endangered species. Other uncertainties arise from what are called "emerging issues" – issues that have not yet appeared on the public agenda. As with events, emerging issues are inherently uncountable, but some are more apparent than others. They may not be unheard of, but they are not receiving the attention they could. The difference comes with a framing event, an occurrence that propels the issue onto the public agenda. Books or studies might be such an event. Dr Jim Hansen's testimony on the reality of ozone depletion before Congress in 1989 was just such an event. 9–11 put terrorism on the world's agenda; Iran and North Korea did the same for nuclear proliferation. Emerging issues have a way of significantly changing the direction of the future after they become framed.

New ideas

New ideas also have power to change the future. Kurt Lewin (1951, 169) suggested that "there is nothing as practical [or as powerful] as a good theory." New Ideas have shaped history – religious ideas contained in Christianity and the other world religions; political and economic ideas of monarchy, democracy, socialism, communism, mercantilism, capitalism; social ideas like human rights, freedom of the individual, freedom of the press and assembly. New ideas in the focal domain can also shape its future – welfare reform, market-oriented solutions for environmental problems, charter schools and vouchers. Where do new ideas come from? Well, everywhere and when they appear, they can have a profound impact on the future – hence their ability to kick off alternative paths to the future.

Key uncertainties

Images of the future are also ideas that shape the future. Elise Boulding (n.d.), herself a proponent of powerful positive images of the future, describes Fred Polak's argument about how images shape the future. According to Polak, one of the founding fathers of Dutch futures studies, the human capacity to create mental images of the "totally other" – that which has never been experienced or recorded – is the key dynamic of history. At every level of awareness, from the individual to the macrosocietal, imagery is continuously generated about the not-yet. Such imagery inspires intentions, which then moves people purposefully forward. Through daily choices of action, individuals, families, organizations, communities, and nations move toward that which they imagine to be a desirable tomorrow.

So the uncertainties about the future are numerous and unknown. A list of the most important uncertainties, however, is a valuable asset because they together identify the most important alternative futures, those with the greatest impact on the domain. The key uncertainties are chosen using two criteria – impact and uncertainty. Impact is straightforward – which trend reversals, unfulfilled plans, potential events, issues or new ideas would change the baseline the most if they were to occur. Uncertainty is used because the purpose of forecasting is to gain knowledge of what is not known—provided it is important enough to be worth knowing.

8. Scenario kernels

All of the elements of the alternative futures module are pulled together into one or more scenario kernels or logics. The alternative scenarios are the most important and different plausible alternative futures of this domain that result from the uncertainties, including major differences from the present, the value of key quantities, and implications for stakeholders. It is important to choose a memorable title, one that can live on in people's memories after the forecast is done.

Leading indicators wrap up the module. While futurists revel in the uncertainties of the long-term future, those items will not be uncertain forever. As the future gets closer, they will resolve themselves into a singular present (or at least that is the way it is thought about). At any rate, events that don't happen, issues that don't appear, ideas that are not created pass off to the side much like the hazards to navigation (rocks, buoys, other ships) that pass off the side of a vessel in motion. So knowing as early as possible how the uncertainties are resolving themselves is the key to navigating the waters of the future.

Leading indicators are the focused information that will tell how an uncertainty is resolving itself. They constitute a set of precursor events or statistics that point toward one alternative rather than another. What are the signs of impending recession? What indicates whether or not the have/have-not gap is growing or shrinking? How does one tell whether other countries resent the US's position in the world more or less? As opposed to scanning, which incorporates everything relevant to change in the domain, leading indicators are very specific, targeted pieces of information with a clear link to one alternative future or another. Some even use a special term for watching leading indicators; they call it monitoring as opposed to scanning. Scanning uses the radar image; monitoring uses the image of pilot or nurse monitoring their instruments for any signs of change. Change (or stability) in the leading indicator gives a clear signal toward the increasing likelihood of one alternative future or another. Leading Indicators are the signposts along the way to whatever future ultimately prevails.

Alternative futures then balance the baseline. The baseline is the expected future if nothing really surprising happens; the alternatives contain the surprises. The actual future is a combination of both. Many elements of the baseline will come about, but not all. Speculating on how the baseline could be wrong is the source of flexibility and creativity in approaching the future. The momentum of the baseline and the surprising developments of the alternatives are both needed to appreciate and prepare for the real future when it finally becomes the new present.

CONCLUSION

The benefit of listing the most important information in the framework categories is more than just a repository for good items. It also requires input and agreement from others. There is nothing like a good list to raise assumptions and resolve issues among a group of people who believe that they agree with each other. For the most part, they probably do, but it's the little disagreements that may grow into broad conflicts down the line. Thus the framework document is more than just a way to categorize information. It is also a method for articulating and reaching consensus on a group's images and drivers of the future. That consensus can be a powerful means to align and work together for their common future. It is also a great platform on which to build strategy and action – a platform that can also be modified as conditions change.

The key deliverables of the process are two types of forecasts: the baseline and alternative futures. The baseline is the extrapolation of present trends, while the alternatives are, well, alternatives to that. Scenarios are a common method used to generate the alternatives.

Building a framework is a useful step to truly understanding the future of a domain and for getting consensus on that understanding as a prelude to action.

RESOURCES

Armstrong, J. S. (ed.) (2001) *Principles of Forecasting: A Handbook for Researchers and Practitioners* (NY: Springer).

- A comprehensive guide to all forms of forecasting, both quantitative and qualitative. Armstrong is a well-respected expert in this area, though he is not a futurist and does not emphasize futures methods.

Bishop, P., Hines, A. & Collins, T. (2007) "The Current State of Scenario Development: An Overview of Techniques," *Foresight*, 9 (1), 5–25.

- Inspired by what they feel is an over-reliance on the popular 2×2 matrix techniques, the authors identify twenty-three other scenario techniques. They are evaluated and then categorized into eight main types.

Hines, A. (2009) "How Accurate Are Your Forecasts? More Accurate Than You Might Think," *World Future Review*, October–November.

- Reviews the forecasts of Hines and his fellow authors, J. F. Coates and J. B. Mahaffie, 15 years on from their book *2025: Scenarios of US and Global Society Reshaped by Science and Technology* to evaluate how they are tracking. The analysis suggests several lessons learned to improve forecasting.

ManyWorlds (2001) *Grasping the Future: Comparing Scenario Planning to Other Forecasting Techniques* (Houston, TX: ManyWorlds).

- Compares and contrasts different techniques for understanding the future, with a specific eye as to how those techniques can be integrated into scenario development. Groups them into two sets of five categories. The first set – counter punchers, extrapolators, pattern analysts, goal analysts and intuitors – examines how the strategies work; the second divides them by philosophical assumptions: (1) directed vs. emergent (2) narrow vs. broad scope (3) mathematical vs. non-mathematical (4) predictive vs. learning/understanding (5) subjective vs. objective.

Ogilvy, J. (2002) *Creating Better Futures: Scenario Planning as a Tool for a Better Tomorrow* (Oxford, UK: Oxford University Press).

- Drawing on his academic background and extensive experience in applying scenario planning in the organizational setting, the author suggests how scenario planning can be adapted as a tool for creating preferred futures for communities.

Schwartz, P. (1996) *The Art of the Long View: Planning for the Future in an Uncertain World* (NY: Doubleday).

* Describes the author's approach and success stories in using scenario planning with organizations, in an engaging, easy-to-read style.

Van Der Heijden, K. (2002) *The Sixth Sense: Accelerating Organizational Learning with Scenarios* (NY: Wiley).

* Builds on his early work on scenario planning and focuses more sharply on how it can improve organizational learning.

Wack, P. (1985) "Scenarios: Uncharted Waters Ahead," *Harvard Business Review*, 63 (5), 78–84.

* A classic article by the pioneer of the Shell scenario technique in the 1970s.

Wilson, I. & Ralston, B. (2006) *The Scenario Planning Handbook* (Mason, OJ: Thomson-South-Western).

* An excellent step-by-step guidebook on how to do scenarios.

Part III
Influencing

Outbound change is the change that people bring about and effect on the world. It gets to the crux of the matter of why one studies the future in the first place: to help create a better future. Thus, planning is typically done in concert with forecasting. Forecasting maps out the future landscape of possibilities and provides a context for planning.

An exclusive focus on inbound change and forecasting may simply be an interesting intellectual activity unless something is done about it. Planning and the related activities are in part dedicated to influencing the future – to creating change.

But don't people influence the future every day? Sure. But usually without much sense of how they will do so. Part III shows how a formal approach to influencing the future can be carried out. Several different approaches are introduced and described. While there are generally agreed-upon principles for these activities, there is a wide range of approaches for carrying them out. The curriculum's approach is to describe the principles and survey the most relevant approaches.

- Chapter 8, Leadership: covers the people who lead the change. They envision a new era, a way which could be radically better, and they propose to move from the old era to that visionary place. But they cannot create the new era on their own. They need others to help. So they enroll them in a campaign to partially dismantle the old era in order to make room for the new.
- Chapter 9, Visioning: covers the various approaches to developing a vision, whether for organization, community, or individual. Visioning is required for transformational change. The vision is an image of what the preferred future will look like in a way that inspires the individuals involved to work towards it. For example, "I have a dream"!

- Chapter 10, Planning: covers systematic approaches to preparing for the future. It builds a bridge from vision to action. Planning looks at the vision in terms of the forecast, and assesses and maps out how to "get there from here."
- Chapter 11, Change Management: covers the process of executing the plan. It is many times longer and more difficult than planning because this is where real change is created. Creating change requires overcoming resistance because people are not only relatively comfortable in the present, but they have also been successful there.

8
Leadership

INTRODUCTION

Plans do not implement themselves; people implement them, and these people are called leaders. Leaders create transformational change by leading organizations, communities or whole societies from one era to the next. Mapping the future is one thing, and a very important thing, but futurists aspire to influence the future as well. Sometimes they advocate for a preferred future, acting as leaders themselves; more often they help others realize their aspiration to accomplish something of significance. While many futurists are more comfortable in the role of provocateur – and that is a valuable and necessary role – sometimes they need to go further and be more proactive by stimulating action – or watch their research and insight put on the shelf to gather dust.

Thus, the curriculum here explores leadership, both from the perspective of helping students' understanding of how leadership works, so that they can more effectively influence leaders, as well as understanding what it takes for them to become effective leaders themselves.

HISTORY

Leadership has fascinated scholars going all the way back to Thucydides (*The Peloponnesian War*), Plato (*The Republic*), Sun Tzu (*The Art of War*), Plutarch (*Lives*), and Machiavelli (*The Prince*). Academic studies of leadership date back to the 1930s, and they often overlap with management studies because they do not distinguish between authority, management, and leadership. As a result, the literature on leadership is vast – large enough to fill a small library by itself. The Library of Congress, for instance, has over 450 titles containing the term "leader" or its cognates. Tens of thousands of journal and popular articles about leadership have also been published. Wikipedia lists 230 degree programs on leadership[1] just in the US. So the topic is too extensive to summarize completely here.

The study of leadership is characterized by eras in which particular research agendas were popular. After almost a century of study, however, no research agenda has proven to be completely satisfying in providing a complete understanding of leadership.[2]

Era 1. Traits

The first approach was simply to try to distinguish what characteristics made leaders different from followers (non-leaders). Leaders were defined as the individuals who were in positions of authority; followers as those not in such positions.

Numerous lists were developed – intelligence, birth order, socioeconomic status, child-rearing practices, capacity, achievement, responsibility, participation, status. The list goes on. In the end, however, the differences between leaders and followers were not strong enough to be sure that there was any real pattern.

Era 2. Situation

Researchers then turned to the situations or context that leaders found themselves in. The purpose was to decide which personality traits were appropriate for which situations. Hersey and Blanchard (1977) proposed a theory of leadership that depended on two dimensions: the competence and the commitment of the followers. Situations range from low competence and commitment, which requires close supervision, through medium levels, which requires high levels of support, to high levels allowing large-scale delegation.

None of these approaches, however, produced strong results. Researchers were not able to empirically support which traits were appropriate for the different situations.

Era 3. Effectiveness

The third attempt changed the focus from traits to behaviors – not what leaders were, but what they did – to be effective. Part of that approach was to distinguish leadership styles. One of the most common distinctions

---

[1] See http://en.wikipedia.org/wiki/Leadership_studies.
[2] The historical treatment is based on a "History of Leadership Research" compiled by SEDL (formerly the Southwest Educational Development Laboratory) in Austin, TX, see http://www.sedl.org/change/leadership/history.html.

was from Lewin, Lippit and White (1939): Autocratic or Authoritative, Participative or Democratic, Laissez-faire or Free rein leaders.

That line of research also differenciated between two types of behaviors – task-oriented and people-oriented (alternatively called initiating structures vs. consideration, instrumental vs expressive needs, and system-oriented vs. person-oriented behaviors). The most popular approach was Blake and Mouton (1964) who proposed the Managerial Grid that crossed the concern for production and the concern for people.

Researchers tried to figure which of these two orientations was more effective in general and in specific situations. In the end, they concluded both were necessary for effective leadership in most situations.

Era 4. Contingency

The next era expanded the focus to the complex interaction of three types of variables: traits, behaviors, and situations. The model gave researchers a lot of room to theorize and conduct research, but once again, in the end, no one could nail down a fixed relationship between any combination of these variables and leader effectiveness.

Era 5. Shared leadership

Researchers in this era moved away from studying the single individual as leader and focused more on the group as effective or not. One person might be in charge, but many leaders may be necessary for a group to achieve maximum results.

This approach has also gone by the title of the Functional Leadership theory. Rather than focus on the one person who is the designated leader, it concentrates on the functions that need to be performed for an effective group. Any number of lists of functions exist, but three common ones are goal direction, group communication, and individual motivation.

Robert Greenleaf's (1977) concept of Servant Leadership fits within this era as well. Greenleaf contends that the best leaders are those dedicated to making the people in the group successful. The leader then serves them by providing what they need to accomplish the task.

Era 6. Managers and Leaders

Burns (1978) distinguished two types of leaders: transactional and transformational leaders. Bennis (1989) famously renamed these Managers and Leaders. Transactional leaders (managers) coordinate people and resources to achieve known goals within an existing mission. Transformational leaders advocate for new goals and missions in a new environment. Nanus (1992) then promoted vision as a necessary component of transformational, or now visionary, leadership.

Ultimately, however, after a mountain of research, it is still hard to make definitive statements about leadership that have a strong empirical basis. Many distinctions exist and some patterns have been identified, but the traits and behaviors of effective leaders remain almost as elusive as ever.

And these are just a smattering of the thousands of studies of leadership. Furthermore, most of them are really more about management, and even supervision, and not about leadership as promoting transformational change at all. So what's the point? Is it even worth including a chapter on leadership in a work on foresight when so much else is written with so little conclusive consensus? Yes, because leadership is too important to leave out of a discussion about creating change. Leaders promote discontinuous, disruptive, transformational change. Futurists cannot ignore that. So while futurists may not be experts on leadership, they should at least acknowledge how important the leader is in helping others anticipate and influence the future.

GENERALIZATION

The first task then is to define leadership, a task that by itself could take a whole chapter. The origin of the word lead, or leader, rests on a geographic analogy. Leaders physically *lead* groups from one place to another; they *showed the way* to the new location. Joseph Rost (1991, 38–44) reports that the physical use of the word dates back to the 14th Century:

> The verb "to lead" comes from the Old English word *leden* or *loedan*, which meant "to make go," "to guide," or "to show the way," and the Latin word *ducere*, which meant "to draw, drag, pull; to lead, guide, conduct." From all accounts, the words *lead, leader*, and *leading* have been used in several European languages with Anglo-Saxon and Latin roots from 1300 to the present.

So leaders show the way – in this case, not from one *place* to another but from one *time* to another, or in our terms from one *era* to another. Leaders guide their followers across the Gap, the transition from one era to another described in Chapter 1. All eras are temporary; they all end eventually. Leaders encourage others (enroll them in a campaign) to leave the old era and move into the new era before the world comes in and announces *Game Over!* By that time, resources are gone; the world is in charge, and no one has much chance to influence the future. A bankruptcy is just such a moment, as is losing a war or an election. The Soviet Union experienced that moment in 1989 when people started streaming out of East Germany and the Berlin Wall came down. *Game Over!*

> Leaders enroll people in a campaign to accomplish something of significance.

Leaders may appear during the crisis to lead people into the new era amidst the wreckage of the old, but by then it is really too late to build much that is positive. The time for leadership is before the end, before the world steps in, while some order and influence remain. But that is also the most difficult time for leaders to exert their influence because few want to believe them. Leaders see the end or the chance for a better future. They have foresight and vision, but convincing people of the reality of that vision, be it positive or negative, is challenging to say the least. The followers do not see the vision, at least initially. They may think that the leader is crazy. They are steeped in the old era, and they are relatively *comfortable* there. They know it's not perfect, but it's okay; it's familiar. They know how to get along there, to cope, and even to be successful. Little in them wants to pick up and move, to leave the comfort of the old era for the promise of the new. The Gap is treacherous and risky; the promise is fleeting, and a positive outcome is anything but guaranteed.

The story of the Exodus is a classic leadership story – the story of the Israelites moving from one place to another, closing one era and opening a new one. But between them and the new era lay the desert, the Gap. Whether it was 40 years or not is immaterial. The Sinai desert is no walk in the park for any length of time:

> The whole congregation of the Israelites set out from Elim; and Israel came to the wilderness of Sin, which is between Elim and Sinai, on the fifteenth day of the second month after they had departed from the land of Egypt. The whole congregation of the Israelites complained against Moses and Aaron in the wilderness. The Israelites said to them, "If only we had died by the hand of the Lord in the land of Egypt, when we sat by the fleshpots and ate our fill of bread; for you

have brought us out into this wilderness to kill this whole assembly with hunger." (*Exodus*, 16: 1–3)

Does that sound familiar? Even though the Israelites were eager to leave Egypt because of the oppression there, that era looked pretty good compared to the Gap. The leader's job, therefore, is to lead people through the Gap and deliver them to the new era. Simple? Yes. Easy? Not at all.

Leadership distinctions

The concept that leaders show the way from one era to another is not the most common use of the term today. In fact, it is more common to speak of leaders as those in charge, whether CEOs, presidents, or generals. That more common use is unfortunate because it robs the word of its distinctive transformational meaning and confuses the issue of just who are leaders and who are not.

In order to clear up the confusion, a three-part distinction building on Bennis's distinction between managers and leaders is proposed. The third category is authorities. Authorities are elected or appointed to be in charge of something. Their job is to make decisions that are binding on those in their jurisdiction. They set policies, establish budgets, hire, fire, and give orders. When the boss decides, that's it. Some may not like the decision, but that doesn't make any difference. Anyone subject to their authority has to abide by it or leave. So authorities are essentially decision-makers. And, what is more, they don't even have to be good decision-makers. Anyone in their position is expected to make binding decisions that others must obey.

Some authorities are also managers, but they do not have to be. Managers organize and coordinate the activities of an organization; they "make the trains run on time." Their job is to achieve goals within the existing system, goals that have been achieved before, goals that people know how to achieve. They may create change, but their change is incremental, within the system, more continuous improvement than transformational change. Creating incremental change is important, even necessary, if a system is to improve and continue to function in a changed world. So managers create change *in* the system; leaders create change *of* the system. Managers may be authorities, and many are, but they do not have to be. Police dispatchers and executive secretaries, for instance, are managers, although they may have little or no authority. Managers may also be transformational leaders but, again, most are not.

So three different functions within an organization are involved in creating change:

- *Authorities* create (or prevent) change by making binding decisions
- *Managers* create change by improving the operation of the existing system
- *Leaders* create change by transforming the system into something else, thereby opening up a new era.

One person might be good at all three functions, such as an authority who is a good manager and who also promotes transformational change. Noted business leaders, like Jack Welch (GE) or the late Steve Jobs (Apple), might be good examples. More often, however, authorities might just be good managers because that is how they were promoted into positions of authority, literally by doing well within the existing system. Conversely, transformational leaders often come from the outside, either from the margins of the existing system or from outside the system entirely. They are more often visionaries who see a transformed future (both good and bad) and encourage others to work for the good in order to avoid the bad or simply the mediocre. They are usually not authorities or even good managers. Rather they will recruit managers to assist in the campaign for change.

As one would expect, authorities and managers are not always happy with leaders. The manager's job is to create and maintain an efficient, high-performing system. They do not like leaders because leaders create disorder, if not chaos, which is exactly what they do not want; they want to preserve the *status quo*. It is no wonder, therefore, that organizations resist leaders and hang on to the old era longer than they should. But if they hold on too long, the world takes over, which no one wants. Thus authorities need leaders to periodically shake things up and move into the new era; it does not mean that they like it!

APPROACH

So how does the leader go about promoting transformational change? As described above, they are not necessarily authorities so they can't command the change. They may not even be good managers. Rather their function is to enroll people in a campaign to accomplish something of significance: the transformational change. They are missionaries of sorts, sharing the vision and inviting others to participate in creating it.

If leaders are also authorities, they can use that authority to support the campaign. But using authority to promote transformational change is tricky and even dangerous. Traversing the Gap requires motivation, creativity, risk taking, and a tolerance for mistakes, even failure. Authorities can command behavior. "Be sure at this time and do these things." Motivation and creativity, on the other hand, are contributed, not commanded. In fact, the attempt to command the change might set up a power struggle that may scuttle the campaign from the beginning.

By the same token, if leaders are good managers, they can organize and coordinate people to promote the change, but accomplishing the change requires more than coordination. Transformational change is not achieved by planning alone. In fact, the process is often quite disorganized, even chaotic. Transformational change is more exploration than development. Explorers do not work off an itinerary. They go one step at a time, feeling the way along a new path. So although having the backing of authority and the skills of management can help in bringing about the change, the leader's contribution of enrolling people in the campaign and keeping them enrolled during the tough times is also essential. It's about winning hearts and minds as much if not more than about schedules and budgets.

The following are a few descriptions of leadership that illustrate how hard yet how essential the function is.

Leading people into new territory

Consider the image of the leader leading people across the Gap into the new era.

Exploring boundaries of the possible

Most organizations have a good idea of what is possible, even preferable, and it's usually pretty narrow. They have a formula for success and a culture that supports that formula. The formula works; it created whatever success the organization enjoys. Leaders propose changing that formula and disrupting the culture, for good reason, to achieve the vision of the new era. As a result, people are understandably reluctant to tinker with what has worked.

Committing to goals they do not know how to achieve

It may sound silly, but even the leaders have to admit that they do not know exactly how to achieve the vision. They may see the first few steps, but it's dark after that. As noted, moving from one era to the next is more exploration than development. There is no blueprint, no plan, no itinerary. Lewis and Clark were classic explorers. They knew they needed canoes for transportation, guns for hunting, utensils for cooking and guides for direction, but they did not know where they would be on any given day, what they would have to do or even whether they would find the intended water route across the United States. (They didn't!) All they could do was prepare, head out, and do the best they could day-by-day – not a comfortable approach for those who might like a little more clarity about what they were getting involved in.

Building bridges when they know only one side of the river

What people know is their side of the river. The current era works, or at least it has worked so far. So the leader comes along and proposes to move to the other side of the river. There is hope and promise perhaps, but there is no evidence that the other side of the river is better or even as good as what people already know. No one has ever been there. So people who promote the campaign to move to the other side have nothing to offer except hope to counter the risk that they will never make it across the river, or if they do, it will be worth giving up what they already have.

Motivating people to do what they don't want to do

In order to achieve what people want to achieve, sometimes they must do things they don't want to do. Few people disagree with the vision. It sounds wonderful. But is it worth the price? Is it worth learning new skills, overcoming unforeseen obstacles, encountering inherent difficulties? Even if the new era is better, do we really want to go through the Gap to get there? Most would prefer not to. Their reaction, "Yes, but ..." Yes, the vision is wonderful, and we would love to live there, but.... The *but* is too high a price to pay for a hope and dream. And the price must be paid upfront, before the hope is realized.

No wonder leadership is so hard! And no wonder that so few actually volunteer to promote the new era. It's just too much trouble.

CONCLUSION

Transformational change requires leaders. Would that the situation was so bad or that the opportunity so great that change would erupt all by itself. Alas, such hope is unfounded. Any significant change always begins with one person (or a few) raising their hand and saying, "This can be better. This needs to be better." In doing so, they are often taking enormous risk. They are stepping out of line. They are going up against the establishment and the status quo. They are disturbing people's comfort zone and their ability to go on with business as usual.

But history is full of those people. They are admired even though most people do not want to be like them. Most people do not want their hard lives, lives of resistance and persecution. But without leaders, the world would not have advanced much beyond basic. It takes great people to create a great organization, community, or society. The term "leader" is reserved for them.

RESOURCES

Bennis, W. (1994) *On Becoming a Leader*, 2nd edn (NY: Perseus Books).

- The seminal book on leadership that made the famous distinction between managers and leaders.

Blake, R. & Mouton, J. (1964) *The Managerial Grid: The Key to Leadership Excellence* (Houston, TX: Gulf Publishing).

- One of the most popular frameworks of different leadership styles that distinguish between the concern for production and the concern for people.

Burns, J. M. (1978) *Leadership* (NY: Harper & Row).

- The most popular distinction between transactional and transformational leadership.

Greenleaf, R. (1983) *Servant Leadership: A Journey into the Nature of Legitimate Power and Greatness* (Mahwah, NJ: Paulist Press).

- The classic statement that leaders (and managers) are there to help their employees be successful rather than to tell them what to do.

Hersey, P. & Blanchard, K. H. (1977) *Utilizing Human Resources: Management of Organizational Behavior*, 3rd edn (Upper Saddle River, NJ: Prentice Hall).

- A popular framework for situational leadership that proposed that leaders behave differently depending on the competence and the motivation of their followers.

Lewin, K., Lippitt, R. & White, R. K. (1939) "Patterns of Aggressive Behavior in Experimentally Created Social Climates," *Journal of Social Psychology*, 10, 271–9.

* The first study that distinguished different leadership styles and discovered that the participative style was sometimes better than the authoritative style that had been common up to that time.

Nanus, B. (1992) *Visionary Leadership* (San Francisco, CA: Jossey-Bass).

* The classic statement of using visioning within a strategic planning framework.

Rost, J. (1991) *Leadership for the Twenty-First Century* (Santa Barbara, CA: Praeger Publishers).

* A study of the history of leadership.

9
Visioning

INTRODUCTION

A vision is the guiding principle in a long-term transformational change undertaken by choice. It captures the essence of the preferred future. It is a simple yet precious commodity, as it can mean the difference between successful and unsuccessful transformational change. Visioning is an intensive process that involves soul-searching and should not be undertaken lightly. If an organization is doing fine, and just needs to make some small changes, there is really no need to re-envision itself.

A vision is an image of the future. It creates an attractive mental picture of an outcome that people can strive for. Most people think of the future in ideas rather than images. Attractive ideas are progress, security, enjoyment; unattractive ones include overpopulation, pollution, sickness, death. None of these are visions, however, because they are not images. What does it look like? How does it feel? What does it taste like, sound like?

The vision is something tangible and concrete – something that people can get excited about. Sports are replete with concrete visions – trophies, medals, endorsements! Politicians work to keep their seat in the legislature. Attorneys see their clients go free or the big check at the end of a long civil suit. Doctors work for the health of their patients; educators the child's visible enjoyment of learning; priests the salvation of their flock. Even the gray world of business livens things up with awards and recognitions and the signs of status in homes, cars, and corporate jets. These are not abstract concepts but powerful images that guide people's actions.

Figure 9.1   Vision statements

HISTORY

Visioning has existed as long as people have. People have always imagined what the future might look like. In some cases, that involved aspiring to a better future. In many cases, historically, the vision of a group of people or society was prescribed by the leadership. Religions, for example, typically prescribed a view of the future to which the followers should aspire. Political ideologies, such as Marxism-Leninism, similarly created a vision of the future society to which members should aspire – or face the consequences of dissent.

The focus here is on the development of a formal, methodological approach to creating visions, whether for societies, communities, organizations, or even individuals.[1] The conceptual roots of visioning, from a foresight perspective, can be traced to Polak's (1973) classic *The*

---

[1] The authors would like to thank the following Association of Professional Futurist colleagues for their participation in a listserv discussion on this topic: Verne Wheelright, Mike Jackson, Oliver Markley, Sue Whitfield, Ruben Nelson, Jennifer Jarratt, Joel Barker, Jay Gary, Chris Stewart.

Image of the Future. He described the capacity to envision the future as a "gradual emancipation process." Where people once saw themselves as agents or transcribers of the will of the gods, the shift was to seeing themselves as creators of their own future. He noted the importance of a guiding image in helping navigate discontinuities or turbulent times (Jarratt, 2010). He felt that the present situation, then the 1950s when his magnus opus was originally written, was challenging in that societies lacked a compelling image of the future.

Around the same time, Robert Jungk initiated the practice of visioning in the Foresight realm with his Future Workshop. Visioning slowly began to be adopted inside organizations in the 1970s and 1980s (Stewart, 2004). Some visioning approaches emerged from the mainstream management and organizational development. Appreciative Inquiry emerged in the 1980s. Peter Senge and colleagues at MIT's Center for Organizational Learning (now SoL – Society for Organizational Learning) were also influential in spreading the word on visioning. They have continued to innovate with their recent work on presencing (Senge et al., 2004).

Foresight developed approaches of its own alongside the above, with some cross-pollination between the two. For instance, futurist Joel Barker's *The Power of Vision* video came out in 1989 and sold 10,000 copies to more than 7,000 organizations and was translated into 15 languages (Barker, 2010). Bezold (2000) was another of the many futurist proponents of visioning in the 1990s, defining it as "a compelling, inspiring statement of the preferred future that the authors and those who subscribe to the vision want to create." He made the useful distinction that "scenarios and forecasts are 'futures for the head,' while visions are 'futures for the heart.' "

Visioning probably hit its high point of popularity with the business world in the early 1990s. Burt Nanus (1992), a business professor and colleague of Warren Bennis at the University of Southern California, wrote his book on *Visionary Leadership* around that time. The literature on the topic increased dramatically and it became something of a management fad. The good part of that fad was that it increased exposure, which spreads the word; the bad part was that it also led to overuse and misuse, so much so that it was often done as a "me-too, check-the-box" activity. The unfortunate result was that the tool often got blamed for its misuse.

Visioning continues to be used today. There has been something of a mild resurgence of its use among communities, with a series of [name of city or geographical area] _____ 2020 activities[2]. Visioning has

---

[2] A number of cities in the US have undertaken visioning activities; they are typically called New York City 2020, Houston 2020.

also been adapted to the personal level by University of Houston futures program graduate Verne Wheelright (2010) with his work on personal futuring.

GENERALIZATION

Creating images of the future is like riding a bicycle – pretty easy once one gets the hang of it. It is also the most powerful way of portraying a goal. While people's intelligence distinguishes them from other animals, they are still a

Attributes of a vision
√ An image (not an idea)
√ About the future (not the past)
√ Attractive, appealing, even compelling
√ Bold and ambitious yet plausible
√ The best we can be or do
√ Unique (if we don't do it, no one will)
√ Motivating, energizing.

visual species. The visual cortex is more primitive and, in many ways, more powerful than the cerebral cortex. Pictures convey meaning in more immediate and compelling fashion. They are ideal for portraying a preferred future.

Attributes of a vision

A successful vision has several attributes that make it work: It is compelling, motivating, aligning, transforming, and differentiating.

Compelling

The vision contains the best future, the one that people can really commit to. It is not only attractive, it is compelling. It draws them like a magnet, almost beyond their control. Visionaries can do nothing but pursue their vision. There are days they perhaps wish they had never had the vision. "Father, let this cup pass from me" is a refrain not only in religion but in all visionary pursuits. At the same time, visionaries cannot imagine their lives without their vision. It becomes a part of them, like another limb. The vision aligns everything, gives a purpose and a context for decision and action every day.

Motivating

The vision may be most prominently spoken by a leader, but it must be owned by all to be successful. Leaders play a crucial role in adopting and implementing a vision, but it's not the role most people think. Most believe that the leader creates the vision. It's her vision, one that she creates and offers to the members on a take-it-or-leave-it basis. Buy in to this vision or find work elsewhere. The actual leader's role is more subtle than that. Leaders speak the vision that is created and owned by everyone. They are spokespersons for the collective. A group does not speak with one voice. Different backgrounds and interests give everyone a different angle on the vision. The leader speaks the common vision. But if that vision is not owned by everyone in the organization, it is dead; it has no effect on the organization's performance. Leaders who speak visions do so in resonance with individual values and visions throughout the organization. Members recognize more than accept it. "Yeah, that's it! That's what I meant." The enthusiasm is contagious; it powers the organization through the turbulence of change.

Aligning

A shared vision is powerful. It aligns the forces generated by many, even thousands of individuals, to pull in the same direction. A vision is like a bar magnet that aligns all the little dipoles to produce an eternal effect. The number of dipoles does not change, but they produce a visible force when they are all pointed in the same direction.

Transforming

Visions are particularly important during turbulent times that require fundamental transformational change. Such change is never easy, nor easily understood. Tearing down the old regime and building the new one is messy. It never goes according to plan because the plan itself is the product of the old order. Such times can become directionless; conflict can overwhelm the best intentions. The vision is the one constant amidst this turbulence. It remains the same, the light on the hill, the pole star. No matter how stormy, the group is working to achieve that goal.

Differentiating

The vision should be unique to the organization and individuals building it. The reason people continue is that they feel an obligation to work toward the vision. "If not us, who?" The most powerful visions are unique to the group that produces them. Generic visions are those that could be held by almost any organization – "The best customer service in the world," "The largest and most profitable company," "A world-class organization" – these are the one-size-fits-all visions of corporate organizations. Not very motivating, are they? Really compelling visions

---

"I have a dream"

Martin Luther King's "I Have a Dream" speech has all the key elements of a vision:

- It is an *image*, not just an idea. The speech is filled with *images* of oppression and freedom
- It is about the *future*, not about the past
- It is attractive, appealing, even *compelling*. Many believe that King was compelled to be a leader; he is clearly trying to compel others to follow him
- It is *bold* and ambitious, yet plausible. His vision for a country free of discrimination is bold, to say the least, but plausible because some progress had been made already
- It is the *best* we can be or do. There could be no higher calling for citizens of a great nation than to build the kind of race relations outlined
- It is *unique*; it is our time. If we don't do it, no one will. The time is now. If we do not act now, then the moment will be lost for a long time
- It is *motivating* and *energizing*. It moves people to do extraordinary things, to be part of something bigger than themselves, indeed to be a part of history.

---

can only be fulfilled by the organization that creates them – for example, Federal Express's "Absolutely, positively overnight" – it is unique to that organization in its field of endeavor.

Vision statements

Those with a vision articulate the vision as a vision statement. The statement is the public manifestation of the more important commodity that people carry around with them – the vision itself. The statement exists on paper but the real vision lives in the hearts and minds of people. The more important of the two is clearly the vision.

The statement itself is only the tip of the iceberg. It is like a map that represents a territory. It is a statement that signifies the commitment of partners to proceed in concert toward a preferred future. The commitment is more important than the statement, the territory more important than the map.

The danger in crafting vision statements is that people take them too seriously. Language is used in two ways – connotative and denotative. The denotative meaning of a word is what it actually stands for; the connotative is what it implies over and above its denotative meaning. The law uses words in their denotative sense. The words of legislation or contracts have power because they are used to resolve conflicts about meaning. What one meant in a contract is unimportant compared to what the contract says.

Literature is clearly the other extreme. Whether Robert Frost actually stopped by a woods on a snowy evening is irrelevant to the meaning of his poem. The words evoke images and feelings. He uses the words to evoke (connote) an experience that cannot be described in strict denotative fashion. In fact, different readers get different meanings from the same poem. That is why poets and artists are reluctant to "explain" their intent in denotative language. It limits the range of experience that the poem can evoke. If they wanted to write connotatively, they would have written a legal brief or a scientific paper.

Vision statements are much more connotative than denotative. They suggest and imply the real vision rather than embody it in the way a constitution or a mission statement specifies exactly what and how the organization is to be conducted. So the US Declaration says "… life, liberty and the pursuit of happiness," and the Constitution says, "All legislative Powers herein granted shall be vested in a Congress of the United States." The first is connotative; the second denotative. The connotative character of the statement leaves room for individual interpretation. Different people can take different angles, place different emphases, and indeed see their individual vision as part of the larger whole. At the same time, the wording is important but not in the way a legal document is. The connotations of the words are more important than what the words actually say.

APPROACH

There are different points in the process where visioning takes place. Some futurists and client prefer to do a vision "first," before doing forecasting. They feel that the forecast can bias the results of the vision, and that it is best to construct it from a clean slate. Others feel that it makes sense to do the vision after the forecast. They argue that crafting a vision based on the most likely alternative futures brings a needed degree of reality to the process. Either way!

Values

Vision is an expression of the organization's and stakeholders' values organized around a mission or purpose. It's the work we're here to do,

Table 9.1 Four types of values

Type	Description
Traditional	Focused around following the rules and fulfilling one's pre-determined role in life
Modern	Focused around achievement, growth, and progress with material goods as status symbols
Postmodern	Focused around the search for meaning in one's life, with less emphasis on material goods and more on experiences
Integral	The leading edge of values change with an emphasis on a more practical and functional approach, with a goal of "making a difference."

Source: Hines (2011).

and, hopefully, the work we want to do together. Understanding the values within the organization, therefore, is an important element of a vision that "sticks." Visions in synch with values will have a greater chance of surviving the inevitable challenges than a vision that does not connect to organizational values.

Values are an individual view about what is most important in life, which in turn guides decision-making and behavior. Simon, Howe & Kirschenbaum, in their classic *Values Clarification*, noted that a value becomes a value when it is felt, analyzed, and expressed in terms of behavior. Thus to really get at core values, which is fundamental to visioning work, the organization should believe it is a core value, feel it at a deep level, and have some evidence of having acted on it (Simon et al., 1972, 10).

The curriculum also teaches a content module around the evolution of values. Hines has built a long-term model of values change (see summary in Table 9.1), based on the work of Inglehart's World Values Survey[3] and Beck's (1996) *Spiral Dynamics*, that gives students a tangible sense of the impact of values and values change.

Background

Visioning is an approach to aligning the organization: its people, its work and its stakeholders. It's about "getting on the same page." It provides an overall sense of direction, which is a powerful tool when everyone agrees on it as an endpoint, even if they disagree on the means (the planning). In fact, it is healthy to have some disagreement and debate on how to achieve the vision.

---

[3] See www.worldvaluessurvey.org.

Where does the vision or direction come from? Good question. Many people would say that it is the leader's responsibility to create the vision. Leaders do have vision, by definition, else they would not be leaders, but people who say the leader must create the vision are usually not meaning the boss or the authority should do so. The boss may be a visionary, but if not, as good as she or he is, they should not be expected to do things that they are not equipped to do.

In point of fact, visions can come from anywhere – a chance remark, a large group meeting, an outside consultant. The mark of a good vision is that it awakens spirit in the members of the enterprise. "Yeah, that's it!" they say. "I can get excited about that." Until that reaction comes among a large diverse group of people in the enterprise, it does not yet have a vision.

Many organizations have vision statements, but they don't have visions. They are not the same thing, just like the map is not the territory. The vision statement may be a statement of the vision, but unless the members of the enterprise "see" the vision, the statement will have little or no effect at all. "The greatest service company in the world" or words to the effect! How many companies have vision statements that sound like that? Too many, but there is no vision there – nothing unique, nothing exciting, nothing that speaks to everyone. It's generic; at best it's a placeholder until the enterprise gets a real vision. Real visions are exciting, energizing. People feel proud and privileged to be part of an enterprise that is striving for such a lofty and worthwhile goal. Unique visions are even more powerful – "If we can't do this, nobody can!"

Other pseudo-visions, such as a billion-dollar company, four million widgets produced, expansion to 50 countries, are really goals; they are not visions. They are goals for top management to work toward, but they carry very little water for most people. A firm's balance sheet is a theoretical concept, at best, for most workers. They don't get out of bed every morning to add another 2% margin to the bottom line. Their units may have their own goals that are more real and meaningful to them. The overall financial position of the company is meaningful to management, but not to many others.

A vision and its statement are only as powerful as the commitment to implement them. They do not create a new reality the way a law or regulation does. People do not have to follow it under threat of punishment. Rather they willingly lend their effort to following the vision if it conforms to their own vision for themselves and their world. Those who do so commit to form a partnership to work together to achieve the vision.

The bonds of partnership result from meaningful dialogue about common interests and values, about disagreements and history, about the possibilities of the future. Partnerships do not arise easily. Often they have to push their way up through a history of neglect, mistrust and disappointment. "Why are you coming to us now?" is a frequent question. "Haven't we done this before?" ask those who have been approached before and been let down.

Those uncomfortable questions need to be asked and answered because fundamental change has to have partners. Few if any organizations can transform themselves from within. The members see the world in only one way. Only by confronting the different perspectives of others can that way be challenged. The others' perspectives act like a mirror, reflecting back the members' world view and preconceptions. Just as one cannot see one's face without a mirror, so they cannot know their paradigms without the reflecting surface of others.

Visions are required when transformational change is needed. In "normal" times – what earlier was referred to as times of equilibrium – there is not a compelling need to do visioning work. Since visioning work is time and resource intense, it should not be undertaken lightly. If things are going along just fine, no need for revision – provided there is not a storm on the horizon.

Senge et al. (1994, 314) suggest that there are five potential starting points for developing a vision. Organizations tend to be at one of these five points. His advice is to gradually shift the organization toward the most desirable of the five points: co creating. The five stages are listed in Table 9.2.

The starting points are arranged along a continuum from lesser to greater degrees of participation by the organizational members.

Table 9.2 Five stages of developing visions

Telling	Selling	Testing	Consulting	Co-creating
The boss decrees the vision and everyone else follows it	The boss knows the vision, but needs to get the organization to buy in	The boss has an idea or ideas about the vision and wants to know the organization's reaction before proceeding	The boss is putting together a vision and wants input from the organization	The boss and the members of the organization build the vision together through a collaborative process

Increasing levels of participation

Source: Senge et al. (1994).

Charlotte Roberts, in the *Fifth Discipline Fieldbook*, suggests the following generic questions should be addressed in doing a visioning activity (Senge, 1994, 337–8):

• Who are the stakeholders? How do we work with them? How do we produce value for them?
• What are the most influential trends in our industry?
• What is our image in the marketplace? How do we compete?
• What is our unique contribution to the world around us? What is the impact of our work?
• How do we make money?
• What does our organization look like?
• How do we handle good or hard times?
• In what ways is our organization a great place to work?
• What are our values? How do people treat each other?
• How do we know that the future of our organization is secure?
• What is our organization's role in the community?

Leadership expert Jim Collins (1991) suggests three attributes for the hedgehog concept, his term for a vision:

• What are we passionate about?
• What can we do better than anyone else?
• What drives our economic engine?

So there are many ways to carry out a visioning activity. The questions provide a basic guide to what needs to be covered, and there are simply different ways to cover that ground, each with its particular emphasis and strengths.

Jim Dator, How to Conduct a Futures Visioning Workshop

Dator has been head of the University of Hawaii Alternative Futures Master's in Political Science since the 1970s. He has devised a two-day visioning workshop that could be characterized as a bottom-up approach.

He asks participants to arrive with personal vision of the topic in question. To stress the importance of the workshop he includes experts or VIPs and he plays a facilitative role that relies on keeping to the process (not getting too deep into the content). He shows some sample visions. The participants share their personal visions in dyads. The small groups report to plenary in order to learn from one another, including walkabouts to see the preliminary visions. The process is repeated for missing elements, and then for side-effects. After voting, the large group agrees on the key components and a smaller team then writes the vision, which is approved by the core team (Dator, 1994).

Marvin Weisbord, Future Search

Weisbord pioneered this visioning workshop approach, building upon the search conference approach developed by Eric Trist and Fred Emery back in 1959. Future search is a visioning process that is unique in its strong focus on letting the group work out its own process. The facilitators stick to process guidance and avoid the temptation to get involved in problem-solving for the group. The goal is for the group to find its own common ground. There are three main principles (Weisbord & Janoff, 2000):

- Get a diverse, representative cross section of the whole system of the organization to participate in the workshop. Group sizes can range from 50–80 participants
- Rather than solve problems or resolve conflicts on the spot, frame issues in a broad global context and focus on the possibilities of the future
- Do the framing in such a way that the participants manage their work themselves, so that they take responsibility for it.

Oliver Markley, Visionary Futures

Oliver Markley, a former Professor and Chair of the Houston Futures program, has pioneered several techniques for creative visioning. The students learn about the techniques and gain experience with at least one. A goal of Markley's work is to enable students to tap their deep intuitive capabilities, which typically rest beneath the conscious level. Thus relaxation techniques are employed to access this level of knowing, and several scripts, such as Futures Time Travel, have been developed to then lead students through a process aimed at exploring the future. This work can also be done with groups, but it depends on a high level of trust between the facilitator and the group (Markley, 1998).

David Cooperrider, Appreciative Inquiry

The Appreciative Inquiry approach to vision is unique in its focus on what the organization is doing well. Whereas many approaches to organization development focus on fixing the problems, Appreciative Inquiry puts the focus on what is working and builds upon those capabilities. The key idea is that most organizations actually have much more potential than they realize and identifying and building on this potential is the best way to construct a positive vision for the future. The problem with problem-solving is that it brings attention to what's wrong, and taps into negative energy. The four key stages are (Cooperrider & Whitney, 1999):

- *Discovery*: mobilizing a whole system inquiry into the positive change core
- *Dream*: creating a clear results-oriented vision in relation to discovered potential and in relation to questions of higher purpose, such as "What is the world calling us to become?"
- *Design*: creating possibility propositions of the ideal organization, an organization design which people feel is capable of magnifying or eclipsing the positive core and realizing the articulated new dream
- *Destiny*: strengthening the affirmative capability of the whole system, enabling it to build hope and momentum around a deep purpose and creating processes for learning, adjustment, and improvisation, like a jazz group over time.

Otto Scharmer, Theory U

Theory U is another of the major approaches that students are introduced to. This approach emerged from the Society for Organizational Learning and is associated with Peter Senge, who collaborated on the work, though it is Otto Scharmer who is driving it. It suggests that the conventional practice of learning from the past is limiting in terms of creating a vision for the future. Theory U suggests it is possible to sense the future that "wants to emerge." The approach relies on a relatively high degree of self-awareness among participants, or at least their willingness to participate in a process that will tap in to it. Seven actions comprise the U process, the first three descending down the left-hand side of the U in Figure 9.2, the fourth in the middle/bottom, and the last three traversing back up the right-hand side of the U (Scharmer, 2007).

CONCLUSION

Visioning is an approach to developing preferred futures. In some cases a vision precedes the forecast – "let's decide what we want to be, and

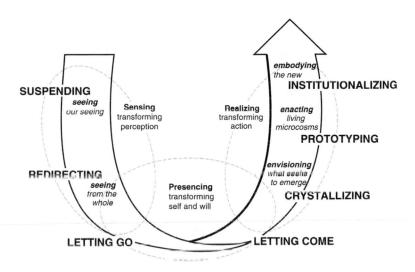

Figure 9.2 Presence: Human Purpose and the Field of the Future
Source: Theory U[4].

then look at the landscape and assess how to get there." In others, the vision comes after the forecast – "let's look at the lay of the land, and then assess where we want to be."

The key idea is to create a crisp, compelling statement of the organization's aspirations for the future, in a way that creates a mental image for those who will work toward it. Its purpose is to be inspirational. Typically, it is a bit of a stretch. If it is too "stretchy" and thus unachievable, it becomes unrealistic and loses its motivational power. If it is comfortable and thus relatively easy to achieve, that too creates a situation where it loses its ability to motivate. Thus, the goal is to find the sweet spot between too easy and too hard. The vision is simply the aspiration. It requires planning to become actualized.

There is no one "right" approach to doing visioning that fits all situations. Different approaches make sense based on the particular context. Students are familiarized with some basic approaches in order to be able to make their choice as to which approach best fits a particular situation.

---

[4] © Peter Senge, C. Otto Scharmer, Joseph Jaworski and Betty Sue Flowers. Available at http://www.solonline.org/repository/download/PresenceUdiagram.pdf?item id=8874346.

RESOURCES

Barker, J. (1989) *Discovering the Future Series: The Power of Vision,* http://www.starthrower.com/joel_barker.htm.

- While probably best known for his groundbreaking "paradigms" work, his video on visioning sold over 10,000 copies and was translated into 15 languages.

Bezold, C. (2000) "The Visioning Method" in R. Slaughter (ed.) *The Knowledge Base of Foresight,* Vol. 2, Millennium Edition (Queensland, Australia: Foresight International).

- Practitioner with long experience working in the visioning space with the Institute for Alternative Futures shares his approach to visioning.

Cooperrider, D. L. & Whitney, D. (1999) "A Positive Revolution in Change: Appreciative Inquiry" in P. Holman & T. Devane (eds) *Appreciative Inquiry* (San Francisco, CA: Barrett-Koehler).

- An excellent introduction to and overview of the key concepts and principles behind the Appreciative Inquiry approach to visioning.

Dator, J. (1994) "How to Conduct a Futures Visioning Workshop." For the Commission on the Future of the Tennessee Judiciary, Fairfield Glade, Tennessee, 8–9 April.

- Describes the process that the author has used with judiciary clients and other groups, operating from his base with the University of Hawaii's Futures Program.

De Geus, A. (1997) *The Living Company* (Cambridge, MA: Harvard Business School).

- A conceptual guide for corporate longevity that covers visioning.

Jungk, R. & Muller, N. (1987) *Future Workshops: How to Create Desirable Futures* (London, UK: Institute for Social Inventions).

- Describes the pioneering process for getting large groups of people working together to envision their preferred futures.

Markley, O. (1998) "I've Seen the Future," *Fast Company,* October/November.

- This *Fast Company* piece popularized his "Virtual Time Travel Approach." The full script, and his other writings on visionary futures, can be accessed at http://www.owmarkley.org/inward/Docs/VisionaryTimeTravelCS.htm.

Nanus, B. (1995) *The Vision Retreat: A Facilitator's Guide* (San Francisco, CA: Jossey-Bass).

- A how-to manual for running a vision retreat.

Polak, F. (1973) *The Image of the Future* (Amsterdam, Netherlands: Elsevier).

- Classic work on the role of the image in envisioning the future.

Scharmer, C. O. (2007) *Theory U: Leading from the Future as it Emerges* (Cambridge, MA: Society for Organizational Learning).

- This comprehensive book brings together the many papers and field experience of Scharmer in developing and applying his Theory U approach to visioning.

Senge, P., Kleiner, A , Roberts, C., Ross, R. & Smith, B. (1994) *The Fifth Discipline Fieldbook* (NY: Currency Doubleday).

- A rich resource work that builds upon the conceptual foundation of *The Fifth Discipline* and is chock-full of tools and techniques for visioning, including a section devoted to the ins and outs of visioning.

Weisbord, M. & Janoff, S. (2000) *Future Search: An Action Guide to Finding Common Ground in Organizations and Communities*, 2nd edn (San Francisco, CA: Berret Koehler).

- The field guide to how to do their visioning approach, known as a Future Search workshop. It covers the key principles, techniques, and provides examples of how it works.

Wheelright, V. (2010) *It's Your Future ... Make it a Good One* (Harlingen, TX: Personal Futures Network).

- Applies the tools of foresight to envisioning one's personal future.

10
Planning

INTRODUCTION

Planning is the activity that most directly involves people with the future. Nations, communities, organizations, and individuals all do some form of planning. Obviously, some do it more systematically than others, and this chapter focuses on how to go about it systematically. Strategic planning is the most commonly known and used approach. Scenario planning has emerged as a variation on how strategic planning is carried out, but it is still strategic planning with scenario inputs.

Planning is the process by which an organization pursues its vision. Ideally, the organization has mapped out the future landscape in the form of alternative futures along with a vision of the future outcome they would prefer. Planning develops the guidebook for achieving that vision. It takes a hard look at the vision in the context of the likely alternative futures, and develops a plan for getting there from here. Strategic planning does not have to start with a vision, however, although  the more transformational the aspirations, the more a vision is required. For less transformational aspirations, simply setting some ambitious goals for the organization can also be considered strategic planning.

Generally, students are taught the basic how-to steps and put them into practice by doing an actual project. This is a subject where effective learning really needs a practical application component. Most students quickly learn that "real life" often deviates from the text or theory fairly quickly. The advice is to understand and know the theory and concepts, and to be prepared to adapt to the circumstances at hand. Knowing when to take shortcuts or when to sidetrack to indulge an influential stakeholder are key skills that can take years of practice to master – if mastery is indeed possible. Just being exposed to these kinds of issues turns out to be an extremely useful practice. Since the goal is to implement the vision and effect positive change in that direction, knowing how to adapt planning in that pursuit is a vital capability.

HISTORY

Introduced to business in the early 1980s, strategic planning was considered to be the *sine qua non* of effective long-term success. The gleam of its once high promise has faded as people realized that it does not contain the magic bullet they were looking for. Since then, organizations have moved off to Total Quality Management (TQM), Business Process Re-engineering (BPR), Enterprise Resource Planning (ERP), Customer Relationship Management (CRM), or whatever is the latest in the alphabet soup of three-letter fads.

Each fad is discredited in turn because it cannot possibly live up to the hyped expectations of its proponents. Of course, those proponents are themselves usually not successful practitioners of the fad but rather consultants and writers who have an interest in over-selling its merits. Nevertheless, each fad does not disappear completely, but rather leaves a residue of common-sense approaches to improve one's business.

Even the now ridiculed time-and motion studies conducted by Frederick Taylor were the basis for the assembly line and modern manufacturing. The Human Relations Movement of the 1930s brought people to the fore as an important, if not the most important component of a successful organization. George Mayo, a founder of the human relations movement, and his followers advocated taking a more humane approach to management. The same can be said for Management by Objectives (MBO), which emerged on the scene in the 1960s under the auspices of Robert McNamara and the Department of Defense. Each team, even today, sets objectives before it begins its work. An obvious improvement, to be sure, and one that was not routinely practiced before that time.

Just as TQM made people more aware of process planning and efficiency and ERP provided the opportunity to coordinate functions across the organization, so strategic planning is a systematic method for analyzing the organization's situation and agreeing on a strategic direction. It is not a magic bullet, but coming to such agreement is an absolute requirement for successful change. Well, perhaps not an absolute requirement. Some organizations succeed because of dumb luck, but one hardly wants to wait around for that to happen!

GENERALIZATION

As noted, the study of the future consists of two main activities: (1) mapping the likely future and other plausible futures; (2) influencing conditions in order to be as close as possible to the preferred future. Planning is central to influencing or changing the future within organizations and in the world in general. The process of creating change and influencing the future involves:

1. understanding expected and plausible future conditions
2. identifying values and preferred futures
3. selecting various approaches (plans) to moving toward the preferred futures
4. implementing the plan to create the desired change(s).

Forecasting is aimed at the first, visioning at the second, planning at the third, and change management at the fourth.

A primary challenge with the planning process is resisting the tendency for it to become overly bureaucratized. In essence, planning can become an end in itself, rather than a means to an end. The intent is to improve strategy and make better decisions in the present that fulfill the strategy and move the organization toward its vision or preferred future. As the process becomes institutionalized, it tends to develop more and more requirements. The focus can shift away from aiding decision-making toward completing the planning process itself. In some cases it evolves into an annual check-the-box activity, and thus loses credibility in the organization. At the same time, increasing requirements, instituted with the noble goal of making the process more effective, increases the size of the planning documents and makes them less user-friendly and actionable. In the worst case, binders full of planning documents gather dust on the shelf. In fact, during the downsizings of the late 1980s and early 1990s, many planning departments were either eliminated or severely cut.

Scenario planning has emerged as a popular way to carry out planning. It was popularized by its successful use by Pierre Wack and colleagues at Royal Dutch Shell in the 1970s. One of the great insights of Wack was to focus the effort as a learning process aimed at influencing the mental models of the leadership team. Thus, the process kept the focus on influencing decision-making, and helped to avoid the tendency for planning processes to become routinized.

Scenario planning faces challenges of its own. As it was adapted for consulting approaches, popularized by several ex-Shell planners at the Global Business Network, it perhaps, in its quest to be user-friendly, overcompensated for the overly detailed processes it set out to replace. In other words, it may have under-emphasized the need for in-depth research. It is not widely publicized that Wack's approach at Shell was tremendously research-intensive and involved a fairly large dedicated staff. He insisted that the team do detailed and deep research in support of the scenarios. Some of that approach was lost in the quest to adopt a process that was more palatable to organizations pressed for time and money.

Thus, the paradox of strategic planning. It requires an extensive commitment of time and resources to be effective. But if that burden is seen as overly intense, organizations shy away from making the commitment; when that happens, the results also can be less than satisfactory. As a result of this paradox, the curriculum teaches the "full" process of strategic planning, with all the conceptual underpinnings and typical process steps, requirements, but recommends that practitioners seek to strike the right balance between rigor and user-friendliness. (Scenario planning is also taught, but since it has its base in forecasting, it is typically taught as part of that course.) This requires an understanding of the organizational culture that one is working with. In other words, there is no one-size-fits-all process that works equally well in every situation. A key lesson is to keep the focus squarely on the mental models of the leadership and to influence their learning and decision-making, and not get caught up in planning for planning's sake. Admittedly, this can be a difficult task.

APPROACH

| "Plans are nothing; planning is everything" – Dwight D. Eisenhower |

Strategic planning as practiced here consists of six principal steps, including an initial step of establishing the planning process. Those steps are, in one sense, a microcosm of the whole futures organization, beginning with understanding the future and finishing with actionable steps. There are a few elements of strategic planning that are unique, but for the most part, the steps reconstruct the categories of future studies itself.

Table 10.1   Steps in strategic planning

Step	Function	Equivalent foresight category
1. Planning to plan	Setting the objectives for the planning process Outlining the approach Securing authorization and buy-in Building the team to carry it out	Framing
2A. Understanding the global future	Mapping and extrapolating macro forces that will provide the context for future success in demographics, technology, economics, politics, and the culture at large	Research, Scanning, Baseline forecasting
2B. Understanding the immediate future	Mapping and extrapolating the forces in the organization's own industry or domain, including customers, competitors, specific technologies, suppliers, regulators, and other stakeholders	Research, Scanning, Baseline forecasting (specific to the immediate environment)
2C. Understanding the organization	Identifying the organization's strategic competencies that make it unique and its strategic weaknesses that make it vulnerable	SWOT (strengths, weaknesses, opportunities, threats) analysis, Stakeholder analysis
3. Setting the direction	Establishing a vision or strategy that will allow the organization to be successful by dominating its immediate environment	Visioning, Strategy formulation
4. Developing the plan	Developing the mission, goals and strategies that will mobilize people and resources toward a common vision and goals	Strategic planning, Goal setting
5. Changing the organization	Transforming (changing) the organization to be able to implement the strategic plan	Change management
6. Managing strategic initiatives and projects	Launching and monitoring strategic initiatives on an annual basis	Implementation

The steps involved in strategic planning form a symmetric hour-glass, shown in Figure 10.1. The first three steps are dedicated to mapping, understanding the future at various levels. The middle step begins influencing the future by establishing the overall strategic direction for the organization. The last three steps start the organization in the direction of its vision and grand strategy.

1. Planning to plan

The first step of any process is, of course, to establish the process in an effective manner. The biggest part of this phase is generating the approval and buy-in of major stakeholders in the purpose and objectives of the planning process. Approvals come from authorities, those who have final say on personnel time and budget. Many authorities will give perfunctory approval, but then fail to follow that up with real support and resources. The real test at the beginning is whether authorities are prepared to commit some or all of people's time to this process or whether people will have to do it as an overload. Many good things are done as an extra responsibility. But extra responsibilities are just that – extra. They tend to be pushed aside when the regular workflow demands full-time commitment.

Figure 10.1 Steps in strategic planning

The other stakeholder group is the members of the organization itself. Many planning processes begin with great fanfare and high hopes only to end in disappointment. Some of the disappointment, unfortunately, is a direct result of the fanfare. Planning is an important activity, and it can produce remarkable results, but it is still planning – it is not doing. The high expectations for planning are based on the assumption that "All we need is to figure out what we want to do, and the rest will take care of itself." That may be true in part, but it is not "all we need." Figuring out what an organization wants to do is a necessary step in its success, but hardly sufficient. People do not automatically spring to the barricades once they are erected. Planning is a small part of the total effort, and it should not be billed as more than that. Executing the plan is much more important, time-consuming, and difficult than planning itself. Some would put planning's contribution to success at less than 10%. Others claim that true transformation takes at least three to five years, most of which is taken up with implementing the plan.

Other than approval and buy-in of the stakeholders, the concrete objectives of this phase are: (1) a plan for the process, including milestones and deliverables; (2) a team to carry out the planning phase. The specifics for the plan and team are discussed in the resources. One of the pitfalls of planning is to make the plan too large. The plan needs to be an outline, a skeleton, with the details filled in as time goes on. The team needs to be a small group of people, committed to the outcome, with the time and resources to complete the planning process. The plan itself should also be more modest than is usually developed. Most plans are gigantic affairs, full of every activity that anyone has ever done or might conceivably do in the future. It is so big that no one understands it, much less is in a position to implement it.

The plan itself should be *thin* – something that everyone in the organization can comprehend, agree with and be able to implement in their own way. The plan is a top-level direction, not the detailed implementation. When asked, everyone in the organization should be able to say what the overall direction and long-term goals are and how they and their unit are contributing to its success. That does not take much paper at all.

2. Understanding the future

The relation of the organization to its environment has been described in Chapter 5, Research. The chapter noted the levels of the broad operating context (the global future), the immediate operating environment, and the level of the organization itself.

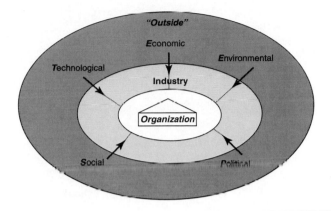

Figure 10.2   Levels of change

The outer layer is the global future. Many people do not pay much attention to the global future because it has little relevance to their day-to-day lives. But strategic planning is not about the day-to-day, but rather about the long-term future. That is where the plan will ultimately have to deliver. It is important therefore to recognize how the global environment is changing and what it might be like when the plan becomes a reality.

This step involves the complete forecasting section of the futures tools: research, baseline and alternative futures forecasting. Those elements are included in the forecasting framework document described elsewhere (see Chapter 7). The plan may also call for scanning so that the understanding of the future developed during the planning phase can be kept up to date with emerging developments.

The outcome of this step is typically a set of opportunities and threats that face the organization in the future. The understanding is more than this, but the opportunities and threats give an early indication of what the strategic direction might be.

The second layer is the organization's immediate environment. It consists mostly of stakeholders – people and organizations that the organization deals with on a daily basis, such as customers, competitors, suppliers and regulators. It is also the geographical, technological and financial facts of that environment. Understanding the immediate environment and its future is just as important as understanding the global future (Porter, 2008, 86).

Stakeholder analysis

Stakeholders are defined as those groups or individuals who may affect or be affected by an organization's strategies and activities.

The first step in stakeholder analysis is to generate a list of people, groups, or institutions who have an interest in the activity of the organization or who it influences to some degree. Next, the list is reviewed and the specific interests of each stakeholder are identified. Since the list can be long, it is usually helpful to sort it according to the priority of the stakeholders' concerns. There are several potential dimensions. Two common ones are their relative degree of interest and power. Sorting the stakeholders along the two dimensions, in a 2×2 matrix, can help the team understand who needs to be included and to what degree of involvement. It also helps the team anticipate the kind of influence, positive or negative, that these stakeholders might have.

The concrete outcome of the analysis of the immediate environment is the organization's mission. A mission is the articulation of the business the organization is in. While "business" has a commercial tone about it, even non-profit organizations have a mission which is their business. Human service agencies help families cope with stress. Foundations dispense money to do good. Schools prepare children and young adults for the future. A pictorial version of the mission is included in the figure below (refer to Appendix 4 for extended analysis).

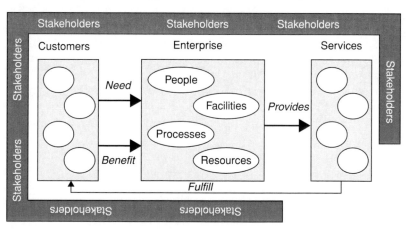

Figure 10.3   The organization model
Source: Bishop, Studies of the Future, UH-Clear Lake.

This diagram also contains a description of the organization itself, the final level of analysis in preparation for setting a direction. The generic mission statement for any organization, then, is to serve one or more sets of customers who have specific needs with a set of products, services, or offerings that fulfill the customer's need, which in turn provides benefit back to the organization and to society in general. Stakeholders also have an interest in and benefit from the success of the organization, but they are not [necessarily] directly served by the organization's products, services, or offerings. So for a public school, the students and their parents are the customers, but the state legislature, the business community, and taxpayers are stakeholders.

The final analysis is based on an internal review of the organization's core competencies and its strengths and weaknesses in facing the future. The competencies will play into selecting a direction since the closer the ultimate direction is to what the organization has been doing, the easier it will be to implement. (At the same time, the direction must also contain new elements or it will merely repeat the conditions and problems of the past.) Strategic competencies are complex sets of skills that the organization does well and that would be hard to duplicate. Maximizing the use of those competencies for long-term success is a good place to look for a new strategic direction.

The strengths and weaknesses lead to the analysis of what the organization must do to be successful in implementing the plan. Playing on the strengths are vital, but overcoming some weaknesses may also be important.

3. Setting the direction

The most important part of the strategic planning process is setting the direction for change. As opposed to the changes from its environment that the organization must anticipate and handle, this is the organization's opportunity to create change on its own (and, secondarily, be a force that others will react to in the future). The direction is the key component of every effective plan, but, ironically, it is often overlooked.

Most plans are directionless or, to say the same thing, they have too many directions. The reason is that most plans are the result of a compromise of interests among management, workers, customers, suppliers, regulators, and other stakeholders. Rather than find a direction that all can support, each group is given a piece of the solution. But the direction that one group wants is not necessarily compatible with the direction that others want – hence the plan ends up with more goals and directions than the organization can handle. What is worse, the many

OR

IBM: *"Let's build a smarter planet"*

Figure 10.4　Greater impact?

goals constitute more of a wish list than a set of targets that the group is committed to achieve. Anything that anyone might someday want to do is put in the plan just in case somebody should someday ask.

The result is a gargantuan document with no chance of changing the future. It is the way of preserving the *status quo* by other means. "We need to plan so we will just recreate what we are doing now with something that maybe someday we might want to do."

The test of a truly effective strategic direction is that (1) it proposes to create real change and (2) it can be expressed in one or two sentences. The direction has to be an "elevator speech" – an explanation that one could give on an elevator as it rises from the first to the fifth floor. If the listener does not leave the elevator knowing what the change is, it's not a strategic direction.

The strategic direction can be embodied in one of two ways, depending on the background of the organization. Business organizations often embody their direction in a grand strategy – how they are going to dominate their market. Prahalad and Hamel (1996) talk about this type of direction in *Competing for the Future*, and which Hamel (2002) expounds on so eloquently in *Leading the Revolution*. Others embody their direction in a vision, a statement of the end-state that they are striving to achieve. (See previous chapter on Visioning.)

The test of an effective strategic direction is whether everyone in the organization understands and is committed to it. One of the authors had lunch once at a medical school's off-site retreat. He sat next to one of the maintenance workers who was as fired up with the direction that that school had adopted as the CEO. They were pursuing a TQM strategy, and he had already integrated the essential components of process improvement into his everyday work. Now that's a vision!

4. Developing the plan

The plan itself is what most people think of when they hear strategic planning. The plan is like a map, a tool for navigating the future. But there are maps, and there are maps. Survey maps, geodetic maps, highway maps are all about known territories. The future, particularly a transformed future, is not nearly so well known. People kid themselves when they think they can plan the unknown future as well as they can plan a cross-country vacation.

Maps of unknown territories are sketchy, sometimes even wrong. So a strategic plan must have the same qualities – put down what is known, don't make too many assumptions, remain flexible, expect surprise, and the like. That doesn't sound like the rigid tomes that most organizations put together, and it isn't. It is a compelling strategic direction with a few additional elements to connect it to everyday work. Figure 10.5 below contains the overall picture of the strategic plan (see also Appendix 4).

The plan is surrounded by the mission, the territory that the organization works in. The mission is like a contract that the organization makes with the world – "If we do this well, you will support us with recognition and resources." So schools educate students, automobile companies provide transportation, armies protect citizens, and so on. The plan may change the mission and adjust the territory, but that should be done

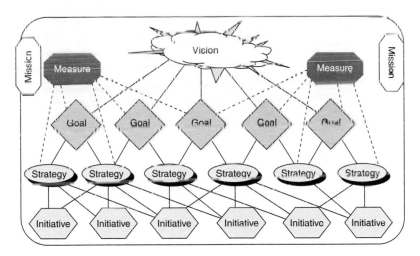

Figure 10.5 Goal hierarchy
Source: Bishop studies of the Future, UH-Clear Lake.

explicitly and with forethought to the consequences. A mission that is too narrow might exclude opportunities that the organization could use; a mission too broad spreads the organization's efforts and decreases the likelihood that it will be successful at any one of them.

The plan is headed, however, by the vision, grand strategy, or hedgehog – the end-state that the organization is striving to achieve. Everything that the organization does should be geared to achieving its vision. One of the most important requirements, perhaps the most important, is that it fulfills its mission in an excellent manner. No visionary company was ever sloppy or ill-prepared to discharge its core responsibility to its customers or to society. The rest of the plan is mobilizing resources to move in the direction of the vision.

The specific changes are expressed as a set of goals. Goals are concrete achievements that can be realized in a specific period of time, as opposed to abstract visionary states that may never be achieved. Visions set directions; goals are the milestones along the way.

Goals are often confused with elements of the mission. So a school may say its goal is to educate students. That sounds like a goal, but it is not in this approach. That is the school's mission – what it does and will always do as long as it exists. A goal is a concrete, achievable accomplishment, not an on-going activity. For that reason, goals are expressed as nouns, not verbs. They are achievements, not activities. One knows when the goals are achieved. It's not just something that is done all the time.

So growth, quality, and recognition are the stuff of goals. Some goals are obvious when they are achieved – a championship is a championship, no doubt about it. Most goals, however, require measures to tell when or to what degree they are achieved. Measures are the observable manifestations of unobservable states. So tests are used to measure intelligence or learning; scales to measure weight; blood pressure cuffs to measure blood pressure. A measurement strategy is essential for goals that are not directly observable else the organization will never know how well it is doing.

Some plans simply track the measures to see how well the organization is doing. Others set a specific target to be achieved. Specific targets can be motivating if they are established with a reasonable basis. Targets are not automatically motivating, however, if they are either too low (easy to achieve) or too high (impossible to achieve). Some reasonable criterion needs to be set, usually based on past experience, in order for the target to be difficult but not impossible to achieve. It should call out the best from people while not making it so difficult that it becomes discouraging.

Goals are the achievements; strategies are the activities that generate the achievements. Goals are nouns; strategies are verbs. The term "strategy" is ambiguous in strategic planning. Even in this approach, strategy might be grand strategy – the overall direction that the plan is designed to achieve or individual strategies that lead to specific goal achievements. In either case, they are activities; it's just the scope that differs.

Strategies are a category of activities that the organization can pursue over the long term to achieve its goals. They are chosen on the basis of their presumed effectiveness given the competencies and resources of the organization.

Strategies are implemented over time in a series of initiatives, short-term projects that put the strategy into action. Many organizations select their initiatives on an annual basis. They make up each year's action plan that implements the strategic plan. Since initiatives are short term, they can be planned in the traditional sense – a series of steps leading to a pre-defined outcome, as shown in Table 10.2.

Table 10.2 Dimensions of an initiative

Step	Description
Charge	Each initiative is charged by the authorities to accomplish a certain objective by the end of the time period. The charge should be ambitious yet reasonable in the time allotted.
Team	Individuals are assembled who have the competencies and resources to accomplish the objective. The team should contain different types of people according to style and background, and they should represent all stakeholders affected in carrying out the charge.
Tasks	The team itself develops a list of tasks that it will undertake to achieve the objective. These tasks are then reviewed and approved by the authorities.
Schedules	The tasks are scheduled into a series of milestones that provide checkpoints on the progress the team is making. These checkpoints are monitored by the authorities or their representatives during the initiative.
Resources	Time, money, equipment, political support or anything else the team needs to achieve its objective. Authorities allocate these resources on the recommendation of the team. Time is usually the most precious commodity. Many initiatives fail because individuals are not given release time from their regular duties to engage in the initiative. As a result, the initiative does not get the attention it needs because team members must place their regular jobs ahead of the initiative in order of priority. The problem is further compounded by the fact that team members are assessed by their immediate supervisors who value the regular job over an organization-wide initiative.

Accomplishing the goals and achieving the vision of a strategic plan, however, involves more than simply initiating a series of projects. If the plan is at all ambitious, it will require the organization to learn new things, adopt new standards and procedures – in general, set off a whole series of fundamental changes. The more ambitious the plan, the more change will be required. While people are usually prepared to change within the traditional boundaries they are used to, visionary goals normally require that the boundaries themselves change.

Change management, then, is the process of equipping the organization with the skills necessary to be successful in achieving its vision. Change of this sort is disruptive, causes anxiety and is implemented only with great difficulty. In the end, however, people report that they have never felt more alive and more involved in the future of the organization. While the traditional ways of doing things are secure, they are not exciting. Encouraging and supporting members of the organization to try the exciting is a difficult yet rewarding task.

CONCLUSION

Planning is a process for achieving a vision or a set of ambitious, long-term goals. It maps out the general activities required to get to the preferred future. It takes the essence of the message of the vision and translates it into concrete plans for realizing the vision. It is a bridge step between the vision and action.

The essence of the plan is typically articulated as a strategy. It is the means to achieve the end of the vision. Since the vision is abstract, it is represented in terms of goals, which provides a tangible target – so the organization knows if they made it. The strategy, thus, aims at the goals. The strategy is articulated in terms of tactics and actions that will be carried out in the action phase.

RESOURCES

Bryson, J. & Einsweiler, R. (eds) (1988) *Strategic Planning: Threats and Opportunities for Planners* (Chicago, IL: American Planning Association Planners Press).

- Strategic planning, methods, and tools for public agencies and non-profit organizations. One of the better "how-to" guides.

Coates, J. (2001) "The Future as a Factor in Business Planning and Management," *Futures Research Quarterly*, 17 (3), 5–11.

- Explains his approach to using foresight as a tool for business planning.

De Geus, A. (1988) "Planning as Learning," *Harvard Business Review*, March–April, 70–4.

- Mentor and guide to the current writers about the learning organization describes his approach to planning, which he developed at Royal Dutch Shell in the 1970s.

Hamel, G. & Prahalad, C.K. (1996) *Competing for the Future* (Cambridge, MA: Harvard Business Press).

- Advice on "how to get to the future first." Suggests that anticipating the future can enable strategic shifts to position organizations to move ahead of their competition.

Hamel, G. (2002) *Leading the Revolution: How to Thrive in Turbulent Times by Making Innovation a Way of Life* (Cambridge, MA: Harvard Business Press).

- A collection of several stories of how grassroots "revolutions" led by inspired individuals helped to enable significant changes in organizational strategies.

Marsh, N., McAllum, N. & Purcell, D. (2002) *Strategic Foresight: The Power of Standing in the Future* (Melbourne, Australia: Crown Content).

- A step-by-step framework, with case studies, of how foresight can aid strategic planning in organizations.

Mintzberg, H. (1994) *The Rise and Fall of Strategic Planning* (NY: Free Press)

- Chronicles why strategic planning fell out of favor by the early 1990s. Mintzberg is the non-planning strategic planner. He argues that CEOs make up strategy as they go along, using experience, opportunity, and insight in a rolling game from which the strategy emerges, almost in hindsight. He believes most strategic planning efforts are useless.

Porter, M. (2008, January) "The Five Competitive Forces that Shape Strategy," *Harvard Business Review*, 79–93.

- The famous "five forces" explained in terms of how they influence strategy.

Schwartz, P. (1996) *The Art of the Long View: Planning for the Future in an Uncertain World* (NY: Doubleday).

* Business book on how to apply scenario planning for strategy development in organizations. Includes how-to advice along with stories of successful applications.

Senge, P., Kleiner, A., Roberts, C., Ross, R. & Smith, B. (1994). *The Fifth Discipline Fieldbook* (NY: Currency Doubleday).

* The bible of the learning organization. *The Fifth Discipline* is the original more academically oriented piece, with the *Fieldbook* focusing on applications and bringing the theory to life with stories and exercises.

11
Change Management

INTRODUCTION

Change management has to do with transformational change. It is not about whether to change staff meetings from one hour to thirty minutes. Or whether to change the make of vehicles purchased for the company fleet. Or whether to redesign the logo (although that could be part of a transformational change process). Transformational change impacts who the organization is and what it does. It most commonly accompanies a visioning process, which, after, considers the very questions of what the organization is all about.

When a visioning process finds it necessary to adjust the vision (see Chapter 9), it next devises the appropriate strategic plan (see chapter 10), and finally crafts a change management process – the focus of Chapter 11.

HISTORY

Change management emerged from the recognition that change wasn't easy. The best-laid plans were not always translating into the anticipated results. Management literature talked about change, but it wasn't until after World War II and the rise of increasingly large and complex organizations that it began to coalesce around a change management theme. Much like foresight, change management has the blessing and curse of drawing upon a wide range of disciplines and theorists—the blessing being the diversity of thought, the curse being that it makes it difficult to distinguish just what change management is and is not.

The curriculum focuses on change management from the perspective of transformational change, but it can be and is used for lesser magnitude change as well. The starting point from which we begin is Everett Roger's model of innovation diffusions, now perhaps the most widely accepted model for explaining how change occurs in a network or organization. He developed the model to explain how new pharmaceuticals diffused in a network of physicians, but it has proved a useful framework to explain the process of adapting to change in many other venues as well.

Figure 11.1 shows how change proceeds along five typical responses to change. The innovators are the first to adopt. They enjoy it, even thrive on it. The early adopters are next. They play a strong "influencer" role on the rest. The innovators often lack credibility with the mainstream, because they like change for the sake of change. The early adopters are more selective, so when they adopt a change, it's a signal to the next group, the early majority, that the change is okay. The late majority follows them and finally the laggards adopt change only when everyone else has and there is no escaping it. Or they sometimes never adopt it.

Hiatt & Creasey (n.d.) note that change management emerged from two streams: engineering and psychology. As one would expect, the engineering approach takes the vantage point of business systems and processes. The psychological approach emphasizes the human aspect. The engineering stream developed approaches like Total Quality Management (TQM), Business Process Re-engineering (BRP), Enterprise Resource

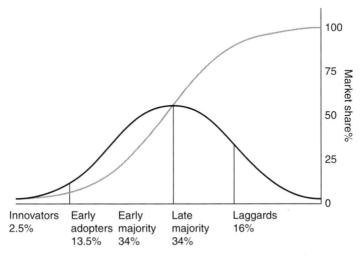

Figure 11.1   Roger's innovation diffusion curve
Source: Tungsten (2009), based on Rogers (1962).

Planning (ERP), Six Sigma, and Lean Manufacturing. Their emphasis is on arranging the adjusting the mechanics of the organizations.

Psychological approaches have become less process focused in comparison to the engineering. Bridges & Brides (2009) are among the most visible advocates for managing the human side of change, or transitions in their parlance. They used the Myers-Briggs personality assessment instrument as a tool to understand people's attitudes toward change – as a way to help manage the process. Many other tools emerged for this purpose, such as the Kirton Adapter-Innovator (KAI) instrument that sorted problem-solving preferences into those who prefer to work within the existing systems and those who would prefer to change it.

John Kotter's (1996) *Harvard Business Review* article on "Leading Change: Why Transformation Efforts Fail," which he later expanded into a book, *Leading Change*, presented an eight-step model for leading change initiatives that helped to catalyze interest and mainstream the practice of change management. Kotter's is perhaps the most frequently cited of the many different step-and-process models that have emerged for change management.

Kotter's eight steps for leading change

1. Establish a sense of urgency
2. Form a powerful guiding coalition
3. Create a vision
4. Communicate the vision
5. Empower others to act on the vision
6. Plan for and create short-term wins
7. Consolidate improvements and produce still more change
8. Institutionalize new approaches.

Jim Collins (2001) catalogued the characteristics of companies that had turned in outstanding stock market performance in his book *Good to Great*. And also of note is Rick Maurer's (1996) excellent treatment of people's response to change in his book *Beyond the Wall of Resistance*.

GENERALIZATION

Strategic foresight requires two parallel skills: anticipating change coming at one from the world and creating change within one's own spheres of influence. This chapter is about the latter.

In the emerging discipline of strategic foresight, the rate of change varies from continuous to discontinuous. In other words, change occurs relatively slowly and predictably over long periods of time, interrupted by rapid, disruptive change. The long periods of continuous change are the eras that are studied in history, a coherent period of time with a unique identity that differs fundamentally from what went before and what happened after. Eras begin and end with disruptions, short periods of rapid change that reset the parameters of the era.

So just as eras occur in the world, they also occur within organizations. New management, an acquisition or merger, a new line of business – all can create a new state of affairs within an organization. The difference, however, is that disruptions within organizations are usually chosen rather than forced by the outside world. Those who choose to create a new era are called transformational leaders. These leaders are not necessarily the managers or authorities in charge of the organization, though they may be. Rather they are people who see the possibility of a new era, commit to move in that direction themselves, and work to persuade others to follow them.

The job of creating a new era is not easy, and it can even be dangerous because the transition from one era to another is treacherous, risky, expensive, time-consuming, and filled with mistakes and setbacks. Joseph Schumpeter called the disruptions between eras "waves of creative destruction." He was talking about the periodic transition from one lead technology to another. Unfortunately, it is not possible to simply leave one era and enter the next one. Rather it is necessary first to abandon, if not destroy many of the good things of the old era in order to make room for the new.

But cannot successful organizations simply build on their strengths and go directly to the new era without having to cross the desert? A good question, and would that it were so. Unfortunately, there seems to be an iron law of change that requires destruction before creation. A new kitchen or a new road requires first tearing out the old one. Starting a new career requires first acquiring the necessary skills and starting at the bottom. A secure retirement requires investing money and taking it out of use for a long time. One step backwards before taking two or more steps forward.

And no one likes that part of transformational change. It is messy, chaotic, disorganized. Perfectly good procedures that have worked for a long time must be abandoned in favor of new, untried procedures. Job skills that made people successful become outmoded. Tasks that were performed efficiently now take longer and cause more problems.

And so people begin to disagree. Why is this taking so long? Why can't we just go back and do it the old way? Why did we start this change in the first place? Long-buried conflicts flare up anew. Some actually try to use the disorganization associated with the change as a chance to advance their own agenda at the expense of others or even of the whole organization. So people who "resist change" may not be so stupid after all. Why would anyone *want* to go through such a period? Actually few people do. But there are good reasons for doing so – the world has changed since the old era began; as a result, the old era has outlived its usefulness; it's time to create a new era with better outcomes, and this is the only way to do so.

Transformational change ...

1. Is rarely chosen; it is almost always forced by external circumstances
2. Always creates disagreements about timing and scope
3. Is always uneven, disorganized, messy, chaotic
4. Always politicizes communication
5. Always changes the relative position of groups
6. Always occurs one person at a time
7. Is never fully adopted by force.

So leaders face enormous resistance when they promote transformational change. Questions and issues arise from all sides:

- What should we abandon (from the old era) and what will replace it?
- How long will this take?
- How expensive is it going to be?
- Can you guarantee that it will be worth it?
- What if we abandon the things of the old era but we are not able to replace it with the things of the new?

All very good questions for which there are no satisfying answers. Transformational change is more like exploration than construction. No one has ever attempted this type of transformation, in this organization, at this time, under these circumstances before. Explorers prepare for their journey as best they can. But if neither they nor anyone else has ever journeyed to their destination before, they clearly cannot have a lock-solid plan. They have to assemble a highly motivated team, be opportunistic and flexible as things happen, and keep their eye on

---

The stages of change

1. Denial. "That will never happen."
2. Anger. "This isn't fair."
3. Bargaining. "OK, just tell me what to do."
4. Depression. "I miss the good old days."
5. Acceptance. "We should have done this a long time ago."

---

the ultimate objective even though the way there may not be entirely clear.

Most attempts to create transformational change fail, but not all. Most venture capital investments also fail, but not all. And the ones that succeed pay for all the rest. Making the successful big investment will make all the difficulties worth it – that is, if we actually do get there! And there's the rub: Destruction happens before creation. The organization has to leave the old era before arriving at the new one. And leaving the old era is no guarantee that it will arrive at the new one, or whether there is even a new one to be arrived at! So leadership is difficult and dangerous, but the reward, when it comes, is enormous.

So if transformation is advisable or even necessary, how does one go about it? The good news is that there are many ways; the bad news is that no one knows which ones work! The authors undertook an informal survey of books about organizational change some years ago and came up with 16 different theories about how organizations change. So the right strategy depends on the situation – the objective, the organization and its culture, the leaders and their skills, and external circumstances. With such variability, it is no wonder that most change initiatives fail.

APPROACH

For better or worse, therefore, the authors have assembled a few principles for creating change that they and others have found useful in promoting transformational change. There are just about as many of these lists in the literature as there are books and articles, but these are the ones recommended here:

1. Have a good reason

As described above, transformational change is a risky and expensive business, and no one should take on the task lightly. So one needs a good reason for promoting change in the first place. What is more, few will enroll in the campaign to create the change unless there is a good reason for doing so.

The rationale is contained in the case for change. It includes the fundamental reason(s) for the change, such as how the world has changed or how the current organizational practices have become obsolete. Jack Welch, the legendary CEO of GE, said, "If the organization is not changing at least as fast as the world, then it will be out of business." The case needs to be compelling, "If we don't do this ..." It also needs to be honest. Simply making stuff up will not work under the scrutiny that the case will receive during the change process.

So the case for change begins from the outside in. While the change may not be forced by circumstances in the world, it is clearly recommended because of them. And the earlier the better! If one waits until the world *requires* the change, it is too late. Game Over! Successful transformational leaders see the changes coming long before anyone else. They begin talking the language of change, slowly, gently, pointing out to those around them that the world is changing.

The ability to see how different the world could become has come to be called foresight. Foresight is essential in creating transformational change. Without it, the change could be foolish, ill-advised or just an ego trip for someone who wants to leave some mark in the history books. The case for change is stated simply as: "The world is changing; we have to change along with it."

2. Be honest about the process

Secondly, the case for change needs to describe the process as clearly as is possible before embarking on the journey. No one can know the exact process ahead of time because the change process is exploration. It is doing some brand-new things at this time in this way. Those who require details are not ready for the journey. When enrolling people the leader must prepare them by emphasizing, without being excessively pessimistic, the challenges that lie ahead.

Unfortunately, the tendency will be to overemphasize the benefits and downplay the difficulties in trying to get people to sign on. That tendency is seen among the many people who try to persuade others to do something, such as sales people, vendors, or political leaders. "All you have to do is ..." Play up the benefits; downplay the costs. But the costs of the change are directly proportional to the scope of the change. There is no free lunch, and no free change. Skilful managers can minimize those costs, but they cannot eliminate them. If the case

Table 11.1   Eight reasons for organizational change

Reason	Description
1. **Crisis** Events occur, and we must react quickly.	Every business is successful until it's not. What's amazing is how often top management is surprised when "not" happens. This astonishment, this belated recognition of dramatically changed circumstances, virtually guarantees that the work of renewal will be significantly, perhaps dangerously, postponed (Hamel & Valikangas, 2003, 3).
2. **Vision** We become strongly committed to implement a change.	There is no more powerful engine driving an organization toward excellence and long-range success than an attractive, worthwhile, and achievable vision of the future, widely shared (Nanus, 1992, 3).
3. **Technology** A technology enables or requires the change.	Transformation is a response to environmental and technological change by different types of organizations (Kilmann & Covin, 1987, 3).
4. **Performance** We move to correct problems when we are not reaching our goals.	Corporate strategy must be the starting point for a reengineering effort because a strategic to-be vision gives the company a consistent course (Carr & Johansson, 1995, 103).
5. **Influence** Influential people, other than authorities, promote the change.	All the successful reorientations we have observed are characterized by an individual leader who is able to serve as a focal point for the change and whose presence, activity, and touch have some special feel or magic (Nadler, 1987, 75).
6. **Benchmarks** Someone outside the organization has adopted the change.	The most efficient way to promulgate effective change is by learning from the positive experience of others ... You learn because another learned first and was willing and able to share that knowledge with you (Brelin & Grayson, 1994, xiv).
7. **Competencies** We develop ourselves and our skills to meet new challenges.	"The best test [of a good servant leader], and most difficult to administer, is: Do those served grow as persons? Do they, while being served, become healthier, wiser, freer, more autonomous, more likely themselves to become servants?" (Greenleaf, 1983).
8. **Dissatisfaction** The level of dissatisfaction builds to breaking point.	Managers often think others need to change, while in fact the need for change frequently lies with the managers themselves. Top-management change is particularly critical when the corporate culture itself is the object of change. The implicit norms and routines of an organization are a result of the prevailing management style. Because it sets the state, either intentionally or through unintentional defensive responses, top management is primarily responsible for the prevailing style. Thus if corporate culture is to change, the behavior of top management needs to change (Beres & Musser, 1987, 169).

for change is not honest about difficulties at the beginning, then the actual difficulties will stall the process in midstream when they become apparent.

3. Articulate a vision

The vision should help the organization to envision the result of the change. For more on visioning, see Chapter 9.

4. Commit to achieve the vision

Commitment means no matter how long it takes and how hard it is, at least for the significant elements of the vision. Most people embark on transformational change with the best intentions. They believe in the worth of their vision, and they are prepared to work for it. But in the end, the work is longer and harder than they anticipated, and they give up. They simply were not prepared for the difficulties involved. We do not blame them. Transformational change is extraordinarily difficult, and it takes a very long time.

On the other hand, lack of commitment is the single most important source of the cynicism that most people have about change. They've been there before – excited about the possibilities, signed on and ready to go, only to be let down when the process fizzles out. Are they going to sign on the next time? Maybe, but they will need a more compelling case. A third time? Or more? After a while, no case for change is good enough. They've been fooled by high-sounding rhetoric before; they will not be fooled again.

So as with the case for change, do not begin a transformational change until there is an open ended commitment to do what it takes to make some observable progress. One does not have to achieve the vision to be successful. Dr King did not see the visionary future of his speech, but he certainly made measurable progress toward it. No one was disappointed in his commitment, nor did they feel let down by his effort. Don't start without a commitment to finish.

5. Communicate!

Everyone knows that communication is essential for the success of any organization – communicating with team members, with bosses, with employees, with customers, with suppliers, with regulators. One can hardly have too much communication, although it does take time to do it well.

Nevertheless, when thinking of communication, people usually only think of it as a one-way process – telling people things in meetings, telephone calls, memos, emails, websites, brochures, newsletters, or ads.

This type of communication is outbound, but the most important communication in transformational change could be inbound, simply listening.

People are ready for the process; they have committed to the vision; they have steeled themselves to the difficulties of change. Now all that has to be done is to *push* it through – push, outbound! No, take a breath and *listen*. Listen to what people want: Why are they part of this organization? What do they like and not like? What are they doing with their lives? And during the change, what warnings are they giving? What problems are they seeing? What suggestions are they making? Part of our commitment, unfortunately, is not to pay any attention to resistance. "Those people are just against the change!" Some, even many may be, but not all. Some are offering genuine information that will be important for a successful outcome.

And even more important, they might be sharing their aspirations, their hopes and dreams. The vision has to touch what is most important to people for it to be motivating and compelling. And the leader cannot touch that unless he or she knows what it is.

And there is a role for outbound communication as well, but again, not what people often think. Most outbound communication is information about the process – details about what is going on, new processes, or new procedures. Those are important, but not as important as continued communication about the vision. Why is all this happening? Why are we doing this? People signed on to work for the vision, but the vision is easily lost in the details and the difficulties. Someone needs to manage the process and communicate the details. The leader's primary communication, in addition to listening, is to continue to focus on the vision. The vision is why all of this is happening, why it started in the first place. The US Public Broadcasting System's documentary on the civil rights movement was entitled *Eyes on the Prize*, an apt phrase for any leader to follow. Focus on the vision, and others will manage the details.

6.   Generate trust

Most of these principles came from an exercise that Bishop conducted for school superintendents (aka chief school administrators) in Texas some years ago. He was asked by a regional service center to offer the superintendents a workshop on change management, but he was asked not to use the term "change management." The superintendents were sick of that term.

It's not ordinary practice so disguise the learning objective in a workshop, but the author went ahead anyway. He created a simple exercise in which the superintendents were to list the change projects they had been part of in two columns – those that had done well and those that had not. (Unfortunately, the second list was longer than the first!) He would then ask them to consider how the two columns differed – what did the good projects do well that the bad projects did not.

Bishop had never done this exercise before so he tried it first on an administrative staff group at the service center before doing it with the superintendents. The staff group came up with four characteristics (key success factors) for the good projects that were not present in the others – vision, commitment, communication, and trust. The next week, the superintendents came up with exactly three of these factors – vision, commitment, and communication. When the author mentioned that the staff group also put trust on the list of key success factors, the superintendents were amazed. "You mean they do not trust us?" A silly question on the face of it!

"No, they do not trust you. You are personally trustworthy people, to be sure; it is your positions they do not trust. They have been disappointed by authorities who promoted change so many times before that they do not trust anyone in your position."

Trust is absolutely necessary in any successful change process because so much is unknown and the process itself is disorganized and confusing. One must be able to trust the leaders and other colleagues, which means one can count on people to tell the truth and to do what they say they will do. When people's words are consistent with what others find out to be true and when they are consistent with what the person eventually does, then they can be trusted. If once they are found to not be telling the truth or they do not do what they say they will do, then they cannot be trusted.

Regrettably, mistrust is much more common in an atmosphere of confusion and cynicism. It takes a long time to build up trust and, unfortunately, only one or two incidents to destroy it. So what is the leader to do? Take the risk and trust until proven otherwise. It is true that some people cannot be trusted, but you do not know who they are until they show it. Fortunately, most people can be trusted so the chances are that giving people the benefit of the doubt initially will reap more rewards than mistrusting everyone from the outset. Yes, some will take advantage of that, and they must be dealt with. But others will respond enthusiastically to the trust that is extended to them.

Without trust, no one follows the leader; no one can count on their team members, and the change process goes nowhere. Trust is the least recognized success factor in transformational change, even as it is the hardest to achieve.

CONCLUSION

Transformational change is the process of creating a new era, in the world for some or in organizations or small groups for most. It begins with one or more leaders who see that the old era is no longer suitable for the present, much less the future. They articulate a vision for the new era and enroll others in the campaign to bring that vision about. They and their followers face enormous obstacles from the skepticism and resistance of the majority to the difficulty of abandoning old practices even before new ones are ready. They engage in that process nevertheless because it must be done sooner or later and they want it done sooner before the world comes in and dictates the terms of the change.

While historical examples are used to illustrate the process, the same principles apply to small organizations, and even to businesses wanting to capitalize on a new opportunity. Change is change whether it is created in the small or the large.

RESOURCES

Collins, J. (2001) *Good to Great* (NY: Harper Business).

* The current reigning bestseller on organizational change. An empirical study of how 11 companies achieved top performance and the lessons learned from that.

Hock, D. (2000) "The Art of Chaordic Leadership," *Leader to Leader*, Winter.

* A somewhat more practical and organizational application of the complexity principles to change.

Kotter, J. (1996) *Leading Change* (Cambridge, MA: Harvard University Press).

* A step-by-step guide to creating transformational change.

Maurer, R. (1996) *Beyond the Wall of Resistance* (Austin, TX: Bard).

- A common-sense guide to dealing with people during transformational change.

Wheatley, M. (1994) *Leadership and the New Science* (San Francisco, CA: Berrett-Koehler).

- Unleashing the power of committed members through the application of complexity science. A breakthrough in how to apply the principles and lessons of complexity in the organizational setting. Somewhat mystical, but a book with excellent insight into why people will or will not support change.

Appendices

Appendix 1. Framework forecasting specification

This appendix contains the exact specifications for the framework forecast.

Forecasting Framework: The basic categories and elements used in forecasting a domain or topic of interest.

- A category is a type of information that plays a specific role in the forecast.
- An element is a specific item within a category.

Contents: Each category should contain:

- at least one element from each of the following societal sectors that are relevant to the domain: demographic, environmental (nature), technological, economic, political and socio-cultural.
- five to ten of the most important items in a standard framework. For more complete frameworks, the category may contain several elements from each sector in a columnar format.

Table A.1 Framework forecasting specification

1. *Domain definition*: A paragraph that defines the scope of the domain, including what is and what is not in the domain. A domain definition may include one or more of the following three levels:	
The organization level	The internal environment of the region, organization, industry, or issue that is to be forecast
The immediate level	The external environment that directly affects the organization in the short or medium term. (The stakeholders within the organization are usually quite conscious of this level of the environment.)
The global level	The external environment that indirectly affects the organization in the long term (includes STEEP)
Geography	The area of the forecast
Time horizon	The future date of the forecast

Table A.1 Continued

2. *Summary*: A short description of the major findings of the study, focusing on interesting or important aspects of the future that the research uncovered. (Not a traditional abstract that merely abbreviates the report.) Develop the summary last as a communication device for people who will receive the framework

3. *Current assessment*: A review of the domain up to and including the present. Each of the following may be divided into any of the three levels (organization, immediate/transaction or global) and/or into the STEEP categories

Current conditions	An overview of how the domain is structured and how it operates. Key quantities that characterize the domain
Stakeholders	The major actors in the domain (individuals and organizations) along with their values, political interests and relationships with one another
Past events	Recent events within the domain that have created the current conditions and stakeholders, with particular attention to recent discontinuities that began and define the current era

4. *Era analysis*: the major differences between the current era and the previous one

Previous era	Current era

5. *Baseline forecast*: material that describes the difference between the present and the expected or most likely future

Constants	Conditions or quantities that are expected not to change before the time horizon
Trends (extrapolations)	Quantities or changes that move incrementally in a specific direction over a long period of time; the value of the quantity and its rate of change (if known). Forecasts of specific quantities and their value at some specific time in the future. Can always say "More" or "Less," or "Increasing" or "Decreasing." Cluster similar alternatives into macro themes
Plans (goals)	Announced intention by any stakeholder to create future change
Cycles	Quantities or changes in the domain that recur, where quantities are in the cycle at present. Can always say "And again..."

(*continued*)

Table A.1 Continued

Projections	Public forecasts that may influence what is expected to happen
Baseline forecast (expected future)	The result of the constants, trends, plans, cycles and projections. A description of the most likely future at a specific time, focusing on the important differences from the present and the implications of those differences for the stakeholders in the domain. The extrapolated value of important quantities in the future if constants, trends, plans, cycles, and projections continue as expected

6. *Baseline analysis*: An expected change in the baseline future

A. Evidence	For the change (as much as is needed)
i. Assumption	Required to use the evidence
1. Alternative	Opposite assumption
a. Reason	For the alternative
b. Reason	For the alternative

7. *Alternative futures*: material that describes the difference between the expected future and other futures that might happen instead

Trend reversals	Trends that go on for a while, but then they may stop or go in the opposite direction
Unfulfilled intentions, plans	Intentions or plans that may not be realized or accomplished
Potential events, wildcards	Expected or unexpected events and wildcards that would disrupt, change, and potentially end the current era. Often appear as a headline in a news source
Issues, conflicts, controversies, dilemmas, choices	Issues that are currently being discussed and those that could become important (emerging) along with the various ways they could be resolved and the implications of each of those ways. In form of: "Should we..." or "Should they..."
New ideas, images, perspectives	People and their ideas that present a new or insightful look at the domain, particularly about its structure, types and rates of change and plausible futures. Something really new or novel, even if unusual

(continued)

Table A.1 Continued

Key uncertainties	The quantities, potential events, issues, and ideas that would have the greatest impact on the future, yet which are least predictable/most uncertain. (The key uncertainties are a selection of the most important items from events, issues and ideas above. Key uncertainties do not contain any new elements that are not listed above.)

8. *Scenario kernels*: One or more alternative futures (scenario logics); scenarios that represent the most important and different plausible alternative futures of this domain that result from the uncertainties, including major differences from the present, the value of key quantities, and implications for stakeholders

Title (of the scenario) Kernel (the logic or plot)	Leading Indicators: Quantities or events that would signal that a key uncertainty is being resolved in one way or another or that one or other scenario is more or less likely to occur

9. *Information*: lists of relevant items in each of the following information categories:

	Research	Scanning
Texts	Overview publications that describe the structure, statistics and/or future of the domain	N/A
Periodicals	Journals or magazines that carry overview or summary material about the domain	Journals or magazines that report on the latest developments in the domain
Organizations	Professional, trade or research organizations and institutes that publish relevant material on the field	
Experts	Knowledgeable people who are often consulted about the domain	
Websites	Sites that contain important information for understanding the future of the domain (portals and destinations)	Sites that carry the latest information about the domain.

Appendix 2. World Futures

This is currently the only regularly scheduled course in the curriculum that deals explicitly with the content about the future. As such, it is a survey of the overall trends and issues that are shaping the world on a global scale. Since the content is updated on a regular basis, as trends and events unfold, this course is treated with a brief overview of how it is taught, rather than going into the specific content.

The key premises of the course are:

* The world of today will be different from the world of tomorrow and is different from the world of yesterday
* The direction of those differences can be anticipated
* The resulting alternative futures can and should be observed, analyzed, discussed and, where practical, acted upon.

Several topical areas are covered:

Demographics	Technology (such as information
Resources (such as food, water,	technology, biotechnology,
energy and the like)	nanotechnology and so on)
Globalization	Economics
Environment	Social (such as lifestyles, values,
Geopolitics	culture and so on)

The course explores the long-term future of the globe. The students are expected, upon completion, to have:

* a comprehension of the major issues affecting the development of the world's future
* an ability to identify emerging global trends and issues
* an ability to analyze global issues, trends, and drivers of change from multiple perspectives
* a competence in futures-based tools and techniques for analyzing the world's future.

Students pick a specific domain and topic to focus a project around. As the semester proceeds, they scan for developments in their domain and their implications for the future. They build up a set of material to use to forecast the baseline or expected future, alternative futures, and then offer a recommendation for improvement in their domain. This is the key work product for the course.

A unique feature of the course is that, for selected topics, students are asked to identify different types of relevant information:

- A dataset, graph or other *empirical data* that illustrates an <u>important change</u>
- An *informative descriptive* piece that <u>analyzes change</u> and provides a forecast of the *expected* future
- An *informative descriptive* piece that <u>analyzes an uncertainty</u> and provides a forecast of an *alternative* future
- A *proposal piece* that contains a specific <u>recommendation, proposal or plan</u> for creating a more *preferable future*.

Appendix 3. Scanning form and explanation

The form was originally developed by Wayne Pethrick while he was a student at the University of Houston-Clear Lake. Wayne is now a futurist with Pitney Bowes.

Title		Author							
Brief source		Date							
STEEP Category/ies		Keywords							
URL									
Type (*bold one*)	Actual event	New trend	New cycle	New plan	Potential event		New information	New issue	
Brief description of the item									
How could the future be different as a result?									
What are the potential Implications for...?	...Stakeholder name:								
Overall effect (*bold one*)	Confirming (baseline scenario)	Creating (a new scenario)	Resolving (between two scenarios)	Impact (0–5)			Plausibility (0–5)		
Baseline, new or resolved scenario(s)				Novelty (0–5)			Timeliness (0–5)		
Scanner				Date Submitted					

Figure A.1   Scanning form

Category definitions:

Title	The title of the piece
Author	The primary author of the piece
Brief source	The name of the journal or organization that released the piece
Date	The date the piece appeared
STEEP categories	The one or more STEEP categories the piece relates to
Keywords	Other important terms that describe the piece
Full citation	The full journal or book citation or the URL

Types:

Actual event	An event that has already happened, but which few people know about and whose implications are not fully developed
New trend	Consistent increase or decrease, more or less of something over time
New cycle	Recurring increase and decrease, more and then less of something over time
New plan	Announced intention to create change in the future
Potential event	A potential happening or occurrence
New information	Information that has just been released
New issue	Debate, conflict, decision, "Should we/they..."
Brief description	A short paragraph describing the event or the new piece of information. What happened or what new information appeared?
What could be different about the future?	A brief comparison about the future before and after this event. How does the future change a result?
What are the implications for ...?	Future consequences of this event for a specific person, group or domain. State the person, group or domain that would be affected
...Name	The name of the person, group, organization, community, country or domain
Overall impact	*Confirming* – confirms the baseline future; supports an existing condition, trend or plan
	Creating – creates a new scenario or plausible alternative future
	Resolving – shows that one scenario is becoming more probable compared to others

Baseline, new or resolved scenario(s)	The scenario that is confirmed (baseline) or created (new) or made more probable (resolved) by this scanning hit
Impact (0–5)	How much is this event or information likely to change the future for that person, group or domain?
Plausibility (0–5)	How likely will this change actually affect the future?
Novelty (0–5)	How new is this event or piece of information to those involved?
Timeliness (0–5)	How much time do those involved have before this item becomes public or is framed in some way?
Scanner	The person submitting the hit
Date submitted	The date the scanning hit was submitted

Appendix 4: Strategic Planning and Change Management

The organization model

Every Enterprise (organization) has a **Mission** – a contract with the World in which the Enterprise agrees to provide certain products and services and the world agrees to grant the Enterprise legitimacy and the resources to carry out its mission. Figure 10.3 (page 260) is a schematic of a generic Mission.

The process begins with a set of **Customers**, individuals or other enterprises that receive its products and services. Serving those customers, even for public sector or non-profit organizations, is the fundamental reason for the Enterprise's existence.

Customers have **Needs**. Identifying Customers' Needs is crucial. It looks easy, but it's not. The common mistake is to confuse a Customer's Need with the product or service that the Enterprise is already offering. So a university might say that their Customers (students) need teachers and courses. No, that's the service or the means for delivering the service. The student really needs knowledge and skill. Immediately, then, one has to question whether teachers and courses are the best way to satisfy that need. (Answer: They do satisfy that need, but there are many other ways, some of which are more effective.) A similar misconception is that Customers need the four million power drills they buy each year. Obvious, right? Not so. They don't need the drills; they need the holes!

Products and/or Services fulfill the Customers' Needs. The Products and Services are the output of the Enterprise. They must satisfy the Customer Needs in the long run or else the Enterprise will eventually lose its legitimacy and disappear.

Finally, the Enterprise thereby derives **Benefit** from satisfying the Customer Needs with its Products and Services. Customers (or someone) eventually "pays for" the Products and Services – often with money, sometimes with political support, recognition or other non-monetary benefits. So there is always quid pro quo, although it can be quite general and amorphous. But in the end, every Enterprise has to get paid or else it won't be able to maintain itself. (Every organism needs to eat or else it will starve to death.)

Stakeholders are individuals and other enterprises that benefit from the success of the Enterprise, but are not served directly by its Products or Services.

The Enterprise also has an internal **Structure** that understands the Customers' Needs, produces the Products and Services and receives the Benefit. The structure consists of People, Facilities/Equipment, Resources and Processes.

Goal hierarchy

(see Figure 10.5, page 263)

- **Enterprise** A group serving a need by investing resources with the purpose of doing some good and deriving some benefit, e.g. a university.
- **Elements** The items an enterprise consists of, operates on, or deals with.
  The external elements of an enterprise are customers, their needs, the products and services that satisfy those needs and the benefits that enterprise derives when it satisfies the needs.
  The internal elements of an enterprise consist of its people, facilities and equipment, resources and processes, e.g. students, etc.
- **Mission** A statement of the purpose of the enterprise, its charter and reason for being, the basis of its legitimacy, e.g. educate students.
- **Vision** An attractive image of preferred future that represents the best that the enterprise can uniquely be or do, e.g. smiling, grateful students.
- **Goal** An external, long-term result that the enterprise wants to achieve, e.g. higher graduate placements.
- **Measure** An observable means of showing how well the enterprise has fulfilled its mission or achieved its goals, e.g. inflation-adjusted, entry-level salaries.
- **Target** A level of the measure that will be feasible, but difficult to achieve, e.g. +25%.
- **Strategy** A long-term, high-level category of internal activities that accomplishes the goals, e.g. partner with local business.
- **Objective** A one-year goal that leads to the long-term goal, e.g. new partner businesses.
- **Project Initiative** A one-year activity that implements the long-term strategy and achieves the short-term objective, e.g. establish internship opportunities with local businesses.

Table A.2   Goal hierarchy

MISSION ELEMENTS	VISION
Customers	An image (not just an idea)
Needs	About the future (not the past)
Products/Services	Attractive, appealing, even compelling
Benefits	Bold, ambitious, yet plausible
People	The best we can be, unique, special
Facilities	Motivating, energizing
Resources	Spoken by leaders, owned by everyone
Processes	
GOAL	**MEASURE**
High level, long term (3–5 years)	Observable
Things, noun oriented	Valid
Externally oriented (only indirectly	Feasible, easily administered
controllable)	Easily recognized
Relatively few in number	
Can be measured	
STRATEGY	**PROJECT ELEMENTS**
High level, long term (3–5 years)	Objectives
Activities, verb oriented	Tasks
Internally oriented (directly	Assignments
controllable)	Milestones
Achieves or partially achieves a goal	Resources
Can be assigned to an individual or	
group	
Fundable	
Relatively few for each goal	

Bibliography

Ackoff, R. & Emery, F. (1972) *On Purposeful Systems* (Salinas, CA: Intersystems Publications).

Aguilar, F. (1967) *Scanning the Business Environment* (NY: Macmillan).

Barker, J. (2010) Personal communication, 3 September.

Beck, D. & Cowan, C. (1996) *Spiral Dynamics: Mastering Values, Leadership, and Change* (Malden, MA: Blackwell).

Beres, M.E. & Musser, S. (1987) "Avenues and Impediments to Transformation: Lessons from a Case of Bottom-Up Change" in R. Kilmann & T. Covin (eds) *Corporate Transformation: Revitalizing Organizations for a Competitive World* (San Francisco, CA: Jossey-Bass).

Berger, P. & Luckman, T. (1967) *The Social Construction of Reality* (NY: Anchor).

Bezold, C. (2000) "The Visioning Method" in R. Slaughter (ed.) *The Knowledge Base of Foresight*, Vol. 2, Millennium Edition (Queensland, Australia: Foresight International); cited in C. Stewart (2004, June) "Deep Visioning: An Action Research Seminar on Visioning and an Integral Visioning Method." Working Paper.

Bishop P., Hines, A. & Collins, T. (2007) "The Current State of Scenario Development: An Overview of Techniques," *Foresight*, 9 (1), 5–25.

Blake, R. & Mouton, J. (1964) *The Managerial Grid: The Key to Leadership Excellence* (Houston, TX: Gulf Publishing).

Boulding, E. (1996) "Toward a Culture of Peace in the 21st Century," *Social Alternatives*, 15 (3), 38.

Boulding, E. (n.d.) *Why Imagine the Future?* http://www.humiliationstudies.org/documents/BouldingWhyImaginetheFuture.pdf.

Brelin, H. & Grayson, J. (1994) "Foreword" in R. Camp *Business Process Benchmarking* (Burr Ridge, IL: Irwin Professional Publishing).

Bridges, W. & Bridges, S. (2009) *Managing Transitions: Making the Most of Change*, 3rd edn (Cambridge, MA: Da Capo Lifelong Books).

Carr, D. & Johansson, H. (1995) *Best Practices in Reengineering: What Works and What Doesn't in the Reengineering Process* (NY: McGraw-Hill).

Carroll, B. (1991) "Shaping the Future with FPS," *G/C/T*, 14(2), 6–8.

Choo, C. W. (2001) "Environmental Scanning as Information Seeking and Organizational Learning," *Information Research*, 7 (1).

Churchman, C. W. (1984) *The Systems Approach* (NY: Dell Publishing).

Clark, R. (2010) *From Zero to Future in 8 Hours: Futures Research Example*. Presentation to Futures Research Class, University of Houston, 15 September.

Collins, J. (2001) *Good to Great* (NY: Harper Business).

Collins, T. & Hines, A. (2010) "The Evolution of Integral Futures," *World Future Review*, June–July, 5–16.

Cooperrider, D. L. & Whitney, D. (1999) "A Positive Revolution in Change: Appreciative Inquiry" in P. Holman & T. Devane (eds) *Appreciative Inquiry* (San Francisco, CA: Barrett-Koehler).

Cornish, E. (2004) *Futuring: The Exploration of the Future* (Bethesda, MD: The World Future Society).

Csikszentmihalyi, M. (1991) *Flow: The Psychology of Optimal Experience* (NY: HarperPerennial).

Daft, R. & Weick, K. (1984) "Toward a Model of Organizations as Interpretation Systems," *Academy of Management Review*, 9 (2), 284–95.

Dator, J. (1994) "How to Conduct a Futures Visioning Workshop." For the Commission on the Future of the Tennessee Judiciary, Fairfield Glade, Tennessee, 8–9 April.

Day, P. & Shoemaker, G. (2006) *Peripheral Vision: Detecting the Weak Signals that Make or Break your Company* (Cambridge, MA: Harvard Press).

De Jouvenal, B. (1967) *The Art of Conjecture* (NY: Basic Books).

Diamond, J. (1999) *Guns, Germs and Steel: The Fates of Human Societies* (NY: Norton).

Forrester, J. (1961) *Industrial Dynamics* (Cambridge, UK: Pegasus Communications).

Galbraith, J. (1985) "The Eight Great Gripes of Gifted Kids: Responding to Special Needs," *Roeper Review*, 8, 15–18.

Giddens, A., Duneier, M., Applebaum, R. & Carr, D. (2009) *Introduction to Sociology*, 7th edn (NY: W. W. Norton).

Godet, M. (2006) *Creating Futures: Scenario Planning as a Strategic Management Tool*, 2nd edn (Paris, France: Economica).

Gordon, T. (2003) "Delphi" in J. Glenn & T. Gordon *Futures Research Methodology, V2.0* (Washington, DC: AC/UNU Millennium Project).

Greenleaf, R. (1983) *Servant Leadership: A Journey into the Nature of Legitimate Power and Greatness* (Mahwah, NJ: Paulist Press).

Hackett, P. & Hunter, P. (n.d.) "Who Governs Britain? A Profile of MPs in the New Parliament" http://www.smith-institute.org.uk/file/Who-Governs-Britain?

Hamel, G. & Prahalad, C.K. (1996) *Competing for the Future* (Cambridge, MA: Harvard Business Press).

Hamel, G. (2002) *Leading the Revolution: How to Thrive in Turbulent Times by Making Innovation a Way of Life* (Cambridge, MA: Harvard Business Press).

Hamel, G & Välikangas, L. (2003) "The Quest for Resilience," *Harvard Business Review*, September.

Hayward, P. (2008) "Pathways to Integral Perspectives," *Futures*, 40 (2).

Hayward, P., Slaughter, R. & Voros, J. (2008) "Integral Futures: Special Issue," *Futures*, 40 (2).

Hersey, P. & Blanchard, K. H. (1977) *Utilizing Human Resources: Management of Organizational Behavior*, 3rd edn (Upper Saddle River, NJ: Prentice Hall).

Heuer, R. (1999) *The Psychology of Intelligence Analysis* (Langley, VA: Center for the Study of Intelligence, Central Intelligence Agency).

Hiatt, J. & Creasey, T. (n.d.) The definition and history of change management: Change Management Tutorial Series, available at http://www.change-management.com/.

Hines, A. (2006, Sept–Oct) "Strategic Foresight: The State of the Art," *The Futurist*.

Hines, A. & Bishop, P. (2007) *Thinking about the Future: Guidelines for Strategic Foresight* (Washington, DC: Social Technologies).

Hines, A. (2007) "Why Foresight? I Can Think of 316 Reasons!" *Changewaves*.

Hines, A. (2010) "Retirement Is an Obsolescent Concept," Special Issue: Golden Boomers, *Adult Career Development Journal*, Summer, 8–17.

Hines. A. (2011) *Consumer Shift: How Changing Values Are Reshaping the Consumer Landscape* (Tempe, AZ: No Limits Publishing).

Inayatullah, S. (1998) "Causal Layered Analysis: Post-Structuralism as Method," *Futures*, 30 (8), 815–29.

Inayatullah, S. (2003) *Futures Research Methodology, V2.0* (Washington, DC: AC/ UNU Millennium Project).

Jarratt, J. (2010) Personal Communication, 3 September.

Kahn, H. (1962) *Thinking about the Unthinkable* (NY: Horizon Press).

Kaufman, D. (1980) *Systems One: An Introduction to Systems Thinking* (Houston, TX: Future Systems).

Kaufman, D. (1981) *Systems Two: The Human Environment* (Houston, TX: Future Systems).

Kilmann, R. & Covin, T. (eds) (1987) *Corporate Transformation: Revitalizing Organizations for a Competitive World* (San Francisco, CA: Jossey-Bass).

Koestler, A. (1990, reprint edn) *The Ghost in the Machine* (NY: Penguin).

Lewin, K., Lippitt, R. & White, R. K. (1939) "Patterns of Aggressive Behavior in Experimentally Created Social Climates," *Journal of Social Psychology*, 10, 271–9.

Lewin, K. (1951) "Field theory" in D. Cartwright (ed.) *Social Science: Selected Theoretical Papers* (NY: Harper & Row).

List, D. (2003) "Three Maps for Navigating the Ocean of Alternative Futures," *Journal of Futures Studies*, 8 (2), 55–64.

Markley, O. (1998) "I've Seen the Future," *Fast Company*, October/November.

Martino, J. P. (1972) *Technological Forecasting for Decision-Making* (NY: Elsevier).

Maurer, R. (1996) *Beyond the Wall of Resistance* (Austin, TX: Bard).

Meadows, D., Meadows, D., Randers, J. & Behrens, William W. (1972) *Limits to Growth: A Report for the Club of Rome's Project on the Predicament of Mankind* (NY: Universe Books).

Meadows, D. & Randers, J. & Meadows, D. (1993) *Beyond the Limits: Confronting Global Collapse, Envisioning a Sustainable Future* (White River Junction, VT: Chelsea Green).

Meadows, D. & Randers, J. & Meadows, D. (2004) *Limits to Growth: the 30-Year Update* (White River Junction, VT: Chelsea Green).

Meadows, D. (2008) *Thinking in Systems: A Primer* (White River Junction, VT: Chelsea Green).

Mills, C. W. (1957) *The Power Elite* (Oxford, UK: Oxford University Press).

Mills, C. W. & Etzioni, A. (1999) *Sociological Imagination* (Oxford, UK: Oxford University Press).

Molitor, G. (Personal Communication) in J. Coates, V. Coates, J. Jarratt & L. Heinz (1986) *Issues Management: How Can You Plan, Organize, and Manage for the Future* (Mt Airy, MD: Lomond).

Morisson, J. L. (1995) "Environmental Scanning" in G. Kurian, & G. Molitor (eds) *Encyclopedia of the Future* (NY: Simon & Schuster), 814–16.

Nadler, D. "Organizational Frame Bending" in R. Kilmann & T. Covin (eds) (1987) *Corporate Transformation: Revitalizing Organizations for a Competitive World* (San Francisco, CA: Jossey-Bass).

Nanus, B. (1992) *Visionary Leadership* (San Francisco, CA: Jossey-Bass).

Nanus, B. (1995) *The Vision Retreat: A Facilitator's Guide* (Indianapolis, IN: Jossey-Bass).

National Research Council (2000) *Beyond Six Billion*, http://www.nap.edu/ openbook.php?record_id=9828&page=39#p200036ecmmm00004.

Nisbet, R. (1979) "The Idea of Progress," *Literature of Liberty: A Review of Contemporary Liberal Thought*, 2 (1).

Passow, A. H. (1988) "Educating Gifted Persons Who are Caring and Concerned," *Roeper Review*, 11, 13–15.

Petersen, J. (1997) *Out of the Blue: Wild cards and other Big Future Surprises: How to Anticipate and Respond to Profound Change* (Toronto, Canada: Madison Books).

Polak, F. (1973) *The Image of the Future* (Amsterdam, Netherlands: Elsevier).

Porter, M. (1979) "How Competitive Forces Shape Strategy," *Harvard Business Review*, March–April, 137–45.

Porter, M. (2008) "The Five Competitive Forces that Shape Strategy," *Harvard Business Review*, January.

Ray, M. & Myers, R. (1988) *Creativity in Business* (Jackson, TN: Main Street Books).

Rogers, E. (1962) *Diffusion of Innovations* (Glencoe, NY: Free Press).

Rost, J. (1991) *Leadership for the Twenty-First Century* (Santa Barbara, CA: Praeger Publishers).

Scharmer, C. O. (2007) *Theory U: Leading from the Future as it Emerges* (Cambridge, MA: Society for Organizational Learning).

Schultz, W. (2004) "Causal Layered Analysis." Lecture, University of Houston-Clear Lake, June.

Senge, P. (1994) *The Fifth Discipline: The Art & Practice of the Learning Organization* (NY: Doubleday).

Senge, P., Kleiner, A., Roberts, C., Ross, R. & Smith, B. (1994) *The Fifth Discipline Fieldbook* (NY: Currency Doubleday).

Senge, P., Scharmer, C.O., Jaworski, J. & Flowers, B. S. (2004) *Presence: Human Purpose and the Field of the Future* (Cambridge, MA: Society for Organizational Learning).

Silverman, L. K. (1994) "The Moral Sensitivity of Gifted Children and the Evolution of Society," *Roeper Review*, 11, 13–15.

Simon, S., Howe, L. & Kirschenbaum, H. (1972) *Values Clarification: A Practical, Action-Directed Workbook* (NY: Warner Books).

Slaughter, R. (1985) "Towards a Critical Futurism," *World Future Society Bulletin*, 18 (4).

Slaughter, R. (1998) "Transcending Flatland: Implications of Ken Wilber's Meta-Narrative for Futures Studies," *Futures*, 30 (6), 519–33.

Slaughter, R. (1999) "A New Framework for Environmental Scanning," *Foresight*, 1 (5), 441–51.

Slaughter, R. (2003) "Integral Operating System," World Futures Society Pre-Conference Course, July, drawing on Inayatullah.

Slaughter, R. (2004) *Futures Beyond Dystopia: Creating Social Foresight* (NY: Routledge/Falmer).

Smil, V. (2006) *Energy: A Beginner's Guide* (London, UK: One World).

Snowden, D. (2000) "Cynefin: A Sense of Time and Space, the Social Ecology of Knowledge Management," in C. Despres & D. Chauvel (eds) *Knowledge Horizons: The Present and the Promise of Knowledge Management* (Oxford, UK: Butterworth Heinemann).

Stewart, C. (2004, June) "Deep Visioning: An Action Research Seminar on Visioning and an Integral Visioning Method." Working Paper.

Taleb, N. N. (2007) *The Black Swan: The Impact of the Highly Improbable* (NY: Random House).

Tallent-Runnels, M. K. & Mullen, G. (2004) "Children's Concerns About the Future: Ten Years Later." Unpublished manuscript.

Tallent-Runnels, M. K. (2005) "Resources for Gifted Students Studying the Future," *Gifted Child Today*, 30 (1).

Toffler, A. (1970) *Future Shock* (NY: Random House).

Toffler, A. (1980) *The Third Wave* (NY: William Morrow).

Torrance, E. P. (1974) "Ways Gifted Children can study the Future," *Gifted Children Quarterly*, 18, 66–71.

Torrance, E. P. (1978) "Giftedness in Solving Future Problems," *Journal of Creative Behavior*, 12, 75–86.

United Way of America (1980) *What Lies Ahead: A Glimpse of the 1980s and the Driving Forces That Will shape the Decade Ahead. An Environmental Scan Report* (Alexandria, VA: United Way of America, Long Range Planning Division).

Weber, M. (1958) "Class, Status and Party" in H. Gerth & C.W. Mills *From Max Weber: Essays in Sociology* (Oxford, UK: Oxford University Press).

Weick, K. (1979) *The Social Psychology of Organizing*, 2nd edn (NY: McGraw-Hill).

Weisberg, R. (1993) *Creativity: Beyond the Myth of Genius* (NY: W. H. Freeman).

Weisbord, M. & Janoff, S. (2000) *Future Search: An Action Guide to Finding Common Ground in Organizations and Communities*, 2nd edn (San Francisco, CA: Berret-Koehler).

Wheelright, V. (2010) *It's Your Future...Make it a Good One* (Harlingen, TX: Personal Futures Network).

Wilber, K. (2001a) *A Brief History of Everything* (Boston, MA: Shambhala).

Wilber, K. (2001b) *A Theory of Everything: An Integral Vision for Business, Politics, Science and Spirituality* (Boston, MA: Shambhala).

Wolfram, S. (2002) *A New Kind of Science* (Champaign, IL: Wolfram Media).

Index